INFORMATION SYSTEMS

Zeeshan Qaiser

TAP

Toronto Academic Press

Information Systems

Zeeshan Qaiser

Toronto Academic Press
224 Shoreacres Road
Burlington, ON L7L 2H2
Canada
www.tap-books.com
Email: orders@arclereducation.com

ISBN: 978-1-77469-789-4

Toronto Academic Press publishes wide variety of books and eBooks. For more information about Toronto Academic Press and its products, visit our website at www.tap-books.com.

ABOUT THE AUTHOR

Zeeshan Qaiser is a dynamic and accomplished professional with over 15 years of experience in the fields of IT, project management, and business development. He is currently serving as the CEO of Axondevs, a leading software development company based in Islamabad, Pakistan. Zeeshan's passion for technology and entrepreneurship led him to co-found Axondevs in 2013, which has since grown into a highly respected and sought-after firm in the software industry. Under his leadership, the company has successfully completed numerous projects for clients in Pakistan, the Middle East, Europe, and the United States. Prior to founding Axondevs, Zeeshan worked as a project manager and IT consultant for several prestigious organizations in Pakistan and the United States. He holds a bachelor's degree in computer science from the University of Central Punjab and a master's degree in business administration from the University of Illinois at Urbana-Champaign. Zeeshan is a forward-thinking and results-driven leader who is constantly seeking new opportunities to innovate and grow. His expertise in software development, project management, and business development, combined with his exceptional communication and leadership skills, make him an invaluable asset to any organization.

Contents

Preface *xvii*
List of Figures *ix*
List of Tables *xi*
List of Abbreviations *xiii*

1 Basic Concepts of Information Systems 1

Unit Introduction **1**
1.1. Information Definition **4**
1.1.1. Data 4
1.1.2. Information 4
1.1.3. Knowledge 4
1.2. System Definition **6**
1.3. Information System (IS) Definition **6**
1.4. Typology of Information Systems (IS) **7**
1.4.1. The Transaction Processing System (TPS) 8
1.4.2. Management Information Systems (MIS) 9
1.4.3. Decision Support Systems (DSS) 9
1.4.4. Executive Support System (ESS) 10
1.5. Decision-Making and Information Systems (IS) **11**
1.6. Information Systems (IS) Applications **15**
1.6.1. Enterprise Resource Planning (ERP) 15
1.6.2. Electronic Commerce 16
1.6.3. Supply Chain Management (SCM) 17
1.6.4. Customer Relationship Management (CRM) 18
1.6.5. Knowledge Management (KM) 19
1.6.6. Business Intelligence (BI) 20
1.7. Information Systems (IS) Security **21**
1.8. Information Systems (IS) Assessment **22**
1.8.1. Efficiency 23
1.8.2. Effectiveness 23
1.8.3. Financial Measures of Managerial Performance 24
1.9. Information Systems (IS) Evolution **25**
1.9.1. The Urbanization of Information Systems (IS) 25
1.9.2. Stages of Urbanization 26
1.10. Summary **28**
Review Questions **28**
Multiple Choice Questions **29**
References **30**

2 Hardware and Software Used in Information Systems 37

Unit Introduction **37**
2.1. Hardware Components **40**
2.2. Processing and Memory Devices: Power, Speed, and Capacity **40**
2.2.1. Processing Characteristics and Functions 41
2.2.2. Memory Characteristics and Functions 42
2.2.3. Multiprocessing 44
2.3. Secondary Storage, Input, and Output Devices **47**

2.3.1. Secondary Storage Devices 47
2.3.2. Input Devices 52
2.3.3. Output Devices 57
2.4. Overview of Software 61
2.5. Systems Software 62
2.5.1. Operating Systems (OSs) 62
2.5.2. Current Operating Systems (OSs) 67
2.6. Utility Programs 70
2.7. Application Software 71
2.7.1. Types and Functions of Application Software 72
2.7.2. Personal Application Software 74
2.7.3. Mobile Application Software 77
2.8. Summary 78
Review Questions 78
Multiple Choice Questions 79
References 80

3 Modeling and Development of Information Systems 89

Unit Introduction 89
3.1. User-Centric Development 92
3.2. Determining Need and Performance Expectations 93
3.3. Characteristic of Good Organizational is Talent 95
3.3.1. Personal Attributes 95
3.3.2. Organizational Environment 96
3.4. Stages in Process Design 97
3.4.1. Requirements Determination 97
3.4.2. Analysis Phase 98
3.4.3. Logical Design 98
3.4.4. Physical Design 99
3.4.5. Process Design 99
3.4.6. Human-Computer System Design 100
3.4.7. Implementation and Testing 100
3.4.8. Maintenance 100
3.5. Modeling a System Design 100
3.6. Stages in is Modeling 101
3.7. System Development Methods 103
3.7.1. First Generation (FG) Methods 103
3.7.2. Second Generation Methods 106
3.7.3. Third Generation Methods 107
3.8. Summary 111
Review Questions 111
Multiple Choice Questions 111
References 113

4 Database Management System 119

Unit Introduction 119
4.1. Data Management 122
4.1.1. Data Entities, Attributes, and Keys 122
4.1.2. The Database Approach 124
4.2. Database Management Systems (DBMS) 126
4.3. Overview of Database Types 126
4.3.1. Flat File 127
4.3.2. Single User 128
4.3.3. Multiple Users 128
4.4. Providing a User View 129
4.4.1. Storing and Retrieving Data 129
4.4.2. Manipulating Data and Generating Reports 130
4.4.3. Popular Database Management Systems (DBMS) 132
4.4.4. Special-Purpose Database Systems 133
4.4.5. Selecting a Database Management System (DBMS) 134
4.5. Database Applications 135
4.5.1. Linking the Company Database to the Internet 135
4.5.2. Data Marts, Data Warehouses, and Data Mining 136
4.5.3. Business Intelligence (BI) 140
4.5.4. Online Analytical Processing (OLAP) 141
4.5.5. Object-Relational Database Management Systems (ORDBMS) 143
4.5.6. Audio, Visual, and Other Database Systems 144
4.6. Summary 146
Review Questions 146

Multiple Choice Questions 147
References 148

5 Role of Telecommunication and Networks in Information Systems 155

Unit Introduction 155
5.1. A Foundation for Telecommunication and Network Management 157
5.2. Telecommunication 159
5.2.1. Types of Telecommunications 159
5.2.2. Components of Telecommunication 160
5.3. Network 160
5.3.1. Types of Networks 160
5.3.2. Components of Networks 161
5.4. Telecommunication and Networks in Information Systems (IS) 162
5.5. Challenges and Risks in Telecommunication and Networks 164
5.5.1. Challenges 164
5.5.2. Risks 164
5.6. Summary 167
Review Questions 167
Multiple Choice Questions 167
References 168

6 Information Systems in Business and Society 171

Unit Introduction 171
6.1. Types of Information Systems (ISS) in Businesses 174
6.2. The Functions of Several is Types in Corporate Groups 174
6.2.1. Transaction Processing Systems (TPSs) 174
6.2.2. Process Control Systems 175
6.2.3. Enterprise Collaboration Systems 175
6.2.4. Management Information Systems (MIS) 175
6.2.5. Decision Support Systems (DSS) 176
6.2.6. Executive Information Systems (EIS) 176
6.2.7. Expert Systems 177
6.2.8. Knowledge Management (KM) Systems 177
6.2.9. Strategic Information Systems (IS) 177
6.2.10. Functional Business Systems 178
6.2.11. Sales and Marketing Information Systems (IS) 178
6.2.12. Manufacturing and Production Information Systems (IS) 178
6.2.13. Finance and Accounting Information Systems (IS) 179
6.2.14. Human Resource Information Systems (HRIS) 179
6.3. Role of is in Society 179
6.3.1. Communication 180
6.3.2. Education 180
6.3.3. Work 180
6.3.4. Entertainment 181
6.3.5. Health and Wellness 181
6.3.6. Privacy and Security 181
6.4. Summary 182
Review Questions 182
Multiple Choice Questions 182
References 183

7 Ethical and Security Issues of Informative System 187

Unit Introduction 187
7.1. Ethical Issues of Information Systems (IS) 189
7.2. Privacy in Information Systems (IS) 189
7.3. Intellectual Property 191
7.4. Accessibility 192
7.4.1. Lack of Accessibility in Information Systems (IS) 192

7.4.2. Failure to Ensure Accessibility 192

7.4.3. Consequences of Inaccessibility 193

7.5. Accuracy 193

7.5.1. Causes of Inaccurate Information 193

7.5.2. Consequences of Inaccurate Information 193

7.6. Security Issues of Information System (IS) 193

7.7. Viruses and Malicious Programs 194

7.8. Phishing 195

7.9. Denial of Service 195

7.10. Botnets 196

7.10.1. Drive-by Download Attacks 197

7.10.2. Working on Drive-by Download Attacks 197

7.10.3. Types of Drive-by Download Attacks 197

7.10.4. Consequences of Drive-by Download Attacks 198

7.11. Ransomware 198

7.11.1. Working of Ransomware 198

7.11.2. Impact of Ransomware 199

7.11.3. Prevention of Ransomware Attacks 199

7.12. Exploit Kits 199

7.13. Advanced Persistent Threat (APT) Attacks 200

7.14. Summary 201

Review Questions 201

Multiple Choice Questions 201

References 203

8 Emerging Trends in Information System 207

Unit Introduction 207

8.1. Cloud Computing 209

8.2. Big Data Analytics 210

8.3. Automation 211

8.4. Artificial Intelligence (AI) 212

8.5. Virtual Reality (VR) 214

8.6. Augmented Reality (AR) 214

8.7. Blockchain Data 215

8.8. Cyber Security 217

8.8.1. Internet of Things (IoT) Security 217

8.8.2. Cybersecurity Awareness Training 218

8.8.3. Zero Trust Security 218

8.9. Summary 219

Review Questions 219

Multiple Choice Questions 219

References 221

INDEX 223

List of Figures

Figure 1.1. The flow from data to information to knowledge

Figure 1.2. Leavitt's diamond: A socio-technical view of IS

Figure 1.3. Information system types according to managerial level

Figure 1.4. Schematic of a transaction processing system

Figure 1.5. An example of an innovative decision support system (DSS) scheme for plant disease management

Figure 1.6. Types of decisions according to managerial level

Figure 1.7. Illustration of a geographic information systems (GIS)

Figure 1.8. Schematic of enterprise resource planning and site components

Figure 1.9. Illustration of the CRM and its components

Figure 1.10. Diagram of knowledge management and its components

Figure 2.1. The input-process-output concept

Figure 2.2. Illustration of the memory vs. storage

Figure 2.3. Schematic of the central processing unit (CPU)

Figure 2.4. Architecture of the multiprocess microprocessor

Figure 2.5. Illustration of the parallel computing

Figure 2.6. Schematic of the grid computing

Figure 2.7. Schematic of the hard disk and its components

Figure 2.8. Illustration of the storage area network (SAN)

Figure 2.9. Image of an optical disk drive

Figure 2.10. Image of a USB flash drive

Figure 2.11. Schematic of the personal computer input devices

Figure 2.12. Illustration of the various types of digital cameras

Figure 2.13. Image of display monitor

Figure 2.14. Illustration of system software

Figure 2.15. Schematic of networking capabilities

Figure 2.16. Picture of window vista

Figure 2.17. Illustration of components of utility programs

Figure 2.18. Schematic of software-as-a-service (SaaS)

Figure 2.19. Floe diagram of word processing

Figure 3.1. Illustration of modeling of information system

Figure 3.2. Schematic of user centric development

Figure 3.3. Image of components of computer-based system

Figure 3.4. Flow diagram of case tool

Figure 3.5. Illustration of system design

Figure 3.6. Illustration of stages of information modeling

Figure 3.7. Image of project management tools

Figure 4.1. Difference between database and DBMS

Figure 4.2. Data management roadmap

Figure 4.3. An example of a data entity

Figure 4.4. eBay assigns an "item number" as a primary key to keep track of each item in its database

Figure 4.5. The database approach to data management

Figure 4.6. Schematic of the Microsoft OneNote

Figure 4.7. Logical and physical access

Figure 4.8. Query by example (QBE) is a method several databases use to produce information and reports

Figure 4.9. A database application provides complex formatting and organization options to output the correct information in style

Figure 4.10. Apple's iTunes software uses a database to access and catalog music

Figure 4.11. Elements of a data warehouse

Figure 4.12. Amazon uses data mining to suggest products attracting site visitors

Figure 5.1. Illustration of telecommunications network – network management architecture

Figure 5.2. Schematic of the wireless communication networks

Figure 5.3. Diagram representing metropolitan area network (MAN)

Figure 5.4. Various cybersecurity attacks in information systems

Figure 5.5. Illustration of internet of things (IoT)

Figure 6.1. Illustration of the different types of information systems in businesses

Figure 6.2. Schematic of management information systems

Figure 6.3. The structure of strategic information systems planning in organizations

Figure 6.4. Schematic of the evolution of the communication

Figure 7.1. Illustration of ethical and security issue of informative system

Figure 7.2. Flow diagram of NORA (non-obvious relationship awareness)

Figure 7.3. Image of NCSA (National Cyber Security Alliance)

Figure 7.4. Picture of web accessibility

Figure 7.5. Illustration of malvertising

Figure 7.6. Schematic of denial-of-service attack

Figure 7.7. Picture of exploit kit

Figure 8.1. Illustration of cloud computing

Figure 8.2. Picture of big data

Figure 8.3. Image of artificial intelligence

Figure 8.4. Schematic of blockchain data

Figure 8.5. Explanation of internet of things

List of Tables

Table 2.1. Comparison for various forms of data storage

Table 4.1. Comparison of data and OLAP

List of Abbreviations

AI	Artificial Intelligence
ALU	Arithmetic/Logic Unit
ANSI	American National Standards Institute
API	Application Program Interface
APT	Advanced Persistent Threat
AR	Augmented Reality
ASP	Application Service Provider
BI	Business Intelligence
CASE	Computer-Aided Software Engineering
CDM	Clinical Data Mart
CD-R	CD-Recordable
CD-RW	CD-Rewritable
CPU	Central Processing Unit
CRM	Customer Relationship Management
DaaS	Database-As-A-Service
DBA	Database Administrator
DBMS	Database Management System

DLP	Data Loss Prevention
DML	Data Manipulation Language
DRM	Digital Rights Management
DSS	Decision Support Systems
DVD	Digital Video Disc
EIS	Executive Information Systems
EPROM	Erasable Programmable Read-Only Memory
ERP	Enterprise Resource Planning
ESS	Executive Support System
ETHICS	Effective Technical and Human Implementation of Computer-based Systems
FBI	Federal Bureau of Investigation
FG	First Generation
GIS	Geographic Information Systems
GUI	Graphical User Interface
HRIS	Human Resource Information Systems
IDC	International Data Corporation
IE	Information Engineering
IEA	International Energy Agency
IS	Information System
ISAC	Information Systems Work and Analysis
ISO	International Standard Organization
IT	Information Technology
ITU	International Telecommunications Union
IUA	International Underwriting Association
JSD	Jackson Systems Development
JSP	Jackson Systems Programming
KM	Knowledge Management
LAN	Local Area Network

LAP	Logical Access Path
LUP	Land Use Plan
MAN	Metropolitan Area Network
MICR	Magnetic Ink Character Recognition
MIS	Management Information Systems
NCSA	National Cyber Security Alliance
OCR	Optical Character Recognition
OLAP	Online Analytical Processing
OLED	Organic Light-Emitting Diode
OLTP	Online Transaction Processing
OMR	Visual Mark Recognition
OPEC	Organization of Petroleum Exporting Countries
OQL	Object Query Language
ORDBMS	Object-Relational Database Management System
OS	Operating System
OSI	Open Systems Interconnection
PAP	Physical Access Path
PIMs	Personal Information Managers
QBE	Query By Example
RAD	Rapid Application Development
RDF	Resource Description Framework
RFID	Radio Frequency Identification
RIA	Rich Internet Application
ROM	Read-Only Memory
SaaS	Software-As-A-Service
SAN	Storage Area Network
SCM	Supply Chain Management
SMBs	Small to Medium-Sized Businesses

SQL	Structured Query Language
SSADM	Structured Systems Analysis and Design Methodology
SSD	Solid-State Storage
SSM	Soft Systems Methodology
STRADIS	Structured Analysis and Design of Information Systems
TCO	Total Cost of Ownership
TDFD	Top-Down Functional Decomposition
TMN	Telecommunication Management Network
TPS	Transaction Processing System
VR	Virtual Reality
W3C	World Wide Web Consortium
WAN	Wide Area Network

PREFACE

The use of information systems (IS) has become an essential aspect of modern-day society. It is evident in all areas of life, including businesses, healthcare, education, and government. The book titled "Information Systems" aims to provide readers with an in-depth understanding of information systems and their impact on various sectors. This book has eight chapters, each exploring different aspects of information systems.

The first chapter of this book discusses the fundamentals of information systems. The chapter aims to provide a comprehensive overview of information systems and their components. This includes hardware, software, data, and processes involved in information systems. The second chapter delves into the hardware and software used in information systems. It explains the various types of hardware and software that are essential in the development and deployment of information systems.

The third chapter focuses on the development process of information systems. It describes the various phases of the development process, such as planning, analysis, design, implementation, and maintenance. This chapter also emphasizes the importance of project management in the development of information systems.

The fourth chapter explores database management systems (DBMS). It explains the various components of database management systems and their functions. It also covers the different types of database models and the challenges associated with managing databases.

The fifth chapter is dedicated to telecommunication and networks. It explains the role of telecommunication and networks in information systems. This includes the different types of networks, such as LAN, WAN, and the internet. The chapter also discusses the latest trends in networking, such as cloud computing and 5G technology.

The sixth chapter is all about information systems in business and society. It explores the different ways information systems are used in various industries, including manufacturing, healthcare, and finance. The chapter also discusses the social implications of information systems and their impact on society.

The seventh chapter is focused on security and ethical issues in information systems. It covers the various security threats and challenges faced by information systems. The chapter also explains the importance of ethical practices in information systems and the role of government regulations.

The final chapter of this book is dedicated to emerging trends in information systems. It discusses the latest technological advancements in the field of information systems, such as artificial intelligence (AI), blockchain technology, and the Internet of Things. The chapter also emphasizes the importance of staying updated with the latest trends in information systems.

In conclusion, the book titled "Information Systems" provides readers with a comprehensive understanding of information systems and their impact on various sectors. This book is written for students, professionals, and anyone interested in the field of information systems. We hope this book will serve as a valuable resource for its readers.

—Author

CHAPTER 1

BASIC CONCEPTS OF INFORMATION SYSTEMS

UNIT INTRODUCTION

Information systems (IS) are an indispensable component of today's businesses and other organizations. They are created with the purpose of making the gathering, storing, processing, and distribution of information inside an organization much simpler. In the modern era of technology, the necessity for organizations to have IS that are both effective and efficient has become of the utmost importance. These systems enable businesses to maintain their competitive edge and adapt quickly to shifting market conditions. The ideas of hardware, software, data, people, and process are the fundamental building blocks of IS. The term "hardware" reflects the tangible elements of a system, including computers, servers, and other electronic gadgets. The programs and apps that grant the computer the ability to carry out a variety of functions are collectively referred to as software. The term "data" refers to the various pieces of information analyzed and saved by the system. The term "people" refers to the individuals who use the system and those who operate and administer it. The terms "procedure" and "protocol" are used to refer to the processes that regulate how the system operates. It is necessary to have a solid understanding of these fundamental ideas to successfully design, implement, and manage IS that cater to the organization's requirements (Stair et al., 2011).

One of the key components of any information systems is hardware. This includes physical components such as computers, servers, storage devices, networking equipment, and peripherals such as printers and scanners. The hardware components of an IS must be carefully chosen and configured to ensure that they work together effectively to achieve the system's goals (Chang, 2008).

Another essential component of an IS is software. This includes the operating system (OS), applications, and other programs that permit users to collaborate with the system. The software must be designed to the user's needs and must be reliable, secure, and easy to use. Data is another critical component of an IS. Data can be structured or unstructured and can take many forms, including text, images, video, and audio. The system should capture, store, retrieve, and process data quickly and accurately (Alter, 2013).

People are also essential to the success of any IS. This includes users, developers, administrators, and support staff. The system must be designed to accommodate the requirements of the people who will use and operate it. Training and support must be provided to ensure that users are comfortable and proficient with the system. Finally, process refers to the procedures and protocols governing the system's functions. This includes everything from how data is entered into the system to how it is processed and analyzed. Effective processes are essential for ensuring that the system operates smoothly and that data is processed accurately and efficiently (Myers & Avison, 2002).

Overall, the basic concepts of IS are interrelated and must be carefully balanced to guarantee that the system meets the organization's needs. By grasping these ideas, organizations may create and maintain efficient IS that support their objectives and keep them competitive in today's quickly evolving business environment (Romney et al., 2012).

Learning Objectives

After this chapter, readers will understand the following:

- Definitions of various terms used in information systems;
- Definition of system and information systems;
- Topology of information systems;
- Relationship between information systems and decision making;
- Various applications of the information systems;
- Security of the information systems;
- Assessment of various information systems;
- Evolution and stages of information system development.

Key Terms

- Decision making
- Information

- Information system (IS)
- IS applications
- IS challenges
- IS evaluation
- IS evolution
- IS security
- IS typology
- System

1.1. INFORMATION DEFINITION

The human mind's content, a systems theorist and professor of organizational transformation, can be split into three divisions which are discussed in subsections.

1.1.1. Data

Data is a fact that is independent of anything else. Data is commonly used to refer to factual facts. This can be a numerical figure or word that is used to recognize, characterize, or represent something, such as a person. The data just exists and has no importance other than that. It can exist in any shape or form, usable or unusable. The data is available in numerous schemes, including text, image, sound, and even video (Goodhue et al., 1992).

KEYWORD

Information is the source of a communication system, whether it is analog or digital.

1.1.2. Information

It combines facts and explanations. Information personifies the idea of a relationship as the relationship between cause and consequence. For instance, the temperature decreased by 15° before it started to rain. When paired with the terms Fahrenheit or Celsius, a temperature value of 100 might have distinct meanings. Additional semantics can be provided if the temperature read is contextualized, such as knowing that it is a liquid, gas, or the annual norm of 20°. Hence, information is significant data due to a relationship. Buckland defines information as "valuable data" that answers the questions "who," "what," "where," and "when " (Buckland, 1991).

1.1.3. Knowledge

Knowledge is an additional semantic level that is extracted from information through a process. This technique is sometimes factual. Mylopoulos defines it as applying data and information; knowledge answers the query "how." For example, what happens to aircraft management in cold weather? Engineers interpret cold through its effect, which is the ice that can build on an airplane, limiting aerodynamic thrust and ultimately impairing the operation of its control surfaces (Mylopoulos et al., 1990).

```
IF temperature <= 0°C THEN cold = true;
```

IF cold = true, THEN tell workers to clear ice from the aircraft.

No doubt, knowledge is a suitable assembly of information that is intended to be beneficial. Knowledge is a predetermined process and is gained by the memorization of facts. It is a pattern that offers an elevated degree of predictability about what is being stated or what will happen next (Figure 1.1).

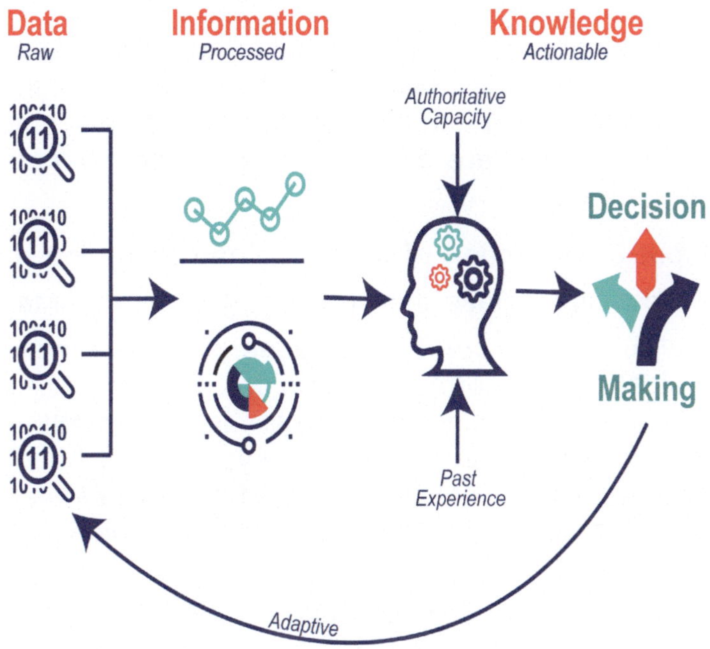

Figure 1.1. The flow from data to information to knowledge.

Source: Internet of Water, Creative Commons License.

For example, if the moisture is extremely high and the temperature decreases dramatically, the atmosphere cannot maintain the humidity long enough for rain to fall (Jurisica et al., 2004).

This knowledge has practical value but incorporating it into a scenario will suggest new knowledge. A pupil, for example, memorizes or accumulates information about the multiplication table. Because this knowledge is in the multiplication table, a learner can answer 2 × 2. Yet, when asked for 1,267 × 300, he cannot respond appropriately since he cannot consult the multiplication table. To precisely answer such a question, authentic intellectual and logical capacity is required, which exists at the next level, i.e., understanding. Most computer lingo programs (modeling, simulation, etc.) rely on stored knowledge (Nakata, 2002).

1.2. SYSTEM DEFINITION

The system is a composite "whole" in which each part communicates with at least one other part. A system's components can be actual or theoretical.

All operating systems (OSs) go along to attain a common system purpose. A system can have several subsystems and it can communicate with other systems (Arnold & Wade, 2015).

It is a group of pieces that operate together to attain a target. The system's operation is evaluated by the components themselves and their interactions. Inputs, processing mechanisms, outputs, and feedback mechanisms are all parts of a system. A system uses input to generate output.

- Input is the action of gathering and recording data.
- Processing entails the processing of inputs into outputs.
- Output is the creation of usable information, which is typically in the form of reports and paperwork. The output of one system might become the input of another system. For example, the output of a system that handles sales orders can be utilized as input to a customer's billing system. Computers generally output to printers and present to monitors.
- Finally, feedback is information from the system that is utilized to change inputs as required (Mihyeon & Amekudzi, 2005).

KEYWORD

Operating system (OS) is system software that manages computer hardware and software resources, and provides common services for computer programs.

1.3. INFORMATION SYSTEM (IS) DEFINITION

An information system (IS) is a group of interlinked components that collect, alter, store, and transmit information while also providing a feedback mechanism. The feedback mechanism aids firms in meeting their targets by boosting profitability, improving customer service, and aiding decision-making and control in enterprises (Westmark, 2004).

Businesses employ IS to enhance revenue and decrease costs (Figure 1.2).

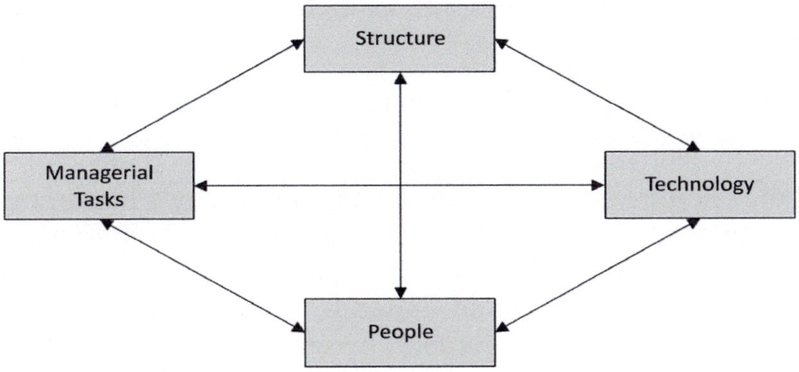

Figure 1.2. Leavitt's diamond: A socio-technical view of IS.

Source: Management Mania, Creative Commons License.

In businesses, IS are arranged around four key principles outlined by Harold Leavitt in the 1960s (Figure 1.2). The design is referred to as the "Leavitt Diamond."

- **Technology:** The hardware, software, and telecommunications equipment needed to gather, operate, store, and disperse information comprise an IS's IT (information technology). Most IS are now IT-based because contemporary IT provides well-organized strategic implementation and productive administration in organizations of all sizes (Knight et al., 2003).
- **Tasks:** These include the activities required to provide a service or product. These activities are aided by exchanging materials, information, and knowledge among the employees.
- **Person:** The people component of an IS includes all individuals connected with the system. These individuals include the managers who determine the system's objectives, the users, and the programmers.
- **Structure:** The interaction between personnel and IS components is known as the organizational structure and IS component. It includes hierarchical structures, relationships, and systems for assessing people (Boaden & Lockett, 1991).

1.4. TYPOLOGY OF INFORMATION SYSTEMS (IS)

A corporation has processes in place to maintain the various managerial levels. These systems include transaction processing systems (TPSs), management information systems (MIS), decision support systems (DSS), and specialized business intelligence (BI) systems.

Remember

Typology of Information Systems categorizes different types of information systems based on their organizational levels, functionalities, and business objectives to support organizational success.

Businesses utilize IS to ensure that reliable and updated information is always on board (Paré et al., 2015).

Professionals at different levels of a company's hierarchy have various information needs, and several types of IS categorize them based on their duties at various organizational structure levels, known as a vertical approach. Indeed, the organization is thought to be a four-tiered management pyramid (Figure 1.3) (Cram & Brohman, 2013):

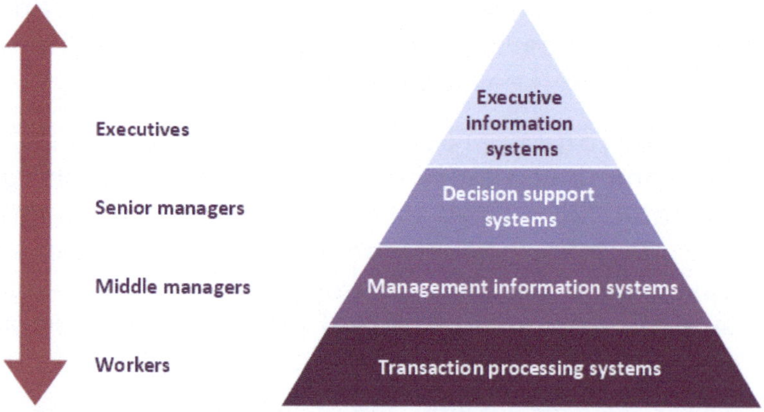

Figure 1.3. Information system types according to managerial level.

Source: Concept Draw, Creative Commons License.

- At the most basic level, employees undertake daily operations such as selling products and providing payment receipts.
- Operational management is where managers manage transaction control and deal with any problems that develop.
- Tactical management has the privilege of deciding on budgets, creating goals, spotting trends, and organizing short-term corporate activity.
- Strategic management is in charge of creating long-term goals (Jiang & Klein, 1999).

1.4.1. The Transaction Processing System (TPS)

Managers require systems that record the essential operations and activities of the firm, such as sales and product flows in a factory, at the operational level. A TPS is a computer system that conducts and records the everyday processes required for managing affairs, such as employee records, payroll, shipping items, record keeping, accounting, and treasury management (Figure 1.4).

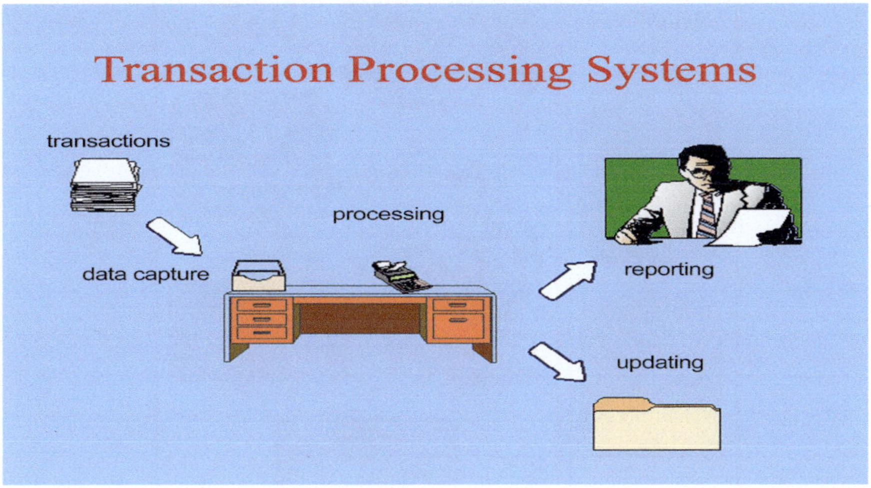

Figure 1.4. Schematic of a transaction processing system.

Source: The University of Baltimore, Creative Commons License.

The major objective of systems at this level is to answer routine inquiries and track transaction flow across the organization (Wang & Kogan, 2018).

1.4.2. Management Information Systems (MIS)

Systems are necessary for middle managers to aid with oversight, control, decision-making, and administrative tasks. Is everything operating properly? is the main query that this kind of system must address.

It gathers data from TPSs and reports on important company operations. Primary transaction data is gathered and processed, and it is shown in reports that are generated regularly (Davis, 2003).

1.4.3. Decision Support Systems (DSS)

For unexpected and rapidly changing circumstances for which there are no completely stated procedures, DSS assists in decision-making. This kind of technology aims to provide answers to issues like; How would doubling sales in December affect production schedules? If the plant timetable were to be postponed by more than six months, what would the amount of return on investment be (Mohemad et al., 2010)? (Figure 1.5).

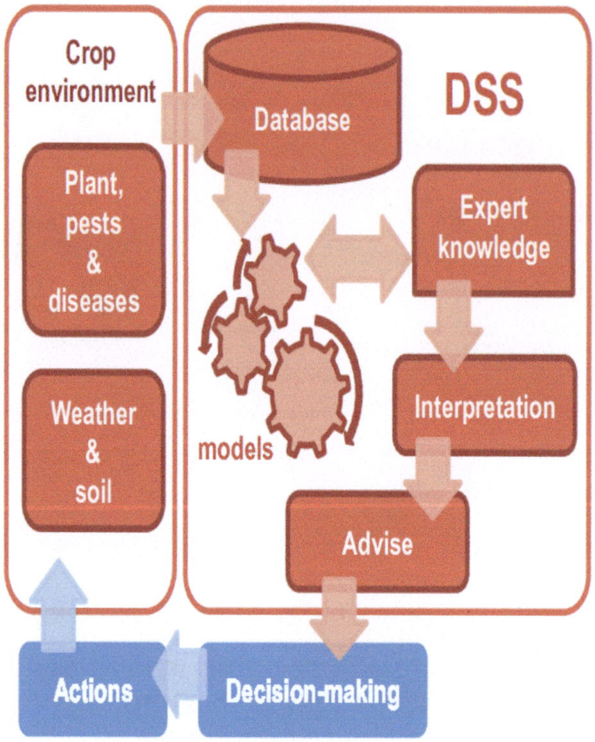

Figure 1.5. An example of an innovative decision support system (DSS) scheme for plant disease management.

Source: Vittorio Rossi et al.; Creative Commons License.

In addition to utilizing internal data from TPS and MIS systems, DSSs also make use of outside resources like stock quotes or rival product prices. These systems examine the data using a variety of models. The system may respond to queries like; which vessel should be allocated and what fill rate should be used to optimize profitability, considering the customer's delivery schedule and the cargo rate offered. What speed will allow a ship to make the most money while making timely deliveries (Eom & Kim, 2006)?

1.4.4. Executive Support System (ESS)

Executive support system (ESS) supports upper management's decision-making. There is no set process to follow to settle a particular issue at this level. Therefore, they address specific decisions that call for judgment, assessment, and a detailed picture of the business environment (Kuo, 1998).

The ESS interface is simple enough for senior managers to grasp, and it uses images and data from various sources. ESS combines aggregate data from MIS and DSS with data from the external environment, such as new taxes or competition data. ESSs generate, filter, and track important data. Because it aids in quickly integrating these top management figures, special attention is paid to how this data is presented. These systems increasingly feature BI analysis tools to pinpoint important trends and projections (Hung, 2003).

1.5. DECISION-MAKING AND INFORMATION SYSTEMS (IS)

Top management in businesses is frequently linked to decision-making. As a result of IS making data accessible at all organizational levels, employees at the operational level are now also in charge of making their own judgments.

Hence, decisions are made throughout the entire organization. Even if some of these judgments are typical, normal, and frequently made, the benefit of changing even one "small" decision may be minimal compared to the value added to the firm by optimizing hundreds of "small" decisions (Hasan et al., 2013).

Decision-making circumstances differ depending on the circumstance. While some choices have a huge impact on the organization and its future, some choices are considerably less significant and have a much smaller impact. The impact of a decision is a criterion that can distinguish between different decision scenarios and the degree of structuring in the decision. Many settings have clearly defined entrances and exits and are quite structured. For instance, it is fairly simple to calculate an employee's pay if we have the necessary input data (for instance, the employee's hourly wage rate and the number of hours worked), as well as all the relevant decision-making rules (for instance, if the employee works more than 40 hours per week, overtime must be calculated), and so on. It is rather simple to create IS that can be utilized to assist decisions in this kind of circumstance (Nowduri, 2011).

In contrast, certain decision-making circumstances are extremely complicated and unstructured, making pinpointing any particular choice rules difficult. Take the assignment to "Create a new convertible vehicle that has a good safety rating and is apparently acceptable to a somewhat large audience" as an illustration. There

Remember

A computer information system is a system that is composed of people and computers that processes or interprets information. The term is also sometimes used to simply refer to a computer system with software installed.

isn't a ready answer for this challenge. Making a design final will include a lot of trade-offs and demand much knowledge and skill (Figure 1.6).

Figure 1.6. Types of decisions according to managerial level.

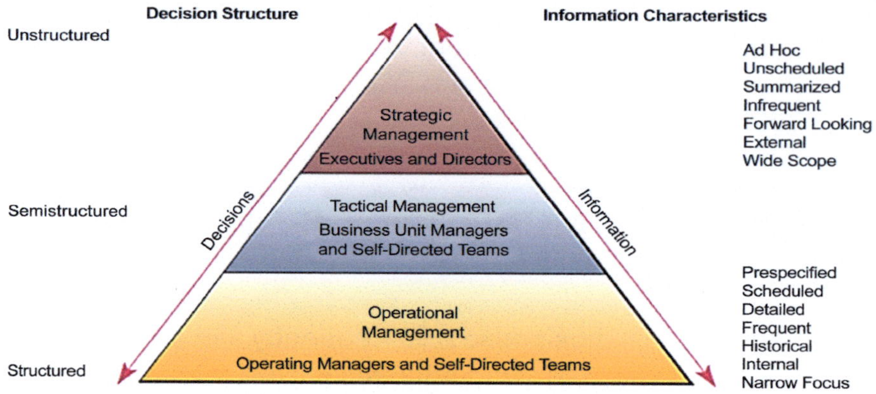

Source: Farha, Creative Commons License.

Generally, structured decisions are more frequent at lower organizational levels while unstructured issues are prevalent at higher company levels (Jankowski, 1995).

Automating a decision is made easier the more organized it is. It generally makes sense to automate the choice of an algorithm that can be utilized to make a well-planned decision and the input data to the algorithm can be gathered at a fair price.

Davenport and Harris put forth a paradigm for classifying decision automation applications. Expert systems are included in most of the systems they describe, frequently in combination with DSS and/or EIS components. Solution Configuration, Performance Optimization, Decision Segmentation, Fraud Detection, Dynamic Forecasting, and Operational Control are some of the categories they offer. As many commercial decision-making circumstances lack a lot of structure, they cannot (or should not) be automated (Kelton et al., 2010).

For instance, if the data were displayed in tabulated form, it would be difficult for users to identify patterns and linkages in the vast amounts of data.

Decision-makers who need to understand the geographic distribution of people or other resources can visualize problems using geographic information systems (GIS). GIS software connects the position information of points, lines, and areas on a map. Some GIS can model data changes and replicate the effects of those changes. GIS, for instance, could aid in determining how quickly the government would respond to events like natural disasters or help banks decide where to establish new locations or ATMs (Sabherwal & King, 1995) (Figure 1.7).

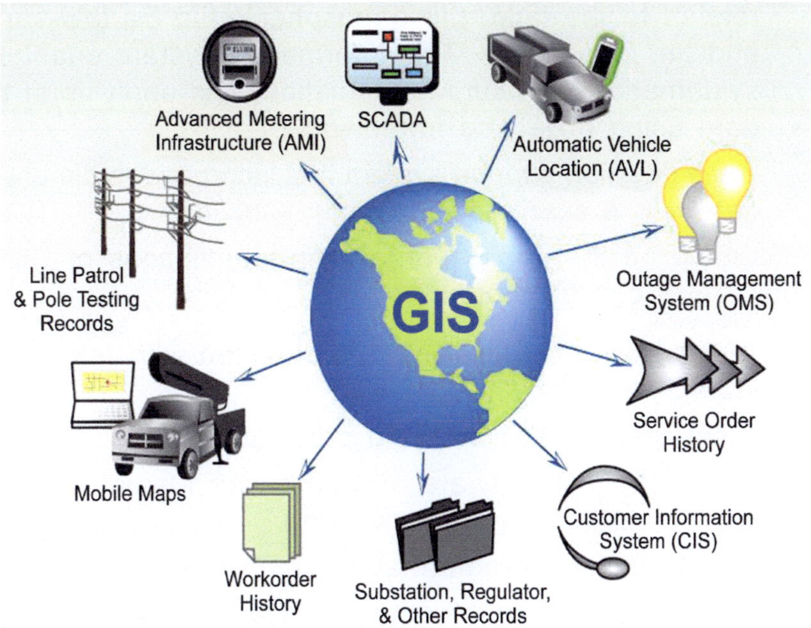

Figure 1.7. Illustration of a geographic information systems (GIS).

Source: IAS Toppers, Creative Commons License.

Geospatial (or geospatial) information includes not only objects that are present (or being planned) in particular places on the surface of the Earth but also things like traffic jams, floods, and other events like outdoor concerts.

Its breadth and level of detail characterize the information given below:

i. The location, scope, and coverage of geographic information are crucial components.

ii. Depending on the application, granularity, such as geometric information, might be clear-cut or fuzzy.

Data that demonstrates a portion of the Earth's surface, administrative and technical entities, and the outcomes of geosciences, economics, and ecological applications are all captured, stored, analyzed, and visualized using GIS (Leidner & Elam, 1993).

i. It is a database-equipped computer system that monitors the geographic distribution of things, actions, or events that are represented by points, surfaces, or lines.

ii. It is an extensive set of tools for gathering, archiving, processing, and visualizing geographical data from the actual world for use in applications (Kingston et al., 2000).

iii. It is an information system that includes all the data related to the land, the atmosphere, the Earth's surface, and the lithosphere. This information system enables the systematic collection, manipulation, and analysis of these data using a defined framework.

iv. It is a decision-support system that incorporates dimensional data into a scenario for problem-solving.

KEYWORD

Thematic analysis is a method for analyzing qualitative data that involves reading through a set of data and looking for patterns in the meaning of the data to find themes.

Depending on the application, multiple definitions of GIS can be used. A GIS can be thought of as:

i. A collection of dimensional information with retrieval and storage functionalities;

ii. A set of computational and practical tools;

iii. A collection of software and hardware elements required for processing geographical data;

iv. A specific form of information technology;

v. A treasure trove of information about geographical issues;

vi. Spatial linkages and structural recognition model (Harris & Weiner, 1998).

A GIS often offers information storage and recovery features, querying, and visualization, transformation, geometric analysis, and thematic analysis.

Moreover, geographic and spatial information is pervasive on mobile devices like cell phones, maps, satellite photos, positioning, routing services, and even 3D simulations. It is becoming popular with customers who are increasingly dependent on it.

Recent technological developments have changed traditional GIS into new types of geographic analysis tools, such as:

i. A client-server architecture was created as a result of web-based and service-oriented methodologies.

ii. The proliferation of mobile technology has caused GIS to become standard on mobile devices such as smartphones, tablets, and laptops (Malczewski, 2006).

1.6. INFORMATION SYSTEMS (IS) APPLICATIONS

Implementing business operations across the business is the primary emphasis of IS applications, which span functional areas.

Some examples of business applications are enterprise resource planning (ERP), supply chain management (SCM), e-commerce, knowledge management (KM), and BI (Farbey et al., 1995). The business application types covered here span the range of managerial tiers, from the executive suite (ESS) to the middle office (MIS and DSS) to the front lines of commerce (ERP and e-commerce).

It's worth noting that some ERP systems, such as the ubiquitous SAP, have software packages that span these diverse domains, such as SCM and customer relationship management (CRM) (Grohmann, 2004).

1.6.1. Enterprise Resource Planning (ERP)

Production, financial and accounting, sales and marketing, and human resource-related business operations can all be combined into a single software system with the help of ERPs. With the integration of a single system and a comprehensive database, information previously dispersed across many separate systems is made available to all business stakeholders (Moon, 2007) (Figure 1.8).

Figure 1.8. Schematic of enterprise resource planning and site components.

Source: Manifera, Creative Commons License.

The processes used by an ERP system, which centralizes data inside an organization, are the processes that the organization must implement. The regulations of the related business processes must be implemented when an ERP provider creates a module. ERP systems are using best management practices. In other words, as a result of integrating ERP, a business also enhances its management. Using an ERP system is a great chance for many businesses to enhance their business processes and software simultaneously. Yet, combining an ERP is a challenge. Are the ERP-integrated procedures superior to the ones that are currently in use? Additionally, what is the process of setting oneself out from the competition if integration is flourishing and the company runs similarly (Jacobs, 2007)?

KEYWORD

Bandwidth refers to the amount of information that something, like a connection to the Internet, can handle at a given time.

ERPs can be customized to fit the unique needs of each firm. ERP systems offer tools for customizing processes for firms that want to keep utilizing their existing ones or even create new ones. However, in the instance of ERP modification, businesses are responsible for upkeep (O'Leary, 2004).

Businesses will need to carefully decide whether to adopt the best practice processes integrated within the ERP system or create their own. If ERP is chosen, just those procedures necessary to maintain its competitive edge should be customized (Marnewick & Labuschagne, 2005).

1.6.2. Electronic Commerce

E-commerce is becoming a bigger part of how businesses interact with their clients. E-commerce boosts the manufacturing and marketing of goods and services and allows market expansion with less financial outlay. Nonetheless, there is a need for globally recognized criteria to guarantee the accuracy of the information and enough telecommunications bandwidth (Vladimir, 1996).

Business-to-Consumer (B2C), Business-to-Business (B2B), and Consumer-to-Consumer are the three main types of e-commerce (C2C):

- **Business-to-Consumer (B2C):** e-commerce entails selling goods and services directly to consumers. A B2C e-commerce example is Amazon, which sells music, software, and books to individual clients (Wigand, 1997).
- **Business-to-Business (B2B):** e-commerce is the exchange of goods and services among companies. B2B e-commerce

is exemplified by the website ChemConnect for purchasing and selling plastics and chemicals.

- **Consumer-to-Consumer (C2C):** e-commerce involves individuals selling to other individuals. For instance, the enormous online auction site eBay enables people to sell their goods to other customers by auctioning them, either to the winning price or through a set price (Kauffman & Walden, 2001).

1.6.3. Supply Chain Management (SCM)

Relationship management with suppliers is made feasible by IS for SCM. With the aid of these systems, suppliers, and distributors can more effectively source, produce, and distribute goods and services by sharing information on orders, production, inventory levels, and product and service delivery.

The main objective is to procure the required number of products from their vendors more quickly and affordably. These systems also increase profitability by allowing managers to plan purchases, production, and distribution efficiency (Saad et al., 2002).

Inaccurate or early information leads to supply chain anomalies such as parts shortages, unused storage spaces, delayed final product storage, or high transportation costs. For instance, manufacturers may keep a surplus of parts on hand because they are unsure of the exact dates of incoming supplier deliveries. Conversely, the producer might only order a modest quantity of raw materials if they are unsure of their exact requirements. Up to 25% of a firm's operating costs are lost due to these supply chain inefficiencies (Habib, 2011).

A producer may successfully employ a tactic known as "just in time" if they have perfect knowledge of the precise number of units of the product that buyers would demand, on what date, and its exact manufacturing rate (just-in-time strategy). Assembled goods would be sent off the assembly line without the requirement for storage as soon as raw materials were acquired precisely when production needed them (Stadtler, 2015).

Unfortunately, there are always unknowns in a supply chain because numerous occurrences, such as late delivery from suppliers, faulty components or nonconforming raw materials, or even faults in the manufacturing process, cannot be expected. Manufacturers frequently handle these variabilities by stockpiling extra materials

Did you Know?

In 1982, Keith Oliver, a consultant at Booz Allen Hamilton, introduced the term "supply chain management" to the public domain in an interview for the Financial Times. In 1983 WirtschaftsWoche in Germany published for the first time the results of an implemented and so called "Supply Chain Management project", led by Wolfgang Partsch.

than they need to deal with these contingencies and keep their clients satisfied. The safety stock serves as a safeguard against any supply chain irregularities. In addition to the cost of handling extra inventory, a poor stock fill rate increases the risk of orders being canceled (Adebayo, 2012).

1.6.4. Customer Relationship Management (CRM)

By combining all corporate operations dealing with customers' sales and marketing, CRM strives to manage client relationships. Revenue, customer happiness, and customer sincerity are to be maximized. Using the data gathered, businesses are better equipped to target, find, and keep the most lucrative clients while improving customer care for current clients and driving up sales (Rababah et al., 2011) (Figure 1.9).

Figure 1.9. Illustration of the CRM and its components.

Source: GRP Consulting, Creative Commons License.

The CRM gathers and combines customer data for the business. It compiles data, analyzes it, and then forwards the findings to other enterprise systems and client touchpoints. A point of contact (also known as a touchpoint) is a way for a vendor to engage with a client through the phone, e-mail, customer care, regular mail, a website, or even a physical store. A solo picture of the firm's customers is provided by well-designed CRM systems, which helps increase sales and provide better customer service. These platforms also give customers a unified perspective of the company regardless of how they interact with it or what they use it for (Bull, 2003).

In order to respond to queries like "What is the worth of a client to the business," "Who are the sincerest customers," "Who are the most lucrative customers," and "What products are profitable customers buying," CRM systems offer data and analytical capabilities (Peppard, 2000).

Companies just use answers to these questions to attract new clients, enhance the quality of their services, assist current clients, cater their offers to individual client preferences, and provide escalating services to keep lucrative clients (Wilson et al., 2002).

1.6.5. Knowledge Management (KM)

Since they have a higher-level understanding of designing, producing, and distributing goods and services, some businesses outperform others. This business expertise can be used to deliver long-term strategic advantages and is tough to imitate. Organizations can better manage procedures for gathering and using knowledge and expertise with the help of KM systems, or KMS. These systems gather all of the firm's pertinent knowledge and experiences and make them accessible to everyone to enhance corporate operations and decision-making (Beesley & Cooper, 2008) (Figure 1.10).

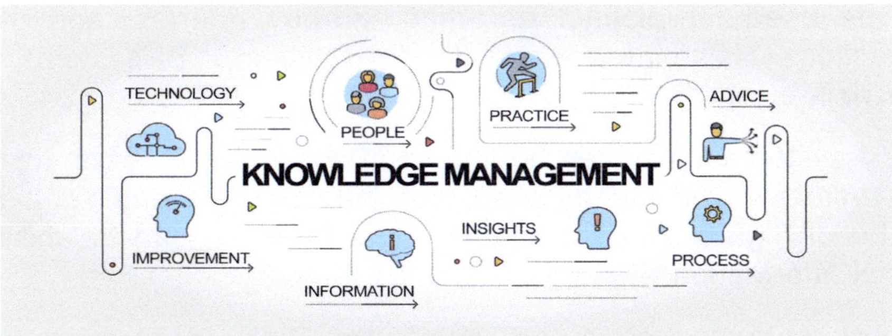

Figure 1.10. Diagram of knowledge management and its components.

Source: John Hovell, Creative Commons License.

Numerous forms of the KM systems exist, but their goals remain the same. The goals of KM are:

i. to permit communication among the workers of a firm; and
ii. to highlight the skills of a few employees and make them accessible to others.

Think about, for instance, a global consulting firm. Thousands of consultants are employed by the organization in numerous nations. Similar to a consultation team in Singapore whose client's issue has already been resolved, a consultancy team in Spain may be working to find a solution to a client's issue. It would be far more beneficial for the Spanish team to utilize the knowledge of the Singapore team rather than design the solution (McInerney, 2002).

One solution to this problem is to keep case histories in a database that employees can access from anywhere in the globe via the internet and look for cases in accordance with their individual needs. The consultants will share experiences and knowledge obtained from each other if the case documentation is of high quality.

Remember

Business intelligence combines business analytics, data mining, data visualization, data tools and infrastructure, and best practices to help organizations make more data-driven decisions.

Sadly, it is frequently challenging to encourage people to contribute significantly to the knowledge base. The work organization must change for such systems to succeed, for example, by introducing a reward system for situations that are well-captured and well-written (Liao, 2003).

1.6.6. Business Intelligence (BI)

Business intelligence (BI) is the broad term for a kind of IS created to assist decision-makers in discovering patterns and discovering connections among vast amounts of data. BI software is frequently used in tandem with sizable databases. The majority of BI systems can be used for distinct reporting, ad-hoc queries, and trend inspections. However, the specific capabilities of BI systems can vary (Isik et al., 2011).

BI systems' utility can be limited in a number of ways, just as KM systems. It is not assured that the collected and kept data will be of high quality. In addition, the database can be missing crucial information.

For instance, ice cream sales are likely to correlate with temperature; however, without temperature data, it might be challenging to find out why ice cream sales have increased or decreased. Even if data analysts are skilled with BI tools, a third issue is their lack of understanding of the operations environment of the firm.

On the other hand, a manager is an expert in the organization but cannot use BI tools. To acquire the most information from a company intelligence system, a team typically consists of a manager and a data analyst (Ramakrishnan et al., 2012).

1.7. INFORMATION SYSTEMS (IS) SECURITY

Information is not always lost when it is stolen, unlike tangible goods. An unauthorized person may upload private information that an organization owns and keep it accessible to the organization, such as a new manufacturing technique.

Information confidentiality is violated when it is disclosed to unapproved parties (Baskerville, 1993). When information integrity is no longer assured, a different sort of system failure occurs. In other words, unauthorized modifications to information occur rather than unauthorized exposure of information. If an intruder were to alter instructions, causing customers to incorrectly set up or even destroy the acquired product, the business website containing information on installing or fixing its products might suffer serious financial consequences (Kankanhalli et al., 2003).

Another sort of information failure is the refusal of access to information or the absence of information. For instance, if a doctor cannot access a patient's test results, the patient may endure needless suffering or possibly pass away. Significant sales could be lost if a business website's website was unavailable for an extended time frame.

It is possible to prevent system failure by taking the necessary action after understanding the likely causes. A wide range of factors could threaten the IS of an organization.

Since they encompass a wide range of activities, human dangers are the most challenging to control. Many pertinent subcategories serve as examples of how the level of information might differ (Karyda et al., 2005):

i. Inadvertent conduct on the part of company employees, technical support staff, and clients;
ii. An individual inside or outside the company engaging in malicious activity.

Additional threat categories include:

i. A natural occurrence, such as a storm, flood, fire, earthquake, or pandemic flu;

TIPS

To avoid financial consequences, organizations should prioritize information security by implementing measures that not only prevent unauthorized disclosure of information but also ensure its integrity to prevent unauthorized modifications.

ii. Environmental factors, including chemical spills and gas explosions;

iii. Danger from technology, including Hardware or software malfunction;

iv. An active threat—a flawed procedure that unexpectedly jeopardizes the privacy, righteousness, or accessibility of information. For instance, an operational strategy that permits application programmers to update software without testing it may cause lengthy outages (Whitman et al., 2001).

KEYWORD

Internet Device means a device that is used to connect to the Internet, including but not limited to a laptop, personal computer, and smartphone.

The many checks used to prevent a failure can be divided into the following categories:

- **Management Processes:** This define system needs, such as privacy, integrity, and information availability, and offer a variety of management controls to guarantee that these specifications are fulfilled.
- **Operational Controls:** This comprises the regular procedures involved in the delivery of information services.
- **Technical Controls:** This relates to the IT infrastructure's technical capabilities built in to enable the greater confidentiality, security, and availability of information services.

According to a commonly used Gartner research report, 80% of critical application service unavailability is directly attributable to people. Technological failures, environmental problems, or natural disasters account for the remaining 20% of all causes.

These errors frequently occur due to program alterations, such as adding new functionality or improper server or internet device configuration.

IT workers must ensure system modifications are prioritized, tested, and communicated to all parties involved (Hsu et al., 2012).

1.8. INFORMATION SYSTEMS (IS) ASSESSMENT

It is possible to quantify and value perceptible benefits. Although imperceptible advantages, such as better decision-making or more effective customer service, cannot be measured right away, they can result in quantifiable long-term gains. Several metrics can be used to assess system performance (Boudreau et al., 2001).

1.8.1. Efficiency

Efficiency is frequently described as "doing the right things." The ratio of output to input can be used to determine efficiency. In other words, a corporation is more efficient if it generates more output from a given number of resources, generates the same amount of output from a given amount of resources with a smaller expenditure, or – even better – generates more output from a given quantity of input. In other words, the business increases productivity while minimizing resource waste in order to increase efficiency (Lvovich et al., 2019).

The manager tunes the inventory system's quantity of the sold item after each sale or order. The manager must review the sales to find out which products have been restocked and sold the most frequently. This significantly minimizes the manager's time needed to handle his stock. Hence, efficiency can be calculated by dividing output by consumption (Vitali & Pernici, 2014).

KEYWORD

inventory system is a process that tracks stock, supplies and sales through an entire supply chain.

1.8.2. Effectiveness

The degree to which system objectives are met is used to gauge effectiveness. It can be computed by dividing the goals attained by the overall number of goals established.

Being effective is defined as "doing the correct thing," "doing what is essential," or "doing what is right." An organization's capacity to meet its stated aims and goals can be used to determine effectiveness. Usually, the most important business is the one that can make and execute the best judgments (Kazanjian & Green, 2002).

A firm might, for instance, develop new products or enhance existing ones based on feedback from its diverse clients and knowledge gathered from sales activities. In other words, IS assist businesses in properly understanding their clientele and satisfying their needs for goods and services. Customers will receive more individualized service from the company if individual customer data is collected (Pitt et al., 1995).

In an effort to anticipate their requirements, the management can ask customers what kinds of goods they would like to purchase in the future. The manager will buy the products the clients want and discontinue ordering unpopular things after the information is acquired.

The formulas we offer here were developed to gauge the efficacy and efficiency of IS utilization. In fact, financial metrics can be used to gauge how much of an influence an IS has on a business (Levy & Ellis, 2006).

1.8.3. Financial Measures of Managerial Performance

Management will undoubtedly want to evaluate if the IS has accomplished its goals after it is put into place. This examination is frequently difficult to complete. The company can make use of financial indicators like ROI, net present value, productivity, and other performance indicators as described in subsections (Sholihin et al., 2010).

KEYWORD

Financial ratio is a relative magnitude of two selected numerical values taken from an enterprise's financial statements.

1.8.3.1. Return on Investment

It is a financial ratio that assesses how much has been made or lost concerning the initial amount spent.

A successful return on investment for an IS suggests that the system can become more effective.

The benefit of employing return on investment is that the expenses and benefits of implementing an IS can be quantified. As a result, this statistic can be used to compare various systems and determine which ones will enable the business to operate more effectively and/or efficiently (Botchkarev et al., 2011).

1.8.3.2. Productivity

For the majority of firms, creating IS that track productivity and control is essential. The ratio of produced output to necessary input is an indicator of productivity. Higher output levels show more Productivity for a given entry level; lower output levels for a given entry-level indicate lower productivity. Productivity ratings do not depend on the number of hours worked. The number of raw materials used, the quality attained, or the turnaround time for the items can all be used as the productivity measures. The value of Productivity must only be evaluated in comparison to previous periods of Productivity, both with other firms in the same industry and according to other characteristics (Huang & Hsu, 2005).

1.8.3.3. Profit Growth

The rise in profit or the growth in realized earnings serves as another gauge of the SI value. For instance, when a mail-order business implements an order processing system, profits increase by 7% over the prior year (Colbert, 1967).

1.8.3.4. Market Share

Market share measures a product or service's sales as a percentage of the total market. Setting up a new online catalog could help the business gain, say, 20% more market share if it boosts sales (Wei & Wang, 2011).

KEYWORD

Total cost of ownership (TCO) is an estimation of the expenses associated with purchasing, deploying, using and retiring a product or piece of equipment.

1.8.3.5. Customer Satisfaction

Although measuring client happiness is challenging, several businesses use internal and external reviews to gauge the performance of their IS. Several businesses employ questionnaires and surveys to find out whether their investments have improved consumer satisfaction (Chikara & Takahashi, 1997).

1.8.3.6. Total Cost of Ownership (TCO)

The total cost of ownership (TCO) is a different metric that the Gartner Group has created to find out the value of IS. Under this method, the whole cost is divided between buying the technology, paying for technical assistance, and paying for overhead. The TCO also includes fees for training. TCO can assist in creating a precise guess of the overall expenses for a variety of systems, from compact laptops to massive mainframes (Degraeve et al., 2005).

1.9. INFORMATION SYSTEMS (IS) EVOLUTION

The development of IT prompts thought about fresh strategies that establish more flexible, more scalable structures to satisfy its agility requirements. One such strategy is the urbanization of IS (Cragg & Zinatelli, 1995).

1.9.1. The Urbanization of Information Systems (IS)

The urbanization of the company's IS is an IT discipline that entails creating the system to ensure that it is consistent with the company's goals and operations—using the opportunities provided by the state-of-the-art in IT while taking into consideration its external and internal limits (Li et al., 2015).

Town planning sets policies and a cohesive, consistent, and advanced framework to which the many stakeholders refer for any investment choice related to the administration of the IS. It is based on several concepts inspired by the urbanization of human habitat, notions that have been reused in IT to codify the IS. To lead the ongoing simplification and consistency of the IS, in other words, is to urbanize.

The difficulties of urbanization include controlling complexity, coordinating, and communicating tasks, taking organizational restrictions into account, and directing technology decisions (Boussis & Nader, 2012).

Did you Know?

According to a report by the United Nations, more than half of the world's population now lives in urban areas, and this trend towards urbanization is driving the growth and development of information systems that support urban infrastructure and services.

1.9.2. Stages of Urbanization

The stages of urbanization are discussed in subsections.

1.9.2.1. Definition of Objectives

Define the project's objectives, define the scope, and create the schedule (Zhou et al., 2015).

1.9.2.2. Existing Situation Analysis

Execute the inventory, plan the project, and deliver the deliverables. List the assets more explicitly and depict the various layers on a map:

- **Business Architecture:** Who performs what, and why? Process descriptions are made using BPMN, EPC formalisms, etc.

This step can call for using experimental techniques because it is challenging. Yet, it does enhance general comprehension and broaden the window for optimization.

- **Functional Architecture:** Which "functional block" will we need to execute the business processes? Here, we are based on a conventional zone system (exchanges, core business, reference data, production data, support activities, and management). The challenge in this step is deciding on the appropriate level of detail while maintaining consistency with corporate procedures. Nonetheless, it offers a hierarchical appearance and makes it simpler to divide the task into smaller portions (Halepoto et al., 2015).

- **Application Architecture:** How are the functionalities accomplished? This action is founded on the traditional N-Tiers classification. Yet, compared to functional architecture, it is more difficult to offer value and solutions. The foundations for realization are laid during this stage (major technological choices, etc.).
- **System Architecture:** It is based on a traditional classification into technical divisions that considers how and where the applications operate (security, storage, etc.). The link between applications and servers is not simple to establish. This step provides structure and concrete and is crucial for determining the system's cost (Mohamad et al., 2012).

1.9.2.3. Identification of the Target IS

It involves the effect on the various tiers, taking into account restrictions (human, material, etc.), creating costed scenarios, and deciding on a target by consensus (Agbola & Agunbiade, 2009).

1.9.2.4. Development of the Trajectory

How to build up an organization, how to structure and then fine-tune budgets, how to create and plan projects, how to specify the support strategy, and what are the players' contributions, duties, and obligations are all parts of the trajectory's development (Qiu et al., 2019).

A land use plan (LUP) is established after this procedure. It is a report that includes the following:

- Analyzes of the orientations selected and the arguments for the choices made;
- A description of zones, communities, and blocks;
- Target and current maps;
- Extra paperwork.

By detailing the actions and their associated costs, improvements will be made to close gaps between the current situation and the urbanization principles. Implementing the urbanization process is exceedingly difficult in practice. On the one hand, a large number of organizational actors must participate, and on the other, the analysis is extensive. Hence, it has to alter, and LUP is no longer always appropriate (Luo et al., 2018).

ACTIVITY 1.1.

Provide two examples of how information systems have improved decision-making processes in a healthcare organization and the security measures in place to protect patient information?

1.10. SUMMARY

As we wrap up this introductory chapter, we will briefly discuss its major notions:

- Data, information, and knowledge are the different levels of information.
- To accomplish a task, each part of the system communicates with another part to form an aggregated "whole."
- A collection of interconnected parts that collect, process, store, and disseminate information to aid in decision-making and control inside an organization is referred to as an information system. A socio-technical system is what an IS is.
- The purpose of information systems is to address a firm's information needs and difficulties.
- A firm has systems to support the various managerial levels.
- Choices may be tactical or strategic in nature.
- Enterprise resource planning (ERP), supply chain management (SCM), customer relationship management, knowledge management, and business intelligence are some of the several business software categories.
- A breach of information's confidentiality, integrity, and accessibility is one of the failures that may have an impact.
- Management controls, operational controls, and technical controls are some of the measures taken to prevent security failures similar to those of the IS.
- The information system's productivity, customer happiness, return on investment, efficiency, and efficacy can all be used to gauge its performance.
- Managing a system's ongoing transformation to ensure consistency is known as urbanization.
- The factors influencing whether an IS is implemented successfully or not are complicated and hotly debated by the numerous parties involved.

REVIEW QUESTIONS

1. What are some of the most important terms used in information systems, and how are they defined?
2. What is the difference between a system and an information system, and how do they relate to each other?
3. What different topologies can information systems have, and how do they affect system performance?
4. How do information systems support decision-making in organizations, and what types of decisions are typically made using these systems?
5. What are some of the most common applications of information systems, and how do they benefit organizations?

6. What are some of the biggest security concerns for information systems, and what measures can be taken to address them?
7. How can the effectiveness of different information systems be assessed, and what factors should be taken into account when conducting such assessments?

MULTIPLE CHOICE QUESTIONS

1. Which of the following terms refers to the physical components of an information system?

a. Data
b. Software
c. Hardware
d. Process

2. What is the difference between a system and an information system?

a. A system is a group of people working together, while an information system is a set of machines.
b. A system is a collection of processes, while an information system is a collection of data.
c. A system is a set of interrelated components working together to achieve a goal, while an information system is a system that collects, stores, processes, and disseminates information.
d. A system is a collection of hardware components, while an information system is a collection of software components.

3. Which of the following is NOT a type of information system topology?

a. Bus
b. Ring
c. Star
d. Square

4. How do information systems support decision-making in organizations?

a. By providing real-time data and analysis tools to support decision making
b. By automating decision making so that human intervention is not required
c. By providing recommendations and suggesting courses of action to decision-makers
d. By removing decision-makers from the decision-making process entirely

5. What are some of the most common applications of information systems?

a. Accounting and finance, human resources, marketing and sales, and supply chain management

b. Biology, physics, chemistry, and mathematics
c. Art, literature, music, and history
d. Politics, law, social sciences, and philosophy

6. **What is one of the biggest security concerns for information systems?**
   a. Inadequate data storage capacity
   b. Insufficient data processing speed
   c. Data loss due to hardware failure
   d. Unauthorized access and data breaches
7. **How can the effectiveness of different information systems be assessed?**
   a. By measuring the speed and capacity of the system's hardware components
   b. By evaluating the accuracy and completeness of the system's data
   c. By assessing the system's ability to support decision-making and business processes
   d. By analyzing the system's software components and the programming languages used to develop them

Answers to Multiple Choice Questions

1. (c); 2. (c); 3. (d); 4. (a); 5. (a); 6. (d); 7. (c)

REFERENCES

1. Adebayo, I. T., (2012). Supply chain management (SCM) practices in Nigeria today: Impact on SCM performance. *European Journal of Business and Social Sciences, 1*(6), 107–115.
2. Agbola, T., & Agunbiade, E. M., (2009). Urbanization, slum development and security of tenure: The challenges of meeting millennium development goal 7 in Metropolitan Lagos, Nigeria. *Urban Population-Environment Dynamics in the Developing World: Case Studies and Lessons Learned*, 77–106.
3. Alter, S., (2013). Work system theory: Overview of core concepts, extensions, and challenges for the future. *Journal of the Association for Information Systems*, 72.
4. Arnold, R. D., & Wade, J. P., (2015). A definition of systems thinking: A systems approach. *Procedia Computer Science, 44*, 669–678.
5. Baskerville, R., (1993). Information systems security design methods: Implications for information systems development. *ACM Computing Surveys (CSUR), 25*(4), 375–414.
6. Beesley, L. G., & Cooper, C., (2008). Defining knowledge management (KM) activities: Towards consensus. *Journal of Knowledge Management, 12*(3), 48–62.

7. Boaden, R., & Lockett, G., (1991). Information technology, information systems and information management: Definition and development. *European Journal of Information Systems, 1*(1), 23–32.

8. Botchkarev, A., Andru, P., & Chiong, R., (2011). A return on investment as a metric for evaluating information systems: Taxonomy and application. *Interdisciplinary Journal of Information, Knowledge, and Management, 6*(6), 245–269.

9. Boudreau, M. C., Gefen, D., & Straub, D. W., (2001). Validation in information systems research: A state-of-the-art assessment. *MIS Quarterly,* 1–16.

10. Boussis, A., & Nader, F., (2012). Urbanization of information systems with a service-oriented architecture according to the PRAXEME approach. *Web and Information Technologies*, 102.

11. Buckland, M. K., (1991). *Information and Information Systems* (No. 25). ABC-CLIO.

12. Bull, C., (2003). Strategic issues in customer relationship management (CRM) implementation. *Business Process Management Journal, 9*(5), 592–602.

13. Chang, K. T., (2008). *Introduction to Geographic Information Systems* (Vol. 4). Boston: McGraw-Hill.

14. Chikara, T., & Takahashi, T., (1997). Research of measuring the customer satisfaction for information systems. *Computers & Industrial Engineering, 33*(3, 4), 639–642.

15. Colbert, B. A., (1967). Pathway to profit: The management information system. *Management Services: A Magazine of Planning, Systems, and Controls, 4*(5), 3.

16. Cragg, P. B., & Zinatelli, N., (1995). The evolution of information systems in small firms. *Information & Management, 29*(1), 1–8.

17. Cram, W. A., & Brohman, M. K., (2013). Controlling information systems development: A new typology for an evolving field. *Information Systems Journal, 23*(2), 137–154.

18. Davis, G. B., (2003). Management information systems (MIS). *Encyclopedia of Computer Science,* 1070–1077.

19. Degraeve, Z., Roodhooft, F., & Van, D. B., (2005). The use of total cost of ownership for strategic procurement: A company-wide management information system. *Journal of the Operational Research Society, 56*(1), 51–59.

20. Eom, S., & Kim, E., (2006). A survey of decision support system applications (1995–2001). *Journal of the Operational Research Society, 57*, 1264–1278.

21. Farbey, B., Land, F. F., & Targett, D., (1995). A taxonomy of information systems applications: The benefits' evaluation ladder. *European Journal of Information Systems, 4*(1), 41–50.

22. Goodhue, D. L., Wybo, M. D., & Kirsch, L. J., (1992). The impact of data integration on the costs and benefits of information systems. *MIS Quarterly,* 293–311.

23. Grohmann, C. H., (2004). Morphometric analysis in geographic information systems: Applications of free software GRASS and R. *Computers & Geosciences, 30*(9, 10), 1055–1067.

24. Habib, M., (2011). Supply chain management (SCM): Theory and evolution. *Supply Chain Management-Applications and Simulations, 10*, 24573.
25. Halepoto, I. A., Sahito, A. A., Uqaili, M. A., Chowdhry, B. S., & Riaz, T., (2015). Multi-criteria assessment of smart city transformation based on SWOT analysis. In: *2015 5th National Symposium on Information Technology: Towards New Smart World (NSITNSW)* (pp. 1–6). IEEE.
26. Harris, T., & Weiner, D., (1998). Empowerment, marginalization, and "community-integrated" GIS. *Cartography and Geographic Information Systems, 25*(2), 67–76.
27. Hasan, Y., Shamsuddin, A., & Aziati, N., (2013). The impact of management information systems adoption in managerial decision making: A review. *The International Scientific Journal of Management Information Systems, 8*(4), 010–017.
28. Hsu, C., Lee, J. N., & Straub, D. W., (2012). Institutional influences on information systems security innovations. *Information Systems Research, 23*(3-part-2), 918–939.
29. Huang, H. H., & Hsu, J. S. C., (2005). An evaluation of publication productivity in information systems: 1999 to 2003. *Communications of the Association for Information Systems, 15*(1), 31.
30. Hung, S. Y., (2003). Expert versus novice use of the executive support systems: An empirical study. *Information & Management, 40*(3), 177–189.
31. Isik, O., Jones, M. C., & Sidorova, A., (2011). Business intelligence (BI) success and the role of BI capabilities. *Intelligent Systems in Accounting, Finance and Management, 18*(4), 161–176.
32. Jacobs, F. R., (2007). Enterprise resource planning (ERP)—A brief history. *Journal of Operations Management, 25*(2), 357–363.
33. Jankowski, P., (1995). Integrating geographical information systems and multiple criteria decision-making methods. *International Journal of Geographical Information Systems, 9*(3), 251–273.
34. Jiang, J. J., & Klein, G., (1999). User evaluation of information systems: By system typology. *IEEE Transactions on Systems, Man, and Cybernetics-Part A: Systems and Humans, 29*(1), 111–116.
35. Jurisica, I., Mylopoulos, J., & Yu, E., (2004). Ontologies for knowledge management: An information systems perspective. *Knowledge and Information Systems, 6*, 380–401.
36. Kankanhalli, A., Teo, H. H., Tan, B. C., & Wei, K. K., (2003). An integrative study of information systems security effectiveness. *International Journal of Information Management, 23*(2), 139–154.
37. Karyda, M., Kiountouzis, E., & Kokolakis, S., (2005). Information systems security policies: A contextual perspective. *Computers & Security, 24*(3), 246–260.
38. Kauffman, R. J., & Walden, E. A., (2001). Economics and electronic commerce: Survey and directions for research. *International Journal of Electronic Commerce, 5*(4), 5–116.

39. Kazanjian, A., & Green, C. J., (2002). Beyond effectiveness: The evaluation of information systems using a comprehensive health technology assessment framework. *Computers in Biology and Medicine, 32*(3), 165–177.

40. Kelton, A. S., Pennington, R. R., & Tuttle, B. M., (2010). The effects of information presentation format on judgment and decision making: A review of the information systems research. *Journal of Information Systems, 24*(2), 79–105.

41. Kingston, R., Carver, S., Evans, A., & Turton, I., (2000). Web-based public participation geographical information systems: An aid to local environmental decision-making. *Computers, Environment and Urban Systems, 24*(2), 109–125.

42. Knight, J. C., Strunk, E. A., & Sullivan, K. J., (2003). Towards a rigorous definition of information system survivability. In: *Proceedings DARPA Information Survivability Conference and Exposition* (Vol. 1, pp. 78–89). IEEE.

43. Kuo, F. Y., (1998). Managerial intuition and the development of executive support systems. *Decision Support Systems, 24*(2), 89–103.

44. Leidner, D. E., & Elam, J. J., (1993). Executive information systems: Their impact on executive decision making. *Journal of Management Information Systems, 10*(3), 139–155.

45. Levy, Y., & Ellis, T. J., (2006). A systems approach to conduct an effective literature review in support of information systems research. *Informing Science, 9.*

46. Li, Y., Lu, Y., Kwak, Y. H., & Dong, S., (2015). Developing a city-level multi-project management information system for Chinese urbanization. *International Journal of Project Management, 33*(3), 510–527.

47. Liao, S. H., (2003). Knowledge management technologies and applications—literature review from 1995 to 2002. *Expert Systems with Applications, 25*(2), 155–164.

48. Luo, T., Xu, M., Huang, T., Ren, X., & Bu, X., (2018). Rethinking the intensified disparity in urbanization trajectory of a Chinese coastal province and its implications. *Journal of Cleaner Production, 195*, 1523–1532.

49. Lvovich, I. Y., Lvovich, Y. E., Preobrazhenskiy, A. P., Preobrazhenskiy, Y. P., & Choporov, O. N., (2019). Modelling of information systems with increased efficiency with application of optimization-expert evaluation. In: *Journal of Physics: Conference Series* (Vol. 1399, No. 3, p. 033079). IOP Publishing.

50. Malczewski, J., (2006). GIS-based multicriteria decision analysis: A survey of the literature. *International Journal of Geographical Information Science, 20*(7), 703–726.

51. Marnewick, C., & Labuschagne, L., (2005). A conceptual model for enterprise resource planning (ERP). *Information Management & Computer Security, 13*(2), 144–155.

52. McInerney, C., (2002). Knowledge management and the dynamic nature of knowledge. *Journal of the American Society for Information Science and Technology, 53*(12), 1009–1018.

53. Mihyeon, J. C., & Amekudzi, A., (2005). Addressing sustainability in transportation systems: Definitions, indicators, and metrics. *Journal of Infrastructure Systems, 11*(1), 31–50.

54. Mohamad, M. I., Nekooie, M. A., Taherkhani, R., Saleh, A. L., & Mansur, S. A., (2012). Exploring the potential of using industrialized building system for floating urbanization by SWOT analysis. *Journal of Applied Sciences (Faisalabad), 12*(5), 486–491.

55. Mohemad, R., Hamdan, A. R., Othman, Z. A., & Noor, N. M. M., (2010). *Decision Support Systems (DSS) in Construction Tendering Processes.* arXiv preprint arXiv:1004.3260.

56. Moon, Y. B., (2007). Enterprise resource planning (ERP): A review of the literature. *International Journal of Management and Enterprise Development, 4*(3), 235–264.

57. Myers, M. D., & Avison, D., (2002). *Qualitative Research in Information Systems: A Reader* (Vol. 1, pp. 1–10). Sage.

58. Mylopoulos, J., Borgida, A., Jarke, M., & Koubarakis, M., (1990). Telos: Representing knowledge about information systems. *ACM Transactions on Information Systems (TOIS), 8*(4), 325–362.

59. Nakata, M., (2002). Indigenous knowledge and the cultural interface: Underlying issues at the intersection of knowledge and information systems. *IFLA Journal, 28*(5, 6), 281–291.

60. Nowduri, S., (2011). Management information systems and business decision making: Review, analysis, and recommendations. *Journal of Management and Marketing Research, 7*, 1.

61. O'Leary, D. E., (2004). Enterprise resource planning (ERP) systems: An empirical analysis of benefits. *Journal of Emerging Technologies in Accounting, 1*(1), 63–72.

62. Paré, G., Trudel, M. C., Jaana, M., & Kitsiou, S., (2015). Synthesizing information systems knowledge: A typology of literature reviews. *Information & Management, 52*(2), 183–199.

63. Peppard, J., (2000). Customer relationship management (CRM) in financial services. *European Management Journal, 18*(3), 312–327.

64. Pitt, L. F., Watson, R. T., & Kavan, C. B., (1995). Service quality: A measure of information systems effectiveness. *MIS Quarterly*, 173–187.

65. Qiu, L., Pan, Y., Zhu, J., Amable, G. S., & Xu, B., (2019). Integrated analysis of urbanization-triggered land use change trajectory and implications for ecological land management: A case study in Fuyang, China. *Science of the Total Environment, 660*, 209–217.

66. Rababah, K., Mohd, H., & Ibrahim, H., (2011). Customer relationship management (CRM) processes from theory to practice: The pre-implementation plan of CRM system. *International Journal of e-Education, e-Business, e-Management and e-Learning, 1*(1), 22–27.

67. Ramakrishnan, T., Jones, M. C., & Sidorova, A., (2012). Factors influencing business intelligence (BI) data collection strategies: An empirical investigation. *Decision Support Systems, 52*(2), 486–496.

68. Romney, M., Steinbart, P., Mula, J., McNamara, R., & Tonkin, T., (2012). *Accounting Information Systems Australasian Edition* (Vol. 1, pp. 1–15). Pearson Higher Education AU.
69. Saad, M., Jones, M., & James, P., (2002). A review of the progress towards the adoption of supply chain management (SCM) relationships in construction. *European Journal of Purchasing & Supply Management, 8*(3), 173–183.
70. Sabherwal, R., & King, W. R., (1995). An empirical taxonomy of the decision-making processes concerning strategic applications of information systems. *Journal of Management Information Systems, 11*(4), 177–214.
71. Sholihin, M., Pike, R., & Mangena, M., (2010). Reliance on multiple performance measures and manager performance. *Journal of Applied Accounting Research, 11*(1), 24–42.
72. Stadtler, H., (2015). Supply chain management: An overview. *Supply Chain Management and Advanced Planning: Concepts, Models, Software, and Case Studies*, 3–28.
73. Stair, R., Moisiadis, F., Genrich, R., & Reynolds, G., (2011). *Principles of Information Systems* (Vol. 1, pp. 1–5). Cengage Learning Australia.
74. Vitali, M., & Pernici, B., (2014). A survey on energy efficiency in information systems. *International Journal of Cooperative Information Systems, 23*(3), 1450001.
75. Vladimir, Z., (1996). Electronic commerce: Structures and issues. *International Journal of Electronic Commerce, 1*(1), 3–23.
76. Wang, Y., & Kogan, A., (2018). Designing confidentiality-preserving blockchain-based transaction processing systems. *International Journal of Accounting Information Systems, 30*, 1–18.
77. Wei, Y. S., & Wang, Q., (2011). Making sense of a market information system for superior performance: The roles of organizational responsiveness and innovation strategy. *Industrial Marketing Management, 40*(2), 267–277.
78. Westmark, V. R., (2004). A definition for information system survivability. In: *37th Annual Hawaii International Conference on System Sciences, 2004; Proceedings of the* (p. 10-pp). IEEE.
79. Whitman, M. E., Townsend, A. M., & Aalberts, R. J., (2001). Information systems security and the need for policy. In: *Information Security Management: Global Challenges in the New Millennium* (pp. 9–18). IGI Global.
80. Wigand, R. T., (1997). Electronic commerce: Definition, theory, and context. *The Information Society, 13*(1), 1–16.
81. Wilson, H., Daniel, E., & McDonald, M., (2002). Factors for success in customer relationship management (CRM) systems. *Journal of Marketing Management, 18*(1, 2), 193–219.
82. Zhou, J., Shen, L., Song, X., & Zhang, X., (2015). Selection and modeling sustainable urbanization indicators: A responsibility-based method. *Ecological Indicators, 56*, 87–95.

CHAPTER 2

HARDWARE AND SOFTWARE USED IN INFORMATION SYSTEMS

UNIT INTRODUCTION

The practical application of technology in today's world is meant to produce tangible commercial benefits, as seen by Turboinstitut. The use of information technology (IT) and the provision of extra processing power can boost worker productivity, open up new company prospects, and enable greater flexibility. Beginning with a definition of hardware, this chapter describes the software and hardware parts of an information system (IS) (Yakubailik et al., 2018).

Hardware describes the actual parts of a computer system that carry out its input, processing, storing, and output functions. In what way hardware can serve the aims of the company and the IS should be the primary factor taken into account by a corporation when making hardware decisions.

People should choose and arrange components while understanding the trade-offs between total system performance and cost, control, and complexity to create an effective and efficient system. Manufacturers, for instance, make an effort to match the components of an automobile to the application for which it is intended. For instance, racing automobiles need particular tires, transmissions, and engine types. When choosing a drivetrain for a racing car, it's crucial to weigh the amount of engine power that can be sent to the wheels against the transmission's cost, control, and number of gears (complexity). In a similar way, businesses set together computers that are useful, efficient, and well-suited to the jobs that need to be done (Thrall, 1999).

The IS solutions that different firms opt for can be fairly different because the business requires, and their significance varies at each organization. To make wise purchase selections, those choosing the computer hardware for their firm must thoroughly understand both current and future business requirements. Take a look at the examples below of how to use business knowledge to make significant hardware decisions:

- The NOAA is a scientific organization whose goals are to conserve and manage coastal and marine resources as well as comprehend and forecast changes in the Earth's ecosystem. To fulfill its mandate, the NOAA creates severe storm warnings and daily weather predictions. The NOAA realized it needed greater computational power and backup storage. In order to handle more precise information and sharpen the resolution of meteorological conditions, it recently updated from a single machine to two more potent computer systems. The two brand-new devices, Stratus and Cirrus, have four times as much computing power as the old one. The Cirrus computer, which is kept in a different location, also serves as a backup for the Stratus computer. The Cirrus can take over in minutes if the Stratus fails.
- With 1.5 million followers and 223 branch locations, the North Carolina State Workers' Credit Union is the 4th-largest credit union in the nation. The credit union constantly seeks ways to cut costs while enhancing client service. Consequently, it made a large investment in computer hardware to upgrade more than 3k desktop computers to modern, affordable, flexible systems.
- On Boston's picturesque waterfront sits the 426-room, four-diamond-rated Seaport Hotel. The guest house installed tablets in each room based on the findings of focus group discussions and guest feedback. These computers enable guests to access current hotel and neighborhood attraction information, obtain traffic updates and weather forecast, have unrestricted Internet, and make free local and long-distance calls online (Ganesh, 2021).

These illustrations show that selecting the appropriate computer hardware necessitates grasping how it relates to the data system and the company's requirements. Moreover, hardware goals complement the data system and the organization's present-day and upcoming demands but are subordinate to them.

Learning Objectives

At the end of this chapter, readers will be able to learn:

- Components of hardware used in information systems;
- Processing and memory devices in information systems;
- Various secondary storage, input, and output devices;
- Overview of the software used in the information systems;

- Operating systems of the software;
- Utility programs and applications of the software in information systems.

Key Terms

- Computing
- Data
- Device
- Hardware
- Memory
- Network
- Operating systems
- Software
- Storage

2.1. HARDWARE COMPONENTS

Hardware components consist of the roles of input, processing, data storage, and output (Figure 2.1).

Figure 2.1. The input-process-output concept.

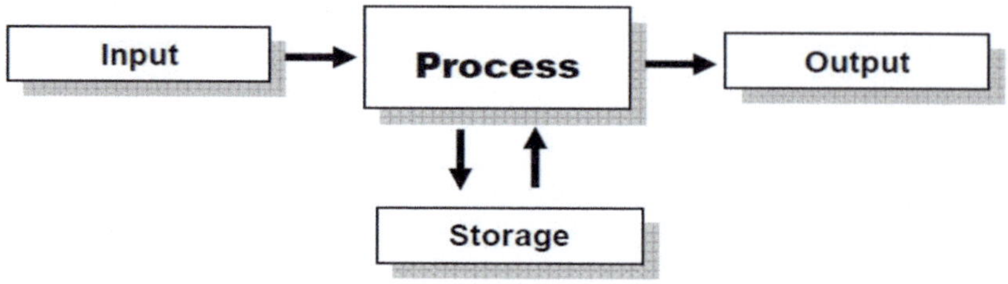

Source: General Note, Creative Commons License.

These elements consist of the CPU, peripheral devices, telecommunications equipment, secondary and primary storage devices, and devices for exchanging data (CPU). The CPU comprises the CU, the ALU (arithmetic/logic unit), and the register storage sections (Herbst et al., 1999).

A crucial component of a computer system is its capacity to process (order and manipulate) data. Processing is carried out through the interaction of one or more central processing units (CPUs) with primary storage. The ALU and the control unit are the two main components of each CPU. Mathematical calculations and logical comparisons are carried out by the ALU. The CU (control unit) coordinates data flow into and out of the ALU, primary storage, secondary storage, and different output devices while progressively accessing and decoding program instructions. The CPU and primary memory, which stores data and program instructions, are closely related.

After learning about the fundamental hardware components and how they work, readers are now prepared to look at processing capacity. These three characteristics determine a hardware device's capabilities (Saputra, 2022).

2.2. PROCESSING AND MEMORY DEVICES: POWER, SPEED, AND CAPACITY

The system unit, also known as the box or cabinet housing the CPU and memory, is where the processing-related parts are kept.

All additional computer hardware, including the keyboard and display, is either linked indirectly or directly to the system unit casing. As mentioned, organizational goals and IS objectives should come first when choosing memory and processing devices. This section looks into the traits of these significant devices (Wright et al., 2013) (Figure 2.2).

Figure 2.2. Illustration of the memory vs. storage.

Source: Christine Taylor, Creative Commons License.

2.2.1. Processing Characteristics and Functions

Organizations measure processing speed using a range of metrics because timely output and effective processing are crucial. These metrics include clock speed and the length of a machine cycle.

2.2.1.1. Clock Speed

The duty cycle, which determines how quickly each CPU generates a sequence of electronic pulses that influences machine cycle time, is produced by each CPU. The electronic cycle, or pulses, of the CPU "clock," determine how the control unit will instruct. The duration of each instruction is at least equal to the time elapsed between pulses. Each command can be carried out more quickly the more often the pulses are sent. Personal computers have clock speeds in the several GHz range or trillions of cycles per second (Raj et al., 2019).

2.2.1.2. Physical Characteristics of the CPU

Physical limitations also affect processor speed. Most CPUs are made up of groups of digital circuits that are printed on silicon chips, or chips, each of which is no larger than the tip of an eraser. The electrical current must move from point A to point B through a material (often silicon) to switch on or off a logic gate within the CPU. Lowering the distances between the spots or the medium's impedance to the electric charge will both increase the rate at which it moves between them (Belo & Marques, 2012) (Figure 2.3).

Figure 2.3. Schematic of the central processing unit (CPU).

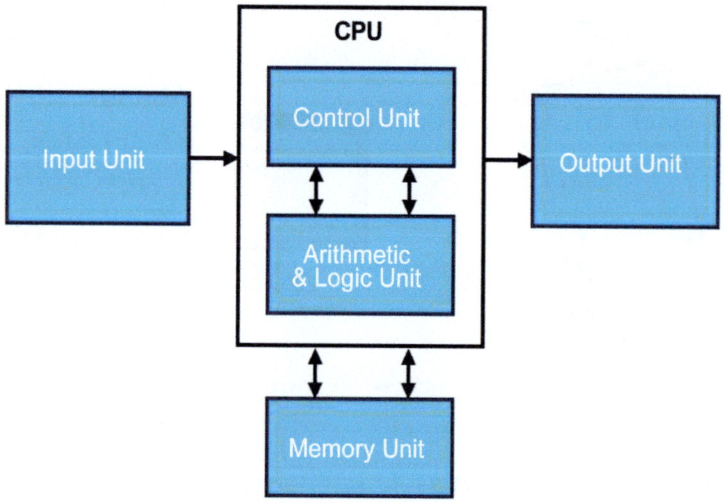

Source: Tutorials Point, Creative Commons License.

2.2.2. Memory Characteristics and Functions

Memory offers the Processor a functioning storage area for program instructions and data by being physically close by (to reduce access time). The main benefit of memory is that it gives the Processor access to data and instructions quickly.

2.2.2.1. Storage Capacity

Memory devices have thousands of transistors engraved on a silicon chip, similar to the CPU. Every circuit conducts electrical current (turned on) or does not (off). Circuit states that are both on and off are used to store data in memory. A character, such as a letter A, is typically represented by 8 bits. A byte is formed by eight bits (B). The most common unit of measurement for storage space is the byte, with one byte standing in for one bit of data. With much more than 126 million objects and 530 kilometers of bookcases, the Library of Congress' collection would need nearly 20 terabytes of digital storage data. Units for assessing computer storage capacity are listed in Table 2.1.

2.2.2.2. Types of Memory

There are numerous types of memory. Random access memory can temporarily store instructions or data (RAM). RAM is transient and brittle; if the current is interrupted or switched off, RAM transistors lose their contents. RAM modules are directly located on the computer's main circuit board or in peripheral cards connecting to the main circuit board. Millions of switches sensitive to electric current shifts make up these RAM chips (Mello et al., 2005). The simultaneous use of many processors to carry out the same activity to quickly get results.

Table 2.1. Comparison for Various Forms of Data Storage

Name	Abbreviation	Number of Bytes
Byte	B	1
Kilobyte	KB	2^{10} or approximately 1,024 bytes
Megabyte	MB	2^{20} or 1,024 kilobytes (about 1 million)
Gigabyte	GB	2^{30} or 1,024 megabytes (about 1 billion)
Terabyte	TB	2^{40} or 1,024 gigabytes (about 1 trillion)
Petabyte	PB	2^{50} or 1,024 terabytes (about 1 quadrillion)
Exabyte	EB	2^{60} or 1,024 petabytes (about 1 quintillion)

Source: Office Depot, Creative Commons License.

KEYWORD

Read-only memory (ROM) is a type of non-volatile memory used in computers and other electronic devices.

Another type of memory is read-only memory (ROM), which is typically nonvolatile. Because the circuit states in ROM are fixed, its information is not discarded if the power is turned off. For information and instructions that don't change over time, such as programs and data from the computer's maker and the commands that tell the computer how to start up when the power is switched on, ROM offers eternal storage.

2.2.3. Multiprocessing

Multiprocessing is the correlation method of two or more instructions, and it takes many different forms.

2.2.3.1. Multicore Microprocessor

A multicore microprocessor integrates two or more independent engines into a single computer to share the workload and increase processing capacity. When compared to its two-lane predecessor, a dual-core processor can accommodate up to twice as many vehicles without requiring each car to travel at twice the speed. A dual-core CPU also makes it possible to do two things simultaneously: play a game and burn a CD. In the market for multicore processors, Intel, AMD, and IBM are vying for first place (Hayashi et al., 2020) (Figure 2.4).

Figure 2.4. Architecture of the multiprocess microprocessor.

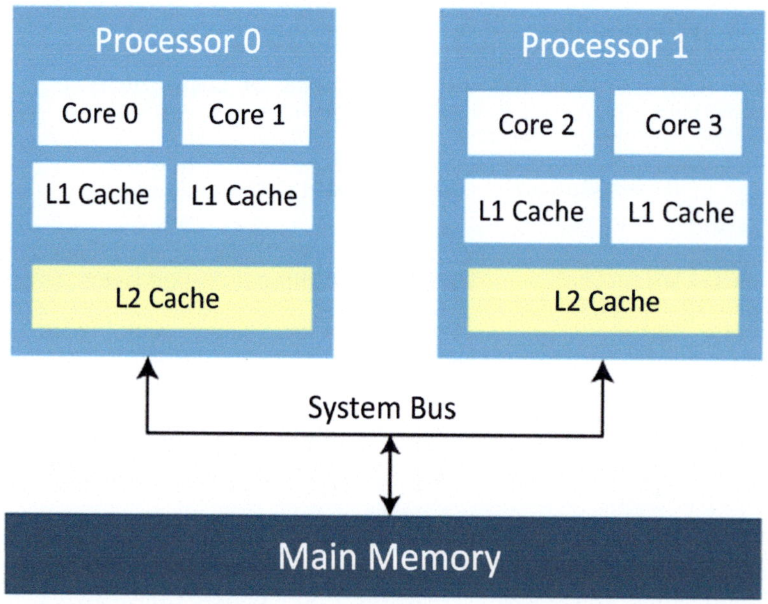

Source: Java Point, Creative Commons License.

By releasing new quad-core chips, Intel and AMD have enhanced dual processors. Four CPUs are combined onto a single chip for the Intel Core i7, allowing them to share an L3 cache. The AMD's quad-core, 3.4 GHz Phenom II X4 Black Edition CPU was just released. Even though the AMD clock speed is somewhat quicker than the Intel Core i7, there is little point in comparing the clock speeds of two CPUs with distinct designs. The CPU must be integrated with the main memory and the other computer components for the system to function. Based on the outcomes of numerous computer benchmarks, the Intel Core i7 processor beats out the AMD Phenom processor. Eight processor cores were featured in the Power7 CPU from IBM. The chip offers a 32-core processor because each core can do four jobs or threads. Electric utilities can process more than 85 million reads per day in a smart grid thanks to this potent processor, up from less than 1 million reads per day in a traditional [power] system (Arvanitis & Krystalli, 2021).

Did you Know?

The global parallel computing market size was valued at USD 9.79 billion in 2020 and is expected to grow at a CAGR of 14.6% from 2021 to 2028, driven by the increasing demand for efficient computing systems in data-intensive applications such as AI, machine learning, and big data analytics.

2.2.3.2. Parallel Computing

Through links that enable many processors to run concurrently or in parallel, parallel processing, another type of multiprocessing, speeds up processing.

The most common parallel computing applications are modeling, simulation, and data analysis. In medicine, parallel computing is utilized to create new imaging systems that can do ultrasound scans more quickly and accurately, allowing clinicians to diagnose patients more accurately. Engineers can build virtual models of new items instead of physical ones, test how they function using parallel computing and then adjust design and material choices as necessary. By simulating the appearance and motion of new designs on digital models, clothes designers can cut the production time for a seasonal apparel collection from six months to just over one month (Udhayakumar & Murugaboopathi, 2020) (Figure 2.5).

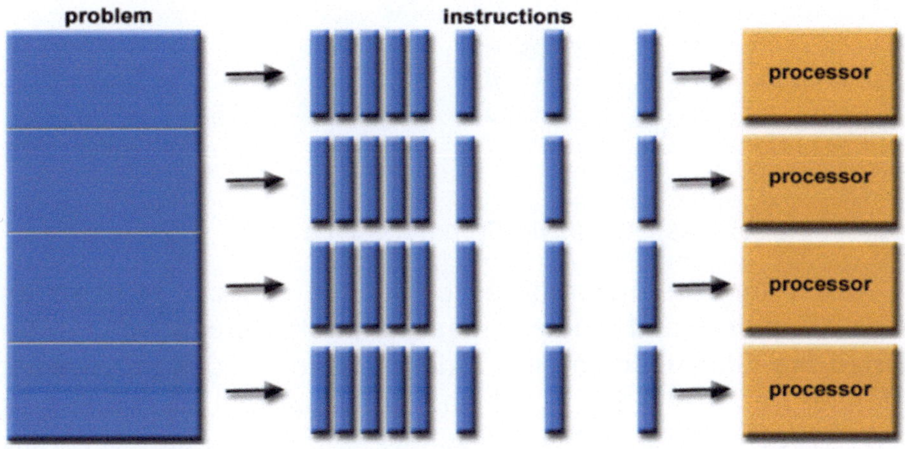

Figure 2.5. Illustration of the parallel computing.

Source: Mobile CSP, Creative Commons License.

2.2.3.3. Grid Computing

Network virtualization entails using several computers, frequently owned by numerous people or organizations, to collaborate to address a common issue. One inexpensive method for parallel processing is called grid computing. The grid comprises several computers—possibly thousands—working together to tackle massive similar processing issues. A central server that serves as the grid leader and network monitor is essential to the success of distributed systems. The computing effort is broken down into smaller tasks by the managing server, which then distributes the work to computers on the grid that (at least momentarily) have the extra processing power. The central server also keeps track of the processing, and if one of the grid members fails to finish a subtask, it will restart or redistribute the task. Once each subtask is completed, the controlling server combines the results, then moves on to the next task until the entire job is finished (Kotenko et al., 2015) (Figure 2.6).

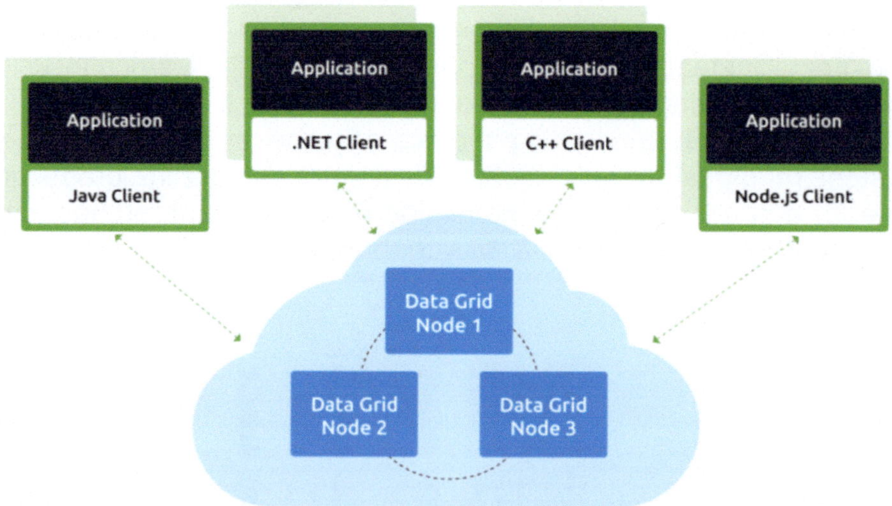

Figure 2.6. Schematic of the grid computing.

Source: Hazel Cast, Creative Commons License.

To tap into the underutilized computing capacity of home and office computers and create a massive public computing grid, IBM started the Global Community Grid initiative in 2004. To evaluate potential treatments for novel and drug-resistant flu viruses like H1N1, researchers at the University of Texas Medical Branch took advantage of the computing capacity of more than 1 million connected devices. According to Stan Watowich, the principal investigator at UTMB, we anticipate identifying novel influenza medication candidates in less than a month. We can focus more intently and swiftly transition from computer calculations to lab testing (Kim & Chung, 2003).

2.3. SECONDARY STORAGE, INPUT, AND OUTPUT DEVICES

As they can see, memory plays a significant role in determining the total power of a computer system. The data and commands the CPU needs to process can only be stored in a small amount of memory. Moreover, more permanent storage of data, commands, and information is required by computers than is possible with main memory. This is accomplished by secondary storage, often known as persistent storage (Lindstrom & Vitter, 1985).

Secondary storage has more capacity, is more cost-effective, and is nonvolatile compared to memory. Most secondary storage options are significantly cheaper than memory. However, secondary storage is much slower than memory due to the electromechanical operations needed. Understanding the essential characteristics of secondary storage media and devices—access method, capacity, and portability—is necessary for making the right choice (Lian et al., 2022).

KEYWORD

Magnetic disk is a storage device that uses a magnetization process to write, rewrite and access data.

2.3.1. Secondary Storage Devices

Magnetic tapes, magnetic discs, and optical discs are the most widely used secondary storage media. While some of these media, like magnetic tape, only permit sequential access, others, like optical and magnetic discs, allow direct and consecutive access.

2.3.1.1. Magnetic Tapes

Magnetic tape is a common secondary storage medium. Magnetic portions of the tape represent bits. A linked list storage media is magnetic tape. Magnetic tape is typically less expensive than disc storage, despite slower access. It is frequently used to back up hard drives and store data off-site for disaster recovery. As technology advances, tape storage systems will have more extensive storage and faster transfer rates. Since dozens of tape cartridges may now be housed in a compact space, large, massive tape drives have indeed been replaced by much smaller tape cartridge devices that are just a few millimeters in diameter. These newer devices require significantly less floor space (Coffman & Hofri, 1986).

2.3.1.2. Magnetic Disks

Iron oxide also coats magnetic discs, which can be Mylar film or thin metal platters. Magnetic discs use tiny, magnetized patches to represent bits, similar to magnetic tape. Companies that must respond promptly to client demands employ magnetic discs and direct access storage technologies that enable swift data retrieval. If the data is saved on a direct access storage device, a manager can quickly determine a customer's credit history or the number of seats left on a specific aircraft (Chen et al., 1994) (Figure 2.7).

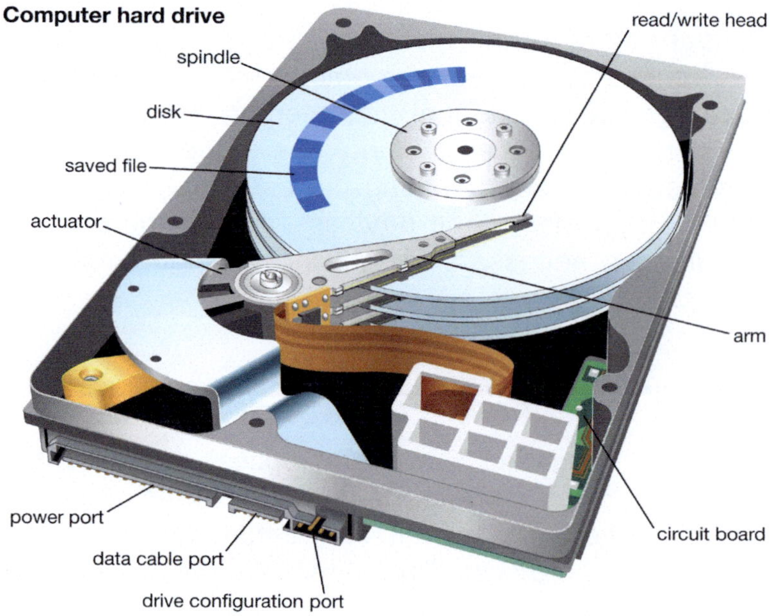

Figure 2.7. Schematic of the hard disk and its components.

Source: Brittanica, Creative Commons License.

2.3.1.3. RAID

Data storage requirements for businesses are growing quickly. Several hundreds of gigabytes are frequently used in modern storage setups. The loss of vital business data can force a company out of business; hence posting the company's data online entails a significant business risk. A disc storage device's most important mechanical parts—the disc drives, the fans, and other input/output devices—can break, which is a source of concern (Coffman & Hofri,

1986). Nowadays, businesses need their data storage systems to be robust, which means they can keep working even if one or more crucial parts fail with little to no performance loss. RAID is a technique for storing data so that the lost data on that drive can be restored during a hard drive failure. In this method, data is distributed uniformly over multiple physical disc drives utilizing the redundant storage method of stripping. For its film production clients and TV, Point360, a post-production firm with headquarters in Burbank, California, edits, masters, reformats, and archives video data. The company adopted a RAID storage solution to increase security and manage the growing storage needs of high-definition video and complex visual effect rendering (McKusick, 1996).

TIPS

Magnetic tapes can be cost-effective for infrequently accessed data, but it's crucial to consider tape durability, longevity, and environmental conditions. Regular testing and maintenance are also recommended to prevent data loss.

2.3.1.4. Virtual Tape

A storage method known as virtual tape makes less often used data appear to be saved on tape cartridges, even though some portions may be kept on faster hard discs. Virtual tape server is another name for software with a data backup system. A comprehensive storage-management system that shifts data to slower but less expensive forms of storage media when individuals utilize the data less frequently can be used with virtual tape. Data access times, the total cost of ownership (TCO), and the floor area required by tape operations can all be decreased thanks to virtual tape technology. More than 400 TB of data related to running this 581-bed academic health hospital are maintained by the IS department at Boston Medical Center. The firm implemented a virtual tape management system to meet stringent regulatory standards, keep data storage expenses in check, and handle a 50% annual data growth rate (Wibawa, 2015).

2.3.1.5. SAN

As seen in Figure 2.8, a SAN (storage area network) connects everything through networks, computer servers, and distributed storage devices. High-speed communications channels are frequently utilized to speed up the storage and retrieval of data. Even though SAN technology is still relatively new, many businesses successfully and effectively store crucial data on it. Almost 7,13,000 Australians subscribe to Austar, a significant pay-TV company that offers digital satellite services. To keep track of every transaction and client interaction, the organization uses a 60-terabyte SAN. According to CIO Dean Walters, all of the information is valuable. We gather much intelligence about our customers' attitudes, openness, and moods through those touch points. We discover crucial information about customers' inclination to stop using the service (Grossman & Silverman, 1973).

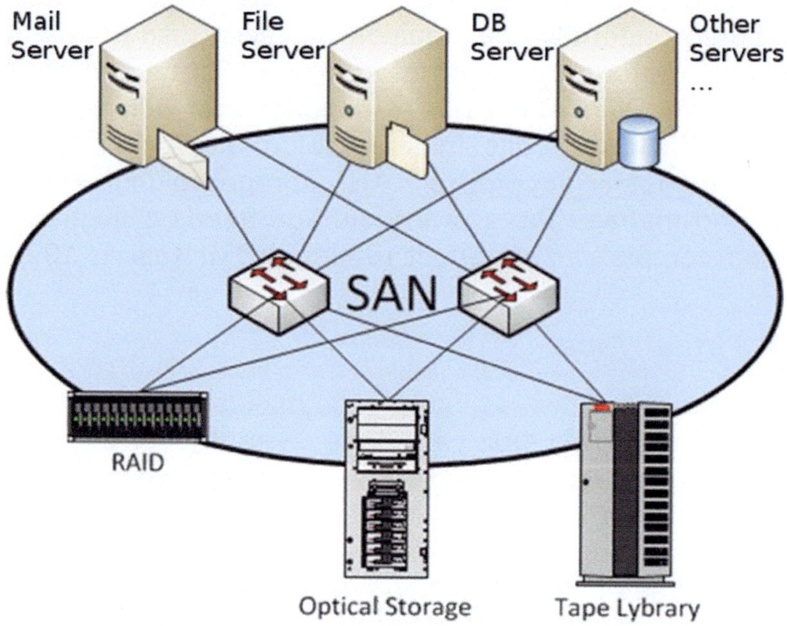

Figure 2.8. Illustration of the storage area network (SAN).

Source: Fiktoria, Creative Commons License.

2.3.1.6. Optical Discs

CD-ROM (compact disc read-only memory) has a 740 MB data storage capacity and is a standard optical disc. A CD-ROM disc is "read-only," meaning it cannot be changed once information is recorded. A tool that can collect data on a disk drive is a CD burner, sometimes a CD recorder. The two most popular types of systems that can print CDs, either once or frequently (CD-RW), are CD-recordable (CD-R) and CD-rewritable (CD-RW) (in the case of CD-RW). CD-RW technology makes data backup on CDs possible for PC users (Grossman & Silverman, 1973).

2.3.1.7. Digital Video Disc (DVD)

A DVD (digital video disc) is a five-inch-diameter disc that resembles a CD-ROM and can hold up to several gigabytes of data or around 135 minutes of digital video (see Figure 2.9). This storage medium is frequently used for movies, video games, and software packages (Christodoulakis, 1984).

Figure 2.9. Image of an optical disk drive.

Source: Tikhomirov Sergey, Creative Commons License.

DVDs have replaced digital audio and rewritable CDs as the popular format for exchanging movies and photographs. A single-sided DVD has a capacity of 4.7 GB, and double-sided DVDs have a total of 9.4 GB, whereas a CD can contain roughly 740 MB of data. Recons can be created on record-only discs or rewritable discs. Rewritable DVD formats are not all interchangeable with one another.

At least three times as much data can be stored on a Blu-ray high-definition video disc than on a DVD. Although this new format may also store computer data, it is mainly used in home entertainment systems to store high-definition video (Arato & Benczur, 1981).

2.3.1.8. Solid-State Secondary Storage Devices

As opposed to optical media, memory chips are where data is kept in solid-state storage (SSD) devices. These memory chips use less power than magnetic data storage devices and offer faster data access. Moreover, SSDs are less brittle than hard disc drives since they contain fewer moving parts. The SSD is recommended for portable laptops because of all these features. The high cost per gigabyte of data storage and the limited capacity of SSDs currently are two drawbacks. As a constantly evolving technology, SSDs will become more affordable and capable (McKellar & Wong, 1978).

One illustration of a frequently used SSD is a USB flash drive. Look at Figure 2.10. External USB flash drives that may be removed and written to are called flash drives. Most are less than an ounce in weight and have storage capacities ranging from 1 GB to 64 GB. Based on a technology known as X4, which stores 4 bits of data in each of the millions of small storage components on a chip called cells, SanDisk creates flash drives with storage capacities of up to 64 GB.

Figure 2.10. Image of a USB flash drive.

Source: SANDISK, Creative Commons License.

With roughly 100 people, Marketing Architects offers its clients radio, television, and telephone marketing programs. The company uses SSD technology to store data to deliver faster response times at lower storage costs than other alternatives (Yue & Wong, 1973).

Secondary storage generally requires more capacity, increased portability, and direct access techniques. While choosing a particular form of storage, the demands of both the business and the individual users should be considered. In general, organizational performance and efficiency can be improved by quickly accessing vast amounts of data and information (Omiecinski et al., 1994).

2.3.2. Input Devices

Input and output devices are typically how people interact with computers for the first time. These gadgets are the system's entry points, allowing them to give the computer information and commands and request output. The computer's UI comprises hardware and software that let them communicate with a computer system, including input and output devices (Jacob, 1996).

While choosing input and output devices, an organization should consider its business objectives, much like determining other computer system components. For instance, several restaurant chains employ computerized terminals or handheld input devices that enable servers to enter orders quickly and correctly. The ability to track stock and promote it to customers has also reduced costs (Jacob et al., 1994). Hundreds of devices can be used for data input, from more general-purpose user input to those with unique purposes for capturing detailed data.

2.3.2.1. Personal Computer Input Devices

A keypad and a computer pointing device are the most popular input devices to enter data, including characters, text, and simple commands. Modern keyboards that are faster, more customizable, and more pleasant are being created by several companies. These keyboards, like the split keyboard, made famous by Microsoft and others, are intended to prevent wrist and hand problems brought on by prolonged keyboard use. They may type text with the keys and draw on the touchpad with the same keyboard (Card et al., 1991) (Figure 2.11).

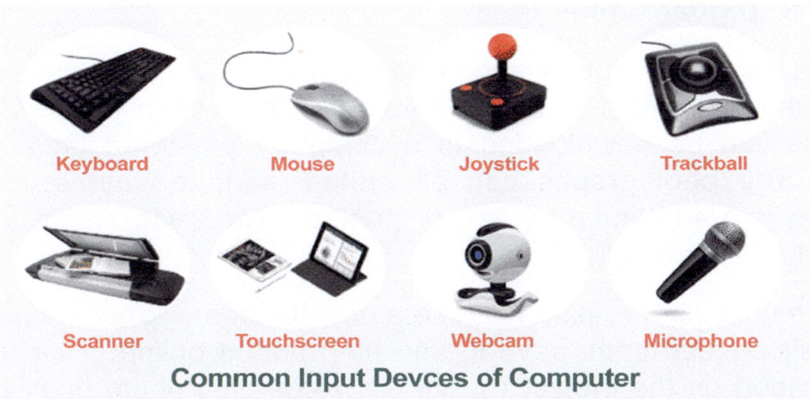

Figure 2.11. Schematic of the personal computer input devices.

Source: Tutorials Mate, Creative Commons License.

Icons, menus, and instructions on the screen are selected using the pointing device to point at and click them. In response, the computer performs various tasks, like data entry into the computer system.

2.3.2.2. Speech-Recognition Technology

With voice-recognition technology, a computer with a microphone or other speech-input device may understand human speech as a substitute for typing in data or receiving directions. Most basic systems have a minimal word vocabulary or need to train to identify their speech patterns.

Modern systems don't require users to break their voices into distinct words to recognize continuous speech. The military and the government use highly sophisticated methods to decipher voices they have never heard before and comprehend various languages (MacKenzie et al., 1991).

Businesses that must deal with consumers regularly are eager to lower their support expenses when enhancing the quality of their services. For instance, SBI Funds Management is an Indian investment management company serving over 5.8 million clients.

The company implemented a speech-recognition technology to replace all the operations that live agents formerly offered. Customers will not need to wait for live agents to become accessible, saving money in addition to that gained from lowering the number of employees. Users communicate with the system using their voice rather than touching the phone's keypad (Mackinlay et al., 1990).

Remember

Digital and digital movie cameras share an optical system, typically using a lens with a variable diaphragm to focus light onto an image pickup device.[4] The diaphragm and shutter admit a controlled amount of light to the image, just as with film, but the image pickup device is electronic rather than chemical.

2.3.2.3. Digital Cameras

Digital cameras capture and store pictures or videos. Images are electronically saved in the camera when they snap pictures. The photos can be downloaded to a computer or stored on a flash card. The photographs can be edited, sent to another place, copied into another program, or printed after being saved to the computer's hard drive.

They could, for instance, use a digital camera to take a picture of their project team, save it, and then post it online or include it in a report on the project's progress. Regarding photo quality and features like zoom, flash, exposure adjustments, special effects, and even video capture, digital cameras have surpassed film cameras used by photographers. They can enhance the image with sound and calligraphy using the appropriate software (Kessler et al., 1995) (Figure 2.12).

Figure 2.12. Illustration of the various types of digital cameras.

Source: Ashley Maas, Creative Commons License.

Full-featured, high-resolution digital camera models are available from Nikon, Canon, Pentax, Casio, Olympus, Sony, Panasonic, and other camera manufacturers for less than $250. For less than $150, some manufacturers offer compact camcorders (Ballagas et al., 2006).

2.3.2.4. Touch-Sensitive Screens

Modern screen technology enables the displays to serve as input and output devices. The software can be run, or a computer activity triggered by touching specific areas of a sensitive screen. Gesture screens are regularly used at gas stations so that clients can choose the grade of gas they want and request an invoice, at fast-food restaurants so that order takers can enter customers' needs, and at hotel information desks so that visitors can ask questions about nearby restaurants and bars, and at theme parks so that visitors can get directions. Also, they are utilized in airport and department store kiosks (Zhai, 1998).

2.3.2.5. Optical Data Readers

Users can scan papers using a specialized scanner called an optical signal reader. OMR (visual mark recognition) and OCR (optical character recognition) are the two types of OCR (optical data readers). When standardized tests use pens to fill in the boxes on OMR paper, commonly known as a "mark sense form," they employ OMR scanners for test marking and other uses. OMR systems, which are used in standardized exams like the GMAT and SAT, are being taken into consideration as a way to record electors' decisions on election day. In contrast, most OCR readers scan and identify characters using reflected light. OCR readers use specialized software to turn typewritten or handwritten documents into electronic data. This information can be shared, altered, and sent to hundreds of people over computer networks after being entered (Wanderley & Orio, 2002).

According to Missouri law, police officers must record information about each traffic stop and report it to the State Attorney General. Using OMR technology, the St. Peters Police Department decided to abide by this. The department created a traffic stop data card, which the officer fills out during each traffic stop, to record the necessary information. The cards are returned and scanned at the end of each shift. The findings are condensed into two formats: an overview report to give the state attorney general the information they need and a more in-depth examination using graphs and charts to ensure the agency is serving the requirements of the people (Kim et al., 2005).

TIPS

MICR lines help facilitate automatic check-clearing when banks send their checks to central processing systems at the end of the day. They are designed to be easily read by people as well, so that check information can be communicated easily.

2.3.2.6. Magnetic Ink Character Recognition (MICR) Devices

Cheques, credit applications, financial records, and other documents in the 1950s overran the banking industry. The industry created magnetic ink character recognition (MICR), a technique for quickly reading this data, to address this overflow and process documents more quickly. A unique magnetic ink is used to write MICR data on the bottom of a check or other form to aid special and routine inspections. This ink has a special character set that people and computers can read when printing data (Wood et al., 2005).

2.3.2.7. Pen Input Devices

Users can execute a command or have the computer perform a task by touching a touch screen with a pen input device. Users can also enter handwritten notes and draw pictures of items and figures. Pen input necessitates specialized hardware and software. Text can be generated from screenwriting using handwriting recognition software. With the help of its hardware partners, Microsoft, with its Tablet PC, can convert handwriting into textual content and store the "digital ink" exactly how it is written. E-mails may be written and delivered using a pen, and users can also annotate Word documents, PowerPoint, and even manual charts on paper. Then, such information can be moved, underlined, searched for, and turned into text. This interface has the potential to be widely used once it is developed. If using a keyboard makes them uncomfortable, pen input may be appealing. The success of pen input hinges on how well and inexpensively handwriting can be read and converted into digital form (Lapointe et al., 2011).

2.3.2.8. Radio Frequency Identification (RFID)

Using a mobile device called a tag, an RFID (radio frequency identification) system transmits data that an RFID reader reads and processes following the requirements of an information system (IS) program. One common use for RFID is adding a microchip to retail products and installing readers inside stores that track the stock on the shelves to identify when frames need replenishment. Remember that the RFID tag chip's EPROM (erasable programmable read-only memory) component stores information about the object to which the tag is connected. Its memory can be updated by a radio-frequency signal as the item's status changes. The information provided by the tag may include identity, geographic data, or specifics about the tagged item, such as the item's date of manufacture, retail price, color, or purchase date (Taveira & Choi, 2009).

> **KEYWORD**
>
> **EPROM (erasable programmable read-only memory)** is memory that does not lose its data when the power supply is cut off.

RFID technology is used at the Newmount Leeville Gold Mine in Nevada to monitor workers, machinery, and vehicles. For the corporation to track where miners are operating and promptly locate them in the event of an accident, RFID tags are installed in the miners' cap lamps and fastened to trucks and equipment. These tags broadcast real-time position data (Tsukada & Yasumura, 2001).

2.3.3. Output Devices

Computer systems deliver information to decision-makers at all organizational levels so they may address a business issue or seize a business opportunity. Moreover, the output of one computer system might serve as the input for another. This output's chosen format could be digital, audio, or visually appealing. Output devices deliver the appropriate information to the appropriate person in the suitable design at the proper time, regardless of the content or form of the output (Jacob et al., 1993).

2.3.3.1. Display Monitors

The outputs from the computer are displayed on a display monitor. Early monitors were called CRTs since they displayed images using a cathode-ray tube. One or more beam of electrons is produced by the cathode ray tubes. A marker on the screen, known as a pixel, illuminates when the beams hit a phosphorescent substance (phosphor) deposited on the inner surface of the screen. A pixel is a small area of color or light that appears on a touchscreen display. There are just two states it can be in: on or off. As the phosphor begins to dim, the beam of electrons sweeps across the screen to strike it, relighting it (Eisenberg, 2002) (Figure 2.13).

Figure 2.13. Image of display monitor.

Source: Tony Hoffman, Creative Commons License.

Many competent cells (pixels) made of electrodes and neon and xenon gases that are electrically converted into plasma (electrically charged atoms and negatively charged particles) in a plasma display are used to produce the display's light. Using the data in the video feed, the plasma display illuminates the pixels to create an image. Red, green, and blue light make up each pixel in a display. The intensity of the lights is adjusted on the plasma display to provide a broad spectrum of colors. Plasma displays can create high-quality images with great resolution and accurate color representation (Burdea et al., 1996).

Liquid crystals, an organic substance that resembles oil and is sandwiched between two polarizers, are used in LCDs to create characters and graphic pictures on a backlit screen. Because they are brighter and flicker-free and don't release the kind of radiation that some CRT users are concerned about, these displays are friendlier on their eyes than CRTs. Also, compared to CRT monitors of the same size, LCD monitors are smaller and consume less than half the energy (Dicarlo & Banajee, 2000).

A layer of organic material is sandwiched between two conductors in an organic light-emitting diode (OLED), which is then layered between a crystal top plate and a glass bottom plate. Bright, electro-luminescent light is created directly from the organic substance when an electric charge is introduced to the two conductors. OLEDs can produce more precise and vibrant colors than CRTs and LCDs, and because they do not need a backlight, their displays can be flexible and only half as thick as LCDs. The fact that OLEDs do not crack when dropped is another significant benefit. By layering transparent OLED films over a conventional LCD panel, OLED technology may also produce 3D video displays that give the illusion of depth without using 3D glasses or laser optics. Both 2D and 3D content can be displayed on the iZ3D monitor. To coincide with the release of James Cameron's film Avatar, the manufacturer sold a 22-inch version of the monitor for $300 (Eisenberg et al., 2003).

Power consumption is crucial when choosing which type of monitor to buy because most users leave their laptops on for hours. LCD monitors typically use between 35% and 50% less electricity than plasma screens, though this varies from model to model (Ware, 1996). Even less power is used by 18 OLED monitors than by LCD monitors (Ware, 1996).

KEYWORD

Organic light-emitting diode is a light-emitting diode in which the emissive electroluminescent layer is a film of organic compound that emits light in response to an electric current.

2.3.3.2. Printers and Plotters

Physical copies are printed on paper using a printer. For forms like blank check forms, invoicing forms, and so forth, printers with different Laser printers are usually faster than inkjet printers and can handle the larger volume. Modern printers enable companies to provide customized printed output for each customer utilizing standard paper and full-color data input (Balasubramanian & Dalal, 1997).

The quantity of sheets printed per minute is often used to gauge a printer's speed (ppm). The quality or resolution of a printer's output, like that of a display screen, is determined by the amount of dots produced per inch (dpi). The print quality of a 600-dpi printer is superior to a 300-dpi printer. Each time a page is printed, the inkjet or laser cartridge consumed is a recurring expense associated with operating a printer. Some can be configured to work with various paper inkjet printers. Laser printers can print in color at 6 to 25 ppm and in black and white at 25 to 60 ppm. For less than $200, one may get an inkjet printer with a black-and-white print speed of 12 to 40 ppm and a color print speed of 5 to 20 ppm (Waal et al., 2007).

Hard-copy output devices called plotters are commonly utilized for general design work. Businesses often use these devices to produce blueprints, schematics, and drawings of new buildings or items on paper or acetate. Typical plot widths are 24 and 36 inches, while the length might range from a few inches to several feet, depending on the situation (Bornman et al., 2001).

Remember

Digital Audio Players revolutionized on-the-go music listening and continue to offer advanced features such as gapless playback and customizable sound settings.

2.3.3.3. Digital Audio Player

A gadget that can store, manage, and play online music files is known as an audio player. A standard format for compressing sound sequences into tiny files without sacrificing sound quality when played is MP3 (MPEG-1 Audio Layer-3). When a sound file is compressed, it takes fewer seconds to download and uses fewer resources on a hard drive.

Downloading music via the World wide web and other sources can be done using a variety of music players that are approximately the size of a pack of cigarettes. These gadgets can store music for hours and have no moving parts. The iPod MP3 device and the iTunes Online Store make it easy to search for music online, listen to a sample, and download it safely and legally. Affordably, Apple entered the digital music business. With a 2.5-inch screen and the ability to play video, the Apple iPod can play some TV shows they may download from the iTunes Music Store. Other MP3 producers include Motorola, whose Rokr device is the first iPhone that works with Dell, Sony, Samsung, iTunes, and Iomega (Hudson, 2004).

The Apple iPod Touch is a music player with a 3.5-inch-wide screen that can also play movies and TV shows, show photos, and access the Internet. As a result, they can use it to access their e-mail, view YouTube videos, and buy music online. The view is automatically adjusted when the display is rotated from portrait to landscape. To fit the lighting conditions, an ambient light sensor modifies brightness (Bawden, 1985).

2.3.3.4. eBooks

An eBooks is a traditional printed book's digital media equivalent. More than 30k free e-books and more than 100k other e-books are available, according to the Project Gutenberg Online Book Catalog.

E-books can be downloaded to personal computers or specialized hardware units called e-book readers from Project Gutenberg (www.gutenberg.org) and many other places. The gadgets cost between $250 and $350 and download files of recent releases and best-sellers are less than $10.00 each. Around 19 eBooks have screens that range in size from 5 to 8 inches, weigh less than three-quarters of a pound, and are an about one-half inch thick. E-books can be readily grasped in one hand because they are more compact than most paperbacks. For readers with impaired vision, the text size can often be enlarged on e-readers (Dixit, 1991).

ACTIVITY 2.1.

How does the choice of hardware components affect the overall performance and capabilities of an information system, and what factors should be considered when selecting hardware components for a specific application?

2.4. OVERVIEW OF SOFTWARE

Computer programs make up the software that manages how computer hardware functions. Programs for computers are collections of instructions. The documentation describes the program functionalities to assist the user in using the computer system. The application displays some documentation on screen, while other forms are found in other sources, like printed manuals. End-User License Agreements are often read and accepted before commercial software is used (EULAs). Before using the program, which can fall under one of two categories: systems or application software, they often need to read the EULA and click an "I agree" button (El-Gayar & Fritz, 2006).

Systems software is a group of applications created to coordinate the operations and features of the devices and different software applications running on the computer system. Each sort of systems software is designed for a specific CPU architecture and hardware category. Applications that assist users in resolving specific computing issues are called application software. Application software often resides on the computer's hard drive before being loaded into memory and executed. Application software may also be kept on CDs, DVDs, USB-powered flash drives, or keychain storage devices (Cox & Gifford, 1997). There is a growing selection of application software available online. A web-delivered software application, often known as an RIA (rich internet application), combines the hardware resources of the PC and Web server to provide beneficial software services via a Web browser interface. When choosing the optimal strategy for procuring application software, an individual, group, or company should carefully assess their needs and goals (Mellado & Rosado, 2012).

2.5. SYSTEMS SOFTWARE

Did you Know?

According to a report by Statcounter, as of January 2022, the most commonly used operating system worldwide on desktop and laptop computers was Windows, with a market share of 76.24%, followed by macOS at 16.35% and Linux at 1.92%.

One of the most important tasks of systems software is managing how computer hardware operates. Application programs also support the ability of systems software to solve issues. Operating systems (OSs) and utility programs are examples of several systems software (Gifford et al., 1985).

2.5.1. Operating Systems (OSs)

A group of software applications known as an operating system (OS) manages a computer's hardware and serves as an interface for application programs.

OSs can control a single computer, a network of computers, or a single computer used by several users. The following are some examples of the many OS, computer, and user combinations (Garmpis, 2011):

- A single user and one computer. One user at a time is permitted under this arrangement, frequently found in personal.
- A single computer shares several users. This setup is characteristic of more giant mainframe computers that support simultaneous use by hundreds of users or even thousands of users.
- Numerous people are using many computers. This system is typical of a computer network, such as a local network with several connected computers or an extensive network

with tens of connected computers worldwide.

- Specialized computers Many computers with specific purposes, like those that operate high-tech military aircraft, spacecraft, image sensors, or home appliances, typically use this type of technology.

The OS, which is essential to the overall operation of the computer system, is often stored on a disc. A computer system's OS is loaded into memory as needed once it has "booted up" or started. Moreover, a USB-connected thumb drive, CD, or DVD can start a computer. Because it can be used to create the computer if the primary hard disc has issues, a storage device with some or all of the OS is frequently called a "rescue disc" (Hasselbring, 2000).

The group of software applications that make up the OS carry out several tasks, such as the following (Figure 2.14):

- Providing networking capability;
- Managing system memory;
- Performing standard computer hardware functions;
- Managing processing tasks;
- Managing files;
- Controlling access to system resources.

Figure 2.14. Illustration of system software.

Source: Bestweb, Creative Commons License.

2.5.1.1. Common Hardware Functions

Certain hardware-related operations that any application must carry out include (Choi et al., 2003):

- Get input from the keypad or another input devices;
- Fetch information from disks;
- Store information on the storage device;
- Display output on a monitor or printer.

A complete set of instructions is necessary for each of these jobs. The OS transforms a simple request into a specific collection of instructions the hardware needs. The OS is a middleman between the software and the hardware. A typical OS carries out hundreds of these activities, converting each one into one or more hardware instructions. When peripheral devices require attention, a mistake, or something unusual occurs in the system, the OS tells the user (Helps & Renshaw, 2004).

KEYWORD

Application Programming Interface (API) is a software interface that allows two applications to interact with each other without any user intervention.

2.5.1.2. User Interface and Input/Output Management

So long as a UI, which enables users to access and engage with the computer system, is one of the most crucial tasks performed by any OS. The early mainframe and laptop user interfaces were command-based (Phani et al., 2007).

With a command-based UI, the computer must be given written commands to perform simple tasks. For instance, the computer would wipe or delete the file 00TAXRTN if the instruction ERASE 00TAXRTN was entered. Some instructions for modifying files and copying data from one directory to another include RENAME and COPY (Olsen et al., 1985). While using a GUI (graphical user interface), humans can communicate commands to the computer system by selecting items from menus and images known as icons. Many believe that GUIs are more straightforward since users intuitively understand the functionality. The most popular GUI available today is Windows from Microsoft. As its name implies, Windows is based on using a window or a section of the display screen set aside for a particular application. Several windows may be visible at once on the screen. Windows 7 offers strong support for interacting with its GUI through touch, building on the iPhone's success, primarily made possible by its distinctive and sophisticated multitouch user interface (Myers et al., 1997).

2.5.1.3. Hardware Independence

Programs must request services from the OS through a predetermined application program interface (API). With APIs, programmers can build application software without being familiar with the OS's inner workings (Layton et al., 2017).

2.5.1.4. Memory Management

The OS also manages memory access and makes the most available memory and storage. Most modern OSs handle the memory more effectively than legacy OSs do. The computer can efficiently execute program instructions and speed up processing thanks to the memory-management feature found in many OSs. Upgrading to a newer OS and adding more memory are two ways to improve the performance of an old computer (Weiss et al., 1986).

Most OSs support VR memory, which allows space on the hard disc to complement RAM's immediate, usable memory range. Paging is a technique used in virtual memory that allows programs or portions of programs to be switched between memory and one or more storage drives. As a result, more jobs can run simultaneously, and the CPU's idle time is decreased (Xiao & Wang, 2019).

2.5.1.5. Processing Tasks

The task-management capabilities of modern OSs control all processing activities. Task management distributes computer resources to maximize the effectiveness of each system's resources. With task management software, multiple users can use the same computer simultaneously, and one user can run numerous programs or tasks simultaneously (multitasking, time-sharing) (Rayner et al., 2007).

KEYWORD

Task management is the process of monitoring your project's tasks through their various stages from start to finish.

Users can utilize multiple applications simultaneously when using an OS with multitasking features. Most computer users don't realize how creative multitasking OSs are since they exploit them to their advantage. Users can work in one application, quickly switch to another, and then promptly return to the original program to continue where they left off without having to exit it. Better yet, while they are working in one program's foreground, one or more other programs may be working silently in the background, sorting databases, printing documents, or carrying out other time-consuming tasks that would otherwise take up all of their computer's resources and prevent them from doing other work. Users can save a significant amount of time and effort by multitasking (Chandrasekaran, 1987).

More than one person can utilize a computer system at once thanks to time sharing. For instance, 15 customer care agents may simultaneously input sales information into a computer system for a mail-order business. In a different scenario, thousands of individuals may be using an online computer service at once to access stock prices and other business news.

Scalability is the capacity of a computer to manage a growing number of concurrent users efficiently. This functionality is essential for systems like mainframe computers or web servers supporting many users. Personal computer OSs rarely need to manage tasks involving numerous users because they are typically designed for a single user (Brysbaert et al., 2000).

2.5.1.6. Networking Capability

Most OSs provide networking features that allow machines to connect in a network to exchange information and use computing resources. Users can set up home or office networking for exchanging Web access, printers, storage, and data on Computers running the Mac, Linux OSs, or Windows. The Home Group feature in Windows 7 makes sharing files, printers, music, and images with others on a local network simple. Larger server OSs are explicitly created for computer networking environments (Lambourne et al., 2010) (Figure 2.15).

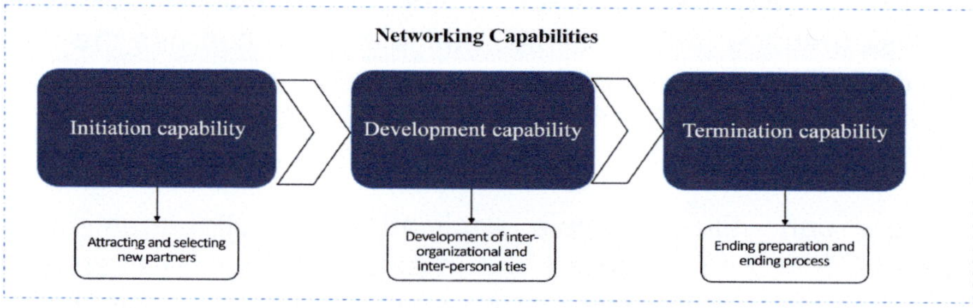

Figure 2.15. Schematic of networking capabilities.

Source: Cristian R. Foguesatto, Creative Commons License.

2.5.1.7. Access to System Resources and Security

Computers regularly handle sensitive data that can be accessible across networks, thus the OS must provide a high level of safeguarding against unwanted access to the data and applications of the users. A login process that requires users to enter an identifying code, such as a username and a match passcode, is often created by the OS. If the passcode does not reflect the identity number or the identifying code is wrong, the users are able to access the computer. Many OSs require users to update their passwords frequently, such as every 20 to 40 days. If a user successfully signs on to the system, the OS restricts access to only those components of the system for which the client has been given permission. Who uses the system, for how long, and by whom is tracked by the OS (Hidayatullah & Ma'Arif, 2017).

2.5.1.8. File Management

The OS controls files to ensure that secondary storage files are accessible when needed and are secured against access by unwanted users. On centrally positioned discs or tape drives, many systems can accommodate numerous users who store their files. The OS keeps track of each file's storage location and authorized users. If multiple users simultaneously seek access to the same file, the System must decide what to do. File management is required even on standalone personal computers with just one user to track where files are, their sizes, when they were generated, and who authored them (Agarwal & Nenkova, 2022).

KEYWORD

File management is the practice of naming, storing, managing, and securing digital files such as documents, photos, and videos on computers.

2.5.2. Current Operating Systems (OSs)

OSs from the past were quite simple. However, more sophisticated OSs have been created, combining sophisticated functions and stunning graphical effects (Peters, 1973).

2.5.2.1. Microsoft PC Operating Systems (OSs)

Personal computer OSs have continuously advanced since a little firm called Microsoft created PC-DOS and MS-DOS to serve the IBM desktop computer released in the 1980s. The command-driven user interfaces of PC-DOS and MS-DOS were challenging to learn and operate. The usability, processing power, dependability, and capacity to support new computer hardware components have increased with each OS version (McKinney et al., 1999).

In the fall of 2001, Microsoft debuted Windows XP, which is said to stand for the fantastic computing experience they will have. Windows' first consumer editions were notoriously unreliable and frequently crashed, necessitating annoying and time-consuming reboots. Microsoft aimed to increase consumer reliability with XP (Novac et al., 2017).

With the intention of delivering an OS that was more stable and secure, Microsoft developed Windows Vista in 2007. Several new features are part of the new OS. Vista's most recent iterations come with a 3D GUI dubbed Aero. Therefore, many users must buy more powerful Computers to meet Windows Vista with Aero's system requirements. One other problem was that some devices and applications made for Windows XP would not function on Vista (Figure 2.16).

Figure 2.16. Picture of window vista.

Source: Office of Information, Creative Commons License.

In 2009, Windows 7, the following version, was introduced with updates and new features. According to most analysts, Windows 7 is "Vista done well." After fixing a few Windows Vista problems, Windows 7 added new windows manipulation features that make it simpler for users to search, access, and operate with data in files. Moreover, it has enhanced apps and home networking capabilities. Netbooks and touch displays are well supported by Windows 7, ushering in a new era of mobile computing devices (Baseman et al., 1995).

2.5.2.2. Apple Computer Operating Systems (OSs)

Apple devices have utilized non-Intel microprocessors created by Apple, Motorola, and IBM and a proprietary Apple OS dubbed the Mac OS. In contrast, IBM system platforms have historically used one of the Windows OSs with Intel CPUs (often referred to as Wintel for this reason). Yet, Intel CPUs are used in newer Apple computers. Apple computers are also prevalent, particularly in publishing, academia, visual design, music, movies, and media, even though Wintel machines still account for most of the commercial PC market (Hagedoorn et al., 2001).

The Apple OSs also have developed throughout the years and frequently offer functionality that Microsoft does not. But, as they battle for consumers, Windows and Mac platforms have been created to share many of the same features. Mac OS X, a brand-new OS for the Mac based on the UNIX platform, was introduced in July 2001. It contained a new user interface that gave users a fresh visual experience. Elements like windows, scroll bars, buttons, and fluid animation were illuminated and partially translucent to improve the user's experience (Harris, 1983).

TIPS

Keep your Microsoft PC operating system updated with the latest security patches and perform regular antivirus scans. Optimizing system settings and minimizing unnecessary applications can also improve performance. Finally, create regular backups of important data.

Apple has repeatedly updated OS X since its first release. The most recent OS X update, Snow Leopard (version 10.6), was made available in 2009 to compete with Windows 7. Snow Leopard comes with Time Machine, a potent backup tool that enables users to restore deleted items and observe how their system appeared in the past. Multiple desktops that let users pose in front of imagined scenery, a robust system search tool, and other new apps are also included with Snow Leopard. Due to the lack of widespread virus or spyware attacks to date, Macs are likewise regarded as being relatively secure (Lorch & Smith, 1998).

Mac users can set up their computer to run both Mac OS X and Windows Vista and then choose which platform to use when they boot their computer because Mac OS X operates on Intel CPUs. Dual booting is a term used to describe such a setup. Macs can dually boot into Windows, but the reverse is not possible. OS X can only be used on Apple devices, according to Apple. However, Linux and other OSs can use dual boot on Windows PCs (Bala et al., 2015).

2.5.2.3. Linux

Linus Torvalds created the Linux OS while he was a student in Finland in 1991. The OS's source code is accessible to everyone and distributed under the GNU General Public License. As a result, it is referred to as an open-source OS. However, this does not imply that Linux and its many variants must be free; businesses and creators are free to charge for a version as long as the programming language is still accessible. Linux is merely an OS's kernel, which controls hardware, maintains files, splits processes, and does other things. Numerous Linux configurations can be used, each with a unique mix of features and programs to create an entire OS. A distribution of Linux is the term used to describe each of these mixtures. Several distributions can be downloaded for free (Wang et al., 2016).

Linux is accessible via various sources, including the Internet. Caldera OpenLinux and Red Hat Linux are two common variations. Several major computer manufacturers, including IBM, Hewlett-Packard, and Intel, support Linux. For instance, IBM employs hundreds of programmers who use Linux. For workstations, distributed systems, and even supercomputers, Linux is a popular OS. There is no lack of developers and engineers for Linux-based systems because most computer science and engineering graduates are conversant with Linux. Open architecture's flexibility makes it simple to adapt Linux to various demands (Appavoo et al., 2005).

KEYWORD

Digital rights management (DRM) enables copyright holders and content creators to manage what users can do with their content, such as how many devices they can access media on and whether they can share it.

Google has created its own OS called Chrome OS, which is based on Linux. Chrome is designed for mobile, PCs, and its primary focus is on Web-based data and services. These services include web surfing, e-mail, social networking sites, and Google online applications (Xiao et al., 2019).

2.6. UTILITY PROGRAMS

Utility software aids in doing maintenance on a computer system or fixing issues. For instance, specific utility programs combine and organize data collections, monitor the progress of computer operations, compress data files before storing or sending them over a network (saving time and space), and carry out other crucial functions. Specific utility software can improve and extend the trouble-free operation of computer systems (Alderighi et al., 1999).

Utility software can also aid in protecting and securing data. Digital rights management (DRM) systems, for instance, are used by the publishing and film industries to stop unauthorized duplication of copyright-protected publications and motion pictures. The intellectual property is stored in files that are encoded so that only versions that have been obtained legitimately can be recognized and played by e-book readers and media players. DRM has drawn criticism for limiting consumers' freedom and rights. Record labels have already abandoned DRM methods to gain the support of their patrons.

Users can buy utility programs individually even though many PC utility apps are pre-installed on computers (Ong et al., 2008) (Figure 2.17).

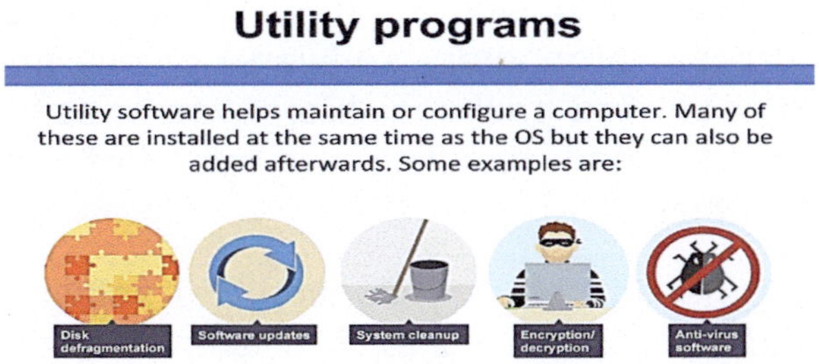

Figure 2.17. Illustration of components of utility programs.

Source: TeachingCS, Creative Commons License.

2.7. APPLICATION SOFTWARE

Application software harnesses the power of a computer to enable people, workgroups, and the entire organization to carry out specified tasks and solve problems. Application programs communicate with the OS, and the OS instructs the computer hardware to carry out the required operations.

Although some programs are more specialized, they all assist them in carrying out common operations like writing and formatting text documents, doing computations, or organizing information. The medical industry uses application software to prolong and save lives. For instance, Swedish Medical Center in Seattle, Washington, employs Oracle content management software to access patient records whenever and wherever required (Dehlinger & Dixon, 2011).

Application software is used for various tasks, from business analysis to enhancing personal efficiency. Application software, for instance, can assist sales managers in tracking sales of a new product in a test market. IntelliVid software watches video feeds from store security cameras and alerts security when a customer acts suspiciously. This book uses application software in most computerized business duties and activities. We start by looking into the many kinds and uses of application software (Aerts et al., 2004).

2.7.1. Types and Functions of Application Software

Application software is the secret to maximizing the capabilities of any computer system. A business can create a unique program for a particular purpose (proprietary software) or buy and employ an already-existing software package. Moreover, specific commercial software can be changed, resulting in a hybrid of commercial and customized methods.

KEYWORD

Business intelligence comprises the strategies and technologies used by enterprises for the data analysis and management of business information

A lot of businesses employ commercial software to support business operations. According to Forrester Research, Microsoft Office is used by 80% of businesses. Important considerations for choosing commercial software also include the following: (i) Can they use the software with the hardware and OS they have chosen? (ii) Would the software satisfy the specified vital business requirements? (iii) Is the developer a trustworthy and financially stable business? and (iv) Are the overall costs of buying, setting up, and sustaining the software positively contrasting with the anticipated business benefits? (Alkhatib, 1992).

Several commercial software packages can be changed, effectively combining commercial and customized methods. To track patients with the H1N1 flu and others who may have been exposed to it, El Camino Hospital in Mountain View, California, modified Microsoft's Amalga e-health management system.

Using an application service provider (ASP) is another way to get a software package specifically designed for them. A business known as an ASP can offer users the software, network access, and computer hardware necessary to execute the software from their premises. An ASP can make a sophisticated business software package simpler so that users can set it up and maintain it more easily. ASPs offer contract modification of commercial software, speed up the rollout of new applications, assist IS managers in avoiding implementation challenges, lessen the requirement for numerous highly qualified IS staff people, and lower project start-up costs. Such a strategy enables businesses to focus more time and resources on more crucial tasks. For instance, to handle its business intelligence (BI), rapid advance, a well-known cash advance service for small to medium-sized businesses (SMBs), employs business objects and crystal reports, software provided by SAP (BI). Real-time access to sales data, partner data, and crucial corporate reporting is provided via the system (Dutke & Reimer, 2000).

The use of an ASP exposes an organization to certain dangers, including the possibility that sensitive data will be compromised due to unauthorized access by employees or by computer hackers; the possibility that the ASP will be unable to keep its computers and network operational as reliably as is required; and the possibility that a natural disaster will render the ASP's data center inoperable, thus temporarily preventing the organization from conducting business. These are all legitimate concerns that need to be addressed by an ASP (Wilkie & Kitchenham, 2000).

Software-as-a-service (SaaS) is a new way of distributing software made possible by the substantial overhead associated with an ASP building, operating, managing, and supporting numerous specialized programs for numerous enterprises. SaaS enables companies to pay a monthly service fee or a per-use price to subscribe to Web-delivered business application software. Like ASP, SaaS vendors host software on their own servers and offer online access. SaaS typically uses a Web browser-based user interface. By distributing its active applications among numerous firms, SaaS can save costs. For instance, an ordinary SaaS supplier may offer customer relationship management (CRM) software to Sears, JCPenney, and Walmart. It is significantly less expensive to offer one excellent SaaS solution to thousands of organizations than to create the software from scratch for each one individually (Kapoor & Agarwal, 2017) (Figure 2.18).

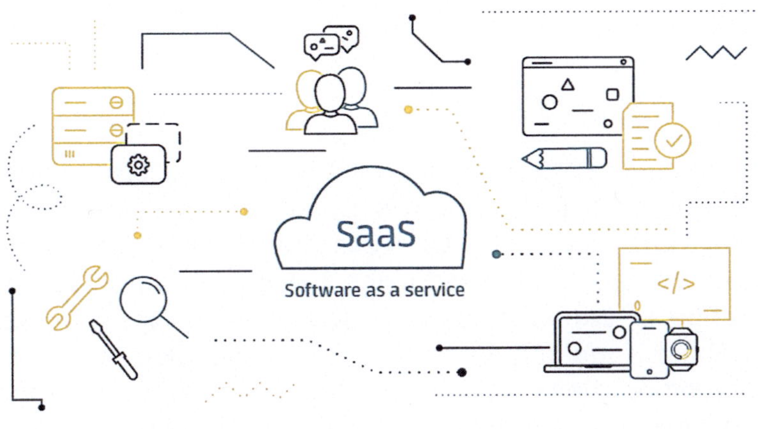

Figure 2.18. Schematic of software-as-a-service (SaaS).

Source: Avsystem, Creative Commons License.

SaaS and new web development tools have given rise to the cloud computing paradigm, a new way of thinking about computing. Using computing resources, such as data storage and software, through the Internet instead of local PCs is called cloud computing. Powerful Web programming languages and methodologies have enabled developers to produce Web-based software that is competitive with installation software. With cloud computing, they use a Web browser to access software downloaded and delivered from a Web server rather than installing, saving, and running it on their machine. Usually, the Web server also houses the data that the software produces. For instance, the Tableau program enables users to import data from databases or spreadsheets to create effective representations that deliver insightful insights. The advantage of cloud computing is that it makes it simple to collaborate with others by sharing papers online (Boehm, 1981).

2.7.2. Personal Application Software

Many computer programs exist that can be used to benefit people at work, home, and school. The features of personalized application software are enumerated. There are probably millions of other private computer programs available besides these general-purpose ones that are designed to carry out more specific tasks, such as helping them with their taxes, getting in shape, losing weight, getting medical advice, writing wills, as well as other official papers, fixing their computer, fixing their car, writing music, and editing their photos and videos. This category of software, often known as user software or personal productivity software, consists of all-purpose tools and applications that cater to user requirements (Van Gorp & Comuzzi, 2013).

Did you Know?

The term word processing appeared in American offices in early 1970s centered on the idea of streamlining the work to typists, but the meaning soon shifted toward the automation of the whole editing cycle.

2.7.2.1. Word Processing

Word processing software can be essential for creating reports, memos, or term papers. Today's personal computers almost all come with word processing software preinstalled. Documents can be created, edited, and printed using these programs. Most provide a wide range of capabilities, including ones for verifying spelling, making tables, inputting formulas, producing pictures, and much more. Like other similar books, this book was written using a word processing program on a home computer (Bergin, 2006).

A group of individuals can use a word-processing tool to work together on a project. For instance, this book's writers and editors tracked and modified the chapter files using Microsoft Word's Transition Words and Reviewing capabilities. With these tools, they can add remarks or edit a document, which a colleague can review and accept or reject (Figure 2.19).

Figure 2.19. Floe diagram of word processing.

Source: Sunybroome, Creative Commons License.

2.7.2.2. Spreadsheet Analysis

People use spreadsheets to create budgets, predict earnings, examine insurance policies, compile income tax information, and evaluate assets. Spreadsheets should be taken into consideration if there are computations and numbers involved. Spreadsheet features include visuals, a constrained database, data analysis, built-in business features, and many others. Current value, internal return rate, and monthly loan payments are only business tasks. Another full function of many spreadsheet systems is optimization. Under certain restrictions, optimization enables the spreadsheet to maximize or minimize a quantity. For instance, a modest furniture producer who creates tables and chairs would desire to increase sales. The limitations might include a finite amount of timber, a certain number of people who can put the chairs and tables together, or a finite number of hardware fasteners that might be needed. The spreadsheet may decide how many chairs and tables to make with labor and material limits to optimize revenues using an optimization capability (Chakravarty et al., 2006).

2.7.2.3. Database Applications

Data storage, manipulation, and retrieval are all made possible by the database software. These applications come in handy when they need to edit a lot of data and create documents and reports. Data combining, editing, and sorting are examples of database manipulations. A database application has many different applications. They can maintain a list of their CD collection, the possessions in their residence, tax information, and expenditures. A student club can utilize a database to keep track of members' names, contact information, and dues payments. A database application in the company can assist with processing sales orders, inventory control, ordering new supplies, sending letters to clients, and paying personnel. Database management systems (DBMS) can be used to keep track of purchases, goods, and clients, evaluate meteorological data to produce forecasts for the coming days and compile the findings of medical research. A database may serve as the user interface for another application. For instance, they can enter and store income tax data in a database application, then export the results to other programs like a spreadsheet or one used for tax preparation (Dehlinger & Dixon, 2011).

Remember

A DBMS may provide an optimization engine, which is used to parse database access language requests and turn them into actionable commands for accessing and modifying data.

2.7.2.4. Graphics Programs

Creating eye-catching graphs, pictures, and drawings using today's graphics software is simple. Develop advertising brochures, promotions, and full-color presentations with graphics software. If they are required to lecture at school or business, they can create and show their slides using a graphics application. They can use a graphics program to assist in creating a PowerPoint, a painting, or an animation. Many types of clip art, including pictures of people meeting, medical devices, telecommunications devices, entertainment, and much more, are included in most (Buchanan, 1993).

2.7.2.5. Personal Information Managers (PIMs)

Individuals, organizations, and groups can use personal information managers (PIMs) to store relevant information, such as a task checklist or a list of names and addresses. These typically offer a spot to write notes and an appointment calendar. Moreover, a PIM's data can be linked. For instance, they can connect a calendar meeting with a sales manager to the manager's contact information in the address book. The address book's entry for the sales manager is accessed and published on the computer monitor when users click the meeting in the calendar. A PIM software program is an example, such as Microsoft Outlook. By enabling users to view calendars, to-do lists, e-mail, social networking sites, contacts, and other data from a single page, Web portals like iGoogle and others facilitate PIM.

They can schedule and organize group meetings using some PIMs. They can upload PIM data and sync it with other network users' calendars and schedules with the same PIM application if a desktop or mobile device is linked to one. Several PIMs also let them organize e-mails to invite people to meetings. Users click a link or button when they receive invitations to be added to the guest list instantly (Aerts et al., 2004).

ACTIVITY 2.1.

How do different types of software used in information systems (such as system software, application software, and utility programs) differ in terms of their purpose and functionality, and what are some examples of each type?

2.7.3. Mobile Application Software

Recall that OS X iOS, Android, and WebOS are OSs created specifically for cellphones. Software developers now have the chance to create programs tailored for mobile use on a small display thanks to the APIs and software developer kits designed for these OSs. And they have. Tens of thousands of programs have been created by outside developers specifically for the iPhone and the mobile user apps that come with the OS. Numerous Apple apps are free; others cost 99 cents and hundreds of dollars. For $999.99, users may prepare for the California bar test with the BarMax iPhone App. Users of Android smartphones can also find 43,000,000 mobile apps in the Android Market. Although the Palm WebOS software development kit was only recently made available, many more applications may soon be available than the present dozens (Offutt, 2002).

2.8. SUMMARY

The chapter "Hardware and Software in Information Systems" is about the components and software that make up modern information systems (IS). An IS is a collection of hardware, software, data, people, and processes that work together to provide useful information for decision making and problem-solving.

The chapter starts by discussing the various hardware components used in IS, such as the CPU, memory devices, motherboard, power supply, and cooling systems. It then covers processing and memory devices in more detail, including their speed and performance, types of memory, and the role of cache memory in performance enhancement. The chapter also explores various secondary storage, input, and output devices, such as hard disk drives, solid-state drives, optical storage devices, keyboard, mouse, scanners, printers, monitors, and speakers.

After discussing the hardware components of IS, the chapter moves on to an overview of software used in IS. It explains the difference between system software and application software, with examples of each. The chapter then delves into OSs, including their definition, function, types, and user interfaces. Finally, the chapter explores utility programs and applications of software in IS, such as system utilities, application programs, and software-as-a-service (SaaS) and cloud-based applications.

REVIEW QUESTIONS

1. What are the different components of hardware used in information systems, and how do they work together to process and store data?
2. What are the processing and memory devices used in information systems, and how do they affect the performance of the system?
3. What are some examples of secondary storage, input, and output devices used in information systems, and how do they work?
4. What is the difference between system software and application software used in information systems, and what are some examples of each?
5. What is an operating system, and why is it important in information systems? What are some common types of operating systems used today?
6. What are some examples of utility programs used in information systems, and how do they help optimize the system's performance?
7. What is software-as-a-service (SaaS), and how does it differ from traditional software applications installed on a computer?
8. What are the key features and benefits of cloud-based applications used in information systems?
9. How can you assess the performance of the hardware components in an information system, and what steps can you take to optimize its performance?

10. What are some potential security risks associated with using software in information systems, and how can you protect against them?

MULTIPLE CHOICE QUESTIONS

1. What is a common input device used in information systems?
   a. Monitor
   b. Printer
   c. Keyboard
   d. Speakers

2. Which of the following is a primary storage device used in information systems?
   a. Hard disk drive
   b. Solid-state drive
   c. USB flash drive
   d. RAM

3. Which of the following is an example of a secondary storage device used in information systems?
   a. RAM
   b. CPU
   c. Hard disk drive
   d. Optical drive

4. What is an operating system?
   a. A type of software application used in information systems
   b. A set of hardware components used in information systems
   c. The user interface used in information systems
   d. The system software that manages hardware and software resources

5. Which of the following is not an example of an operating system?
   a. Windows
   b. Mac OS
   c. Linux
   d. Microsoft Office

6. Which of the following is a type of utility program used in information systems?
   a. Word processor
   b. Spreadsheet software

c. Antivirus software

d. Presentation software

7. What is software-as-a-service (SaaS)?

a. A type of system software used in information systems

b. A type of cloud-based application used in information systems

c. A type of application software installed on a computer

d. A type of programming language used in information systems

8. What is the function of a device driver in information systems?

a. To manage the operating system

b. To manage input and output devices

c. To manage storage devices

d. To manage application software

9. Which of the following is a benefit of cloud-based applications in information systems?

a. Improved system security

b. Reduced hardware costs

c. Increased system speed

d. Improved user interface

10. Which of the following is a potential security risk associated with using software in information systems?

a. Malware infections

b. Hardware failure

c. Network congestion

d. System crashes

Answers to the Multiple-Choice Questions

1. (c); 2. (d); 3. (c); 4. (d); 5. (d); 6. (c); 7. (b); 8. (b); 9. (b); 10. (a)

REFERENCES

1. Adler, R. M., (1995). Emerging standards for component software. *Computer, 28*(3), 68–77.
2. Aerts, A. T. M., Goossenaerts, J. B., Hammer, D. K., & Wortmann, J. C., (2004). Architectures in context: On the evolution of business, application software, and ICT platform architectures. *Information & Management, 41*(6), 781–794.

3. Agarwal, O., & Nenkova, A., (2022). Temporal effects on pre-trained models for language processing tasks. *Transactions of the Association for Computational Linguistics, 10*, 904–921.
4. Alderighi, L., Gans, P., Ienco, A., Peters, D., Sabatini, A., & Vacca, A., (1999). Hyperquad simulation and speciation (HySS): A utility program for the investigation of equilibria involving soluble and partially soluble species. *Coordination Chemistry Reviews, 184*(1), 311–318.
5. Alkhatib, G., (1992). The maintenance problem of application software: An empirical analysis. *Journal of Software Maintenance: Research and Practice, 4*(2), 83–104.
6. Appavoo, J., Auslander, M., Butrico, M., Da Silva, D. M., Krieger, O., Mergen, M. F., & Xenidis, J., (2005). Experience with K42, an open-source, Linux-compatible, scalable operating-system kernel. *IBM Systems Journal, 44*(2), 427–440.
7. Arato, M., & Benczur, A., (1981). Dynamic placement of records and the classical occupancy problem. *Computers & Mathematics with Applications, 7*(2), 173–185.
8. Arvanitis, P., & Krystalli, P., (2021). Mobile assisted language learning (MALL): Trends from 2010 to 2020 using text analysis techniques. *European Journal of Education, 4*(1), 13–22.
9. Bala, K., Sharma, S., & Kaur, G., (2015). A study on smartphone based operating system. *International Journal of Computer Applications, 121*(1), 2–10.
10. Balasubramanian, R., & Dalal, E., (1997). Method for quantifying the color gamut of an output device. In: *Color Imaging: Device-Independent Color, Color Hard Copy, and Graphic Arts II* (Vol. 3018, pp. 110–116).
11. Ballagas, R., Borchers, J., Rohs, M., & Sheridan, J. G., (2006). The smart phone: A ubiquitous input device. *IEEE Pervasive Computing, 5*(1), 70–77.
12. Baseman, K. C., Warren-Boulton, F. R., & Woroch, G. A., (1995). Microsoft plays hardball: The use of exclusionary pricing and technical incompatibility to maintain monopoly power in markets for operating system software. *The Antitrust Bulletin, 40*(2), 265–315.
13. Bawden, D., (1985). Computer output devices: A tutorial review. *Journal of Information Science, 11*(1), 1–8.
14. Belo, O., & Marques, A., (2012). Archiving business operational data heritage. *Procedia Technology, 1*, 107–111.
15. Benlian, A., & Hess, T., (2011). Comparing the relative importance of evaluation criteria in proprietary and open-source enterprise application software selection–a conjoint study of ERP and office systems. *Information Systems Journal, 21*(6), 503–525.
16. Bergin, T. J., (2006). The origins of word processing software for personal computers: 1976–1985. *IEEE Annals of the History of Computing, 28*(4), 32–47.
17. Boehm, B. W., (1981). An experiment in small-scale application software engineering. *IEEE Transactions on Software Engineering*, (5), 482–493.

18. Bornman, E., Alant, E., & Meiring, J., (2001). The use of a digital voice output device to facilitate language development in a child with developmental apraxia of speech: A case study. *Disability and Rehabilitation, 23*(14), 623–634.
19. Brysbaert, M., Van, W. I., & De Deyne, S., (2000). Age-of-acquisition effects in semantic processing tasks. *Acta Psychologica, 104*(2), 215–226.
20. Buchanan, R. L., (1990). Using spreadsheet software for predictive microbiology applications. *Journal of Food Safety, 11*(2), 123–134.
21. Buchanan, R. L., (1993). Developing and distributing user-friendly application software. *Journal of Industrial Microbiology and Biotechnology, 12*(3–5), 251–255.
22. Buncic, P., Sanchez, C. A., Blomer, J., Franco, L., Harutyunian, A., Mato, P., & Yao, Y., (2010). CernVM–a virtual software appliance for LHC applications. In: *Journal of Physics: Conference Series* (Vol. 219, No. 4, p. 042003).
23. Burdea, G., Richard, P., & Coiffet, P., (1996). Multimodal virtual reality: Input-output devices, system integration, and human factors. *International Journal of Human-Computer Interaction, 8*(1), 5–24.
24. Capra, E., Francalanci, C., & Slaughter, S. A., (2012). Is software "green"? Application development environments and energy efficiency in open source applications. *Information and Software Technology, 54*(1), 60–71.
25. Card, S. K., Mackinlay, J. D., & Robertson, G. G., (1991). A morphological analysis of the design space of input devices. *ACM Transactions on Information Systems (TOIS), 9*(2), 99–122.
26. Chakravarty, S., Dogan, K., & Tomlinson, N., (2006). A hedonic study of network effects in the market for word processing software. *Decision Support Systems, 41*(4), 747–763.
27. Chandrasekaran, B., (1987). Towards a functional architecture for intelligence based on generic information processing tasks. In: *IJCAI* (Vol. 87, pp. 1183–1192).
28. Chen, P. M., Lee, E. K., Gibson, G. A., Katz, R. H., & Patterson, D. A., (1994). RAID: High-performance, reliable secondary storage. *ACM Computing Surveys (CSUR), 26*(2), 145–185.
29. Choi, H. R., Kim, H. S., Park, B. J., Park, N. K., & Lee, S. W., (2003). An ERP approach for container terminal operating systems. *Maritime Policy & Management, 30*(3), 197–210.
30. Christodoulakis, S., (1984). Estimating block selectivities. *Information Systems, 9*(1), 69–79.
31. Coffman, E. G., & Hofri, M., (1986). Queueing models of secondary storage devices. *Queueing Systems, 1*, 129–168.
32. Corral, L., Sillitti, A., & Succi, G., (2015). Software assurance practices for mobile applications: A survey of the state of the art. *Computing, 97*, 1001–1022.
33. Cox, A. B., & Gifford, F., (1997). An overview to geographic information systems. *The Journal of Academic Librarianship, 23*(6), 449–461.

34. De Waal, E. E., Kalkman, C. J., Rex, S., & Buhre, W. F., (2007). Validation of a new arterial pulse contour-based cardiac output device. *Critical Care Medicine, 35*(8), 1904–1909.
35. Dehlinger, J., & Dixon, J., (2011). Mobile application software engineering: Challenges and research directions. In: *Workshop on Mobile Software Engineering* (Vol. 2, pp. 29–32).
36. Denaro, G., Polini, A., & Emmerich, W., (2004). Early performance testing of distributed software applications. In: *Proceedings of the 4th International Workshop on Software and Performance*,1, 94–103
37. Dicarlo, C. F., & Banajee, M., (2000). Using voice output devices to increase initiations of young children with disabilities. *Journal of Early Intervention, 23*(3), 191–199.
38. Dixit, S. S., (1991). Quantization of color images for display/printing on limited color output devices. *Computers & Graphics, 15*(4), 561–567.
39. Dutke, S., & Reimer, T., (2000). Evaluation of two types of online help for application software. *Journal of Computer Assisted Learning, 16*(4), 307–315.
40. Ebert, C., & Jones, C., (2009). Embedded software: Facts, figures, and future. *Computer, 42*(4), 42–52.
41. Eisenberg, M., (2002). Output devices, computation, and the future of mathematical crafts. *International Journal of Computers for Mathematical Learning, 7*, 1–44.
42. Eisenberg, M., Eisenberg, A., Hendrix, S., Blauvelt, G., Butter, D., Garcia, J., & Nielsen, T., (2003). As we may print: New directions in output devices and computational crafts for children. In: *Proceedings of the 2003 Conference on Interaction Design and Children* (Vol. 1, pp. 31–39).
43. El-Gayar, O., & Fritz, B. D., (2006). Environmental management information systems (EMIS) for sustainable development: A conceptual overview. *Communications of the Association for Information Systems, 17*(1), 34.
44. Ganesh, E. N., (2021). Study of self organizing wireless hardware and software parts of the network sensor networks. *Current Trends in Information Technology. Programmed Efficiently. The Execution of the Data, 11*(3), 12–16.
45. Garmpis, A., (2011). Design and development of a web-based interactive software tool for teaching operating systems. *Journal of Information Technology Education: Research, 10*(1), 1–17.
46. Gifford, D. K., Baldwin, R. W., Berlin, S. T., & Lucassen, J. M., (1985). An architecture for large scale information systems. *ACM SIGOPS Operating Systems Review, 19*(5), 161–170.
47. Grossman, D. D., & Silverman, H. F., (1973). Placement of records on a secondary storage device to minimize access time. *Journal of the ACM (JACM), 20*(3), 429–438.
48. Hagedoorn, J., Carayannis, E., & Alexander, J., (2001). Strange bedfellows in the personal computer industry: Technology alliances between IBM and Apple. *Research Policy, 30*(5), 837–849.

49. Harris, J. R., (1983). Apple computer, Inc. v. franklin computer corp.-does a ROM a computer program make. *Jurimetrics J., 24*, 248.
50. Hasselbring, W., (2000). Information system integration. *Communications of the ACM, 43*(6), 32–38.
51. Hayashi, V. T., Arakaki, R., & Ruggiero, W. V., (2020). OKIoT: Trade off analysis of smart speaker architecture on open knowledge IoT project. *Internet of Things, 12*, 100310.
52. Helps, C. R. G., & Renshaw, S. A., (2004). Design of a flexible case-study instructional module for operating systems for information technology. In: *Proceedings of the 5th Conference on Information Technology Education, 1*, 56–59.
53. Herbst, K., Littlejohns, P., Rawlinson, J., Collinson, M., & Wyatt, J. C., (1999). Evaluating computerized health information systems: Hardware, software and human ware: Experiences from the Northern Province, South Africa. *Journal of Public Health, 21*(3), 305–310.
54. Hidayatullah, A. F., & Ma'Arif, M. R., (2017). Pre-processing tasks in Indonesian Twitter messages. In: *Journal of Physics: Conference Series* (Vol. 801, No. 1, p. 012072). IOP Publishing.
55. Hudson, S. E., (2004). Using light emitting diode arrays as touch-sensitive input and output devices. In: *Proceedings of the 17th Annual ACM Symposium on User Interface Software and Technology* (Vol. 1, pp. 287–290).
56. Jacob, R. J., (1996). Human-computer interaction: Input devices. *ACM Computing Surveys (CSUR), 28*(1), 177–179.
57. Jacob, R. J., Leggett, J. J., Myers, B. A., & Pausch, R., (1993). Interaction styles and input/output devices. *Behavior & Information Technology, 12*(2), 69–79.
58. Jacob, R. J., Sibert, L. E., McFarlane, D. C., & Mullen, Jr. M. P., (1994). Integrality and separability of input devices. *ACM Transactions on Computer-Human Interaction (TOCHI), 1*(1), 3–26.
59. Kapoor, R., & Agarwal, S., (2017). Sustaining superior performance in business ecosystems: Evidence from application software developers in the iOS and Android smartphone ecosystems. *Organization Science, 28*(3), 531–551.
60. Keller, A., & Hüsig, S., (2009). Ex ante identification of disruptive innovations in the software industry applied to web applications: The case of Microsoft's vs. Google's office applications. *Technological Forecasting and Social Change, 76*(8), 1044–1054.
61. Kelly, D. F., (2007). A software chasm: Software engineering and scientific computing. *IEEE Software, 24*(6), 120–119.
62. Kessler, G. D., Hodges, L. F., & Walker, N., (1995). Evaluation of the CyberGlove as a whole-hand input device. *ACM Transactions on Computer-Human Interaction (TOCHI), 2*(4), 263–283.

63. Kim, M. S., & Chung, S. C., (2003). Identification of nonlinear characteristics for precision servomechanisms. In: *Proceedings of the ASPE 2003 Annual Meeting* (Vol. 1, pp.167–170).
64. Kim, Y. S., Soh, B. S., & Lee, S. G., (2005). A new wearable input device: SCURRY. *IEEE Transactions on Industrial Electronics, 52*(6), 1490–1499.
65. Kotenko, I., Saenko, I., & Ageev, S., (2015). Countermeasure security risks management in the internet of things based on fuzzy logic inference. In: *2015 IEEE Trustcom/BigDataSE/ISPA* (Vol. 1, pp. 654–659).
66. Lambourne, K., Audiffren, M., & Tomporowski, P. D., (2010). Effects of acute exercise on sensory and executive processing tasks. *Med. Sci. Sports Exerc., 42*(7), 1396–402.
67. Lapointe, J. F., Savard, P., & Vinson, N. G., (2011). A comparative study of four input devices for desktop virtual walkthroughs. *Computers in Human Behavior, 27*(6), 2186–2191.
68. Layton, K. J., Kroboth, S., Jia, F., Littin, S., Yu, H., Leupold, J., & Zaitsev, M., (2017). Pulseq: A rapid and hardware-independent pulse sequence prototyping framework. *Magnetic Resonance in Medicine, 77*(4), 1544–1552.
69. Lian, X., Liu, C., Fu, J., Liu, X., Ren, Q., Wan, X., & Wang, L., (2022). Design of plasmonic enhanced all-optical phase-change memory for secondary storage applications. *Nanotechnology, 33*(49), 495204.
70. Lim, S. L., Bentley, P. J., Kanakam, N., Ishikawa, F., & Honiden, S., (2014). Investigating country differences in mobile app user behavior and challenges for software engineering. *IEEE Transactions on Software Engineering, 41*(1), 40–64.
71. Lindstrom, E. E., & Vitter, J. S., (1985). The design and analysis of bucketsort for bubble memory secondary storage. *IEEE Transactions on Computers, 34*(03), 218–233.
72. Lorch, J. R., & Smith, A. J., (1998). Apple Macintosh's energy consumption. *IEEE Micro, 18*(6), 54–63.
73. MacKenzie, I. S., Sellen, A., & Buxton, W. A., (1991). A comparison of input devices in element pointing and dragging tasks. In: *Proceedings of the SIGCHI Conference on Human Factors in Computing Systems* (Vol. 1, pp. 161–166).
74. Mackinlay, J., Card, S. K., & Robertson, G. G., (1990). A semantic analysis of the design space of input devices. *Human–Computer Interaction, 5*(2, 3), 145–190.
75. Maggio, M., Hoffmann, H., Santambrogio, M. D., Agarwal, A., & Leva, A., (2010). Controlling software applications via resource allocation within the heartbeats framework. In: *49th IEEE Conference on Decision and Control* (Vol. 1, pp. 3736–3741).
76. McKellar, A. C., & Wong, C. K., (1978). Dynamic placement of records in linear storage. *Journal of the ACM (JACM), 25*(3), 421–434.
77. McKinney, C. J., MacCormac, E. R., & Welsh-Bohmer, K. A., (1999). Hardware and software for tachistoscopy: How to make accurate measurements on any PC utilizing the Microsoft windows operating system. *Behavior Research Methods Instruments and Computers, 31*, 129–136.

78. McKusick, M. K., (1996). Secondary storage and filesystems. *ACM Computing Surveys (CSUR), 28*(1), 217–219.

79. Mellado, D., & Rosado, D. G., (2012). An overview of current information systems security challenges and innovations. *J. UCS Special Issue; Journal of Universal Computer Science, 18*(12), 1598–1607.

80. Mello, D., Cordiano, F., Gerosa, A., Padalino, M., Gagliano, C., Renna, G., & Franco, G., (2005). In-line monitor introduction to prevent metallic contamination in wet bench. In: *Solid State Phenomena, 108*, 637–642.

81. Mohanty, A., Alam, A., Sarkar, R., & Chaudhury, S., (2021). Design and development of digital game-based learning software for incorporation into school syllabus and curriculum transaction. *Design Engineering, 8*, 4864–4900.

82. Myers, B. A., McDaniel, R. G., Miller, R. C., Ferrency, A. S., Faulring, A., Kyle, B. D., & Doane, P., (1997). The amulet environment: New models for effective user interface software development. *IEEE Transactions on Software Engineering, 23*(6), 347–365.

83. Nagappan, M., & Shihab, E., (2016). Future trends in software engineering research for mobile apps. In: *2016 IEEE 23rd International Conference on Software Analysis, Evolution, and Reengineering* (Vol. 5, pp. 21–32).

84. Novac, O. C., Novac, M., Gordan, C., Berczes, T., & Bujdosó, G., (2017). Comparative study of Google Android, Apple iOS and Microsoft Windows phone mobile operating systems. In: *2017 14th International Conference on Engineering of Modern Electric Systems (EMES)* (pp. 154–159). IEEE.

85. Offutt, J., (2002). Quality attributes of web software applications. *IEEE Software, 19*(2), 25–32.

86. Olsen, Jr. D. R., Dempsey, E. P., & Rogge, R., (1985). Input/output linkage in a user interface management system. *ACM SIGGRAPH Computer Graphics, 19*(3), 191–197.

87. Omiecinski, E., Lee, L., & Scheuermann, P., (1994). Performance analysis of a concurrent file reorganization algorithm for record clustering. *IEEE Transactions on Knowledge and Data Engineering, 6*(2), 248–257.

88. Ong, M. E. H., Tan, E. H., Yan, X., Anushia, P., Lim, S. H., Leong, B. S. H., & Anantharaman, V., (2008). An observational study describing the geographic-time distribution of cardiac arrests in Singapore: What is the utility of geographic information systems for planning public access defibrillation? (PADS Phase I). *Resuscitation, 76*(3), 388–396.

89. Peters, P. A., (1973). Advanced logging system-II: Balloon logging: A look at current operating systems. *Journal of Forestry, 71*(9), 577–579.

90. Phani, A. M. R. V. A., Kumar, D. J., & Kumar, G. A., (2007). *Operating Systems for Wireless Sensor Networks: A Survey Technical Report*, *3*, 1–30.

91. Raj, J. R. F., Vijayalakshmi, K., & Priya, S. K., (2019). Medical image denoising using multi-resolution transforms. *Measurement, 145*, 769–778.

92. Rayner, K., Li, X., Williams, C. C., Cave, K. R., & Well, A. D., (2007). Eye movements during information processing tasks: Individual differences and cultural effects. *Vision Research, 47*(21), 2714–2726.
93. Saputra, F., (2022). The role of human resources, hardware, and databases in mass media companies. *International Journal of Advanced Multidisciplinary, 1*(1), 47–55.
94. Shin, I., (2006). Adoption of enterprise application software and firm performance. *Small Business Economics, 26*, 241–256.
95. Stytz, M. R., (2004). Considering defense in depth for software applications. *IEEE Security & Privacy, 2*(1), 72–75.
96. Taveira, A. D., & Choi, S. D., (2009). Review study of computer input devices and older users. *Intl. Journal of Human–Computer Interaction, 25*(5), 455–474.
97. Thrall, S. E., (1999). Geographic information system (GIS) hardware and software. *Journal of Public Health Management and Practice, 5*(2), 82–90.
98. Tsukada, K., & Yasumura, M., (2001). Ubi-finger: Gesture input device for mobile use. In: *Ubicomp 2001 Informal Companion Proceedings, 11*, 4–10.
99. Udhayakumar, U., & Murugaboopathi, G., (2020). Enhanced security using hybrid parallel integrity key data service access control method in virtual cloud. *Journal of Green Engineering, 10*(2), 342–359.
100. Van, G. P., & Comuzzi, M., (2013). Lifelong personal health data and application software via virtual machines in the cloud. *IEEE Journal of Biomedical and Health Informatics, 18*(1), 36–45.
101. Wanderley, M. M., & Orio, N., (2002). Evaluation of input devices for musical expression: Borrowing tools from HCI. *Computer Music Journal, 26*(3), 62–76.
102. Wang, H., Chen, Z., Xiao, G., & Zheng, Z., (2016). Network of networks in Linux operating system. *Physica A: Statistical Mechanics and its Applications, 447*, 520–526.
103. Ware, C., (1996). Multimedia output devices and techniques. *ACM Computing Surveys (CSUR), 28*(1), 181–183.
104. Weiss, B., Weisz, J. R., & Bromfield, R., (1986). Performance of retarded and nonretarded persons on information-processing tasks: Further tests of the similar structure hypothesis. *Psychological Bulletin, 100*(2), 157.
105. Wibawa, I. N. G. S., (2015). Hierarchy and characteristic of storage devices. *International Research Journal of Management, IT and Social Sciences, 2*(3), 1–4.
106. Wilkie, F. G., & Kitchenham, B. A., (2000). Coupling measures and change ripples in C++ application software. *Journal of Systems and Software, 52*(2, 3), 157–164.
107. Wood, E., Willoughby, T., Rushing, A., Bechtel, L., & Gilbert, J., (2005). Use of computer input devices by older adults. *Journal of Applied Gerontology, 24*(5), 419–438.
108. Wright, C. D., Hosseini, P., & Diosdado, J. A. V., (2013). Beyond von-Neumann computing with nanoscale phase-change memory devices. *Advanced Functional Materials, 23*(18), 2248–2254.

109. Xiao, G., Zheng, Z., Yin, B., Trivedi, K. S., Du, X., & Cai, K. Y., (2019). An empirical study of fault triggers in the Linux operating system: An evolutionary perspective. *IEEE Transactions on Reliability, 68*(4), 1356–1383.

110. Xiao, Y., & Wang, W. Y., (2019). Quantifying uncertainties in natural language processing tasks. In: *Proceedings of the AAAI Conference on Artificial Intelligence* (Vol. 33, No. 1, pp. 7322–7329).

111. Yakubailik, O. E., Kadochnikov, A. A., & Tokarev, A. V., (2018). Web geographic information system and the hardware and software ensuring rapid assessment of air pollution. *Optoelectronics, Instrumentation and Data Processing, 54*, 243–249v.

112. Yamada, S., & Osaki, S., (1985). Software reliability growth modeling: Models and applications. *IEEE Transactions on Software Engineering*, (12), 1431–1437.

113. Yue, P. C., & Wong, C. K., (1973). On the optimality of the probability ranking scheme in storage applications. *Journal of the ACM (JACM), 20*(4), 624–633.

114. Zhai, S., (1998). User performance in relation to 3D input device design. *ACM SIGGRAPH Computer Graphics, 32*(4), 50–54.

CHAPTER 3

MODELING AND DEVELOPMENT OF INFORMATION SYSTEMS

UNIT INTRODUCTION

The process of planning, developing, and applying computer-based solutions that tackle a specific issue or answer a specific need is known as the information development of a system, including modeling. This procedure usually consists of numerous steps, each requiring a unique combination of tools and skills (Robey et al., 1993).

The examination of the issue or need constitutes the initial step in the creation of an information system (IS). It includes determining the requirement of the system, comprehending the business operations that such a system would serve, and determining the project plan. It's an important stage since it establishes the groundwork for the remainder of the development phase and assures that such a system would meet the requirements of its target purposes (Siau et al., 2010).

After the objectives have been figured out, the next step is developing a system. Creating a comprehensive strategy for the company and the system's operation is a necessary step in this process. During this phase, the group will be accountable for creating diagrams and models meant to reflect the various parts of the whole and how these components relate to one another.

Stage three consists of putting the system into action. It includes building the coding for the network, integrating it into the other systems currently in place, and analyzing it to ensure it works as designed. Also, the data will be migrated at this phase, end-users and administrators will be trained, and the system's safety will be evaluated.

The third stage is care and upkeep, often known as maintenance and assistance. After the network has been put into place, it will call for regular support and maintenance to ensure it keeps performing as intended and satisfies the ever-evolving requirements of the people using it. During this stage, you will monitor the network, make updates and enhancements, and provide customers with technical help (De Castro et al., 2011).

Using a variety of modeling approaches to construct representations of the data system being produced is what is meant by "modeling" IS. The above models could be represented visually in various ways, such as flowcharts, illustrations, or even prototypes. The goal of modeling is to provide developers with a tool that will assist them in better understanding the system being constructed and locating any potential problems or possibilities for enhancement (Mylopoulos et al., 1990). The creation of new IS could use a wide variety of modeling approaches, such as data flow charts, entity-relationship illustrations, and case modeling, to name just a few examples of these approaches. The modeling approach that is selected will be determined by the requirements of the project as well as the personal choices of the developers on the team.

Developing and modeling information management entails going through several phases and employing various methods to produce computer-based solutions catering to certain requirements or issues. A diverse team with competence in software design, project planning, and design for user experiences is required for the process (Faraj & Sambamurthy, 2006). Begin, every business already possesses some IS, whether it relies on paper files and pencils, an entirely automated one, or a hybrid. As a result, developing an IS requires work on an existing system. This work includes mapping the framework, automating it, and ensuring it follows the users' requirements. As a result, the process begins by attempting, in its initial phase, to ascertain the breadth and nature of a new system that the user desires. First, before the system is created and implemented, the following phase analyzes the need in two portions to permit comprehensive validation and verification (Haag et al., 1998) (Figure 3.1).

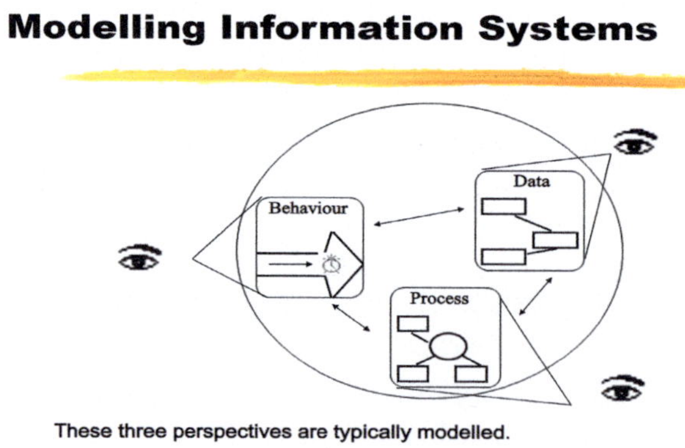

Figure 3.1. Illustration of modeling of information system.

Source: Sliderplayer, Creative Commons License.

Learning Objectives

At the end of this chapter, readers will be able to learn the following:

- Development of the information systems;
- Importance of users in the development of information systems;
- Determination of users' needs and expectations for the development of IS;
- Various characteristics of good organizational IS talent;
- Stages of the design process of IS;
- Modeling of the system design;
- Different stages are involved in the modeling of an IS;
- Methods and generations of development of an IS.

Key Terms

- Development
- Development methods
- Development stages
- Logical design
- Maintenance
- Modeling
- Performance
- Process design
- System design

3.1. USER-CENTRIC DEVELOPMENT

The users' demands, performance goals, criteria, or other requirements are central to developing IT systems ideas. The degree to which an information system's (IS) fundamental users inside an organization are satisfied can determine whether it is successful or unsuccessful. The user's needs must be met either by the database for it to serve its intended purpose; alternatively, the user would continue using his system. The fundamental idea behind this idea is that every subsystem uses the same database to fulfill its informational requirements. The merging of divisions and responsibilities will result in a further important benefit. Every department thus acquires a greater awareness and understanding of how its activities and intentions affect others through business through its exposure to and interaction with the company's overall data resources (Khan et al., 2010).

Why it is crucial to study and plan IS before building them is a key query that may be raised. Why are you unable to create the IS yourself? The primary causes are:

- It's crucial to create the information systems which users require. You won't know what people need when you don't begin with some analysis and strategy.
- Building information systems lacking adequate "blueprints" is a resource wastage because doing so takes longer and produces worse outcomes (Baby & Kannammal, 2020).

Information demands are met through research and development. Interest groups (or user groups) should typically be involved with the project if it is necessary to develop models explaining the IS the users require. Design and analysis activity is also important because it teaches participants much about the newest IS. They understand how IS function and is necessary to use them effectively. One approach to gaining such expertise is participating in analytical and design processes (Bilgram et al., 2008) (Figure 3.2).

Figure 3.2. Schematic of user centric development.

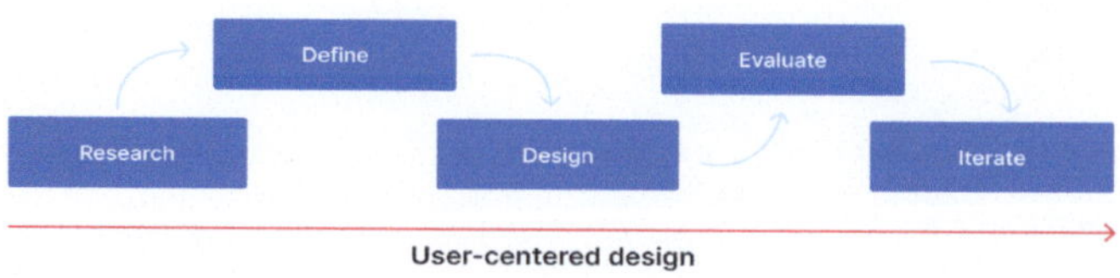

Source: reveal, Creative Commons License.

3.2. DETERMINING NEED AND PERFORMANCE EXPECTATIONS

Each business has a current structure; therefore, system conversion is a step in the IS development phase. The conversion process generally entails the following steps:

- System description (narrative or pictorial);
- Input documents (item description, layouts, etc.);
- Output documents (report formats, output requirements, etc.);
- File design (involves the system design process);
- Program logic (using flow charts or other methods) (Voss et al., 1998);
- Computer programs (COBOL, DYNAMO, BASIC, PASCAL, FORTRAN, to name a few);
- System verification;
- Documentation (Diede et al., 2000).

Possible issues with database construction standards often involve interdepartmental communication and agreement. They could consist of the following:

- A unit desiring to maintain data security may enter incorrect information.
- The erroneously recorded information's "multiplier effect" immediately impacts some other divisions using the data.
- User divisions must agree mostly on when a transaction must be represented in data entry due to the "dimension of time" of data input (Vetter & Worley, 2002).
- The "inter-departmental agreement" is necessary for the level of information to be present in physical database pieces.

A few of the system's intended characteristics would include the following in light of the issues mentioned above which have been noted:

- Simplicity or ease when using or managing (using graphic user interface-based entry and retrieval systems) (Whitman, 1996).
- Firewalls and security mechanisms that are adequate for preventing unauthorized entry (both within the organization and on the web).

Did you get it?

According to a 2020 survey by the International Data Corporation (IDC), spending on software development and deployment tools is expected to reach $15.8 billion by 2024.

- A strict operating system (OS) is the foundation for the many managements structure carried out at various levels.

A list of certain performance indicators would be necessary to grasp the objectives or needs of the constructed system. An assessment of the difference between both the new and the old is made when expenses or benefits are calculated. In all other terms, we can track the numerous changes made across the system or the changes in the system's overall output. The former is ideal.

It is generally uncommon to measure the entire system at the network level. The following broad ideas should be considered when developing a system:

- **System Integrity:** Well, how, if at all, are the subsystems also linked to the main system? How adaptable is the framework? How simple is it to further develop the system?
- **Operating Integrity:** How competent are the system's operators also? Which backup is accessible to avoid a system failure in the case of key personnel absence or equipment malfunction (Batara et al., 2017)?
- **Internal Integrity:** How effectively would the system carry out its intended function? The reliability of output results How resistant to human error, trickery, sabotage, or robbery is the system?
- **Procedural Integrity:** How well-written are the systems and procedures? Are policies written in a way that encourages employees to obey them? How thoroughly are protocols adhered to in actuality? What safeguards guarantee that protocols are followed?
- **Change Analysis:** It should be completed before performing information management design. Alteration analysis involves the investigation of appropriate adjustments to an enterprise's operations in actual circumstances. Before addressing an issue, describe it using a change analysis, especially when you have information management demands or difficulties in efficiently developing IS. Before performing data-oriented work, issue tasks need to be finished.
- **Problem-Oriented Work:** The term "information management development" relates to the portions of development whose goal is to outline whatever the information management would accomplish from the perspective of their consumers. The development components that aim to create technological solutions

KEYWORD

Information management (IM) is the collection and management of information from one or more sources and the distribution of that information to one or more audiences.

for this standard are called data-oriented work. Working with data requires an issue definition as a starting point (Webster & Rashotte, 2010). At the first stage of the design process, the idea has been further described (i.e., requirements analysis).

3.3. CHARACTERISTIC OF GOOD ORGANIZATIONAL IS TALENT

There are several management-related reasons why a manager requires information. The kind of requirement that individuals will require at various periods and for various reasons mostly depends on two things that we will quickly discuss: their management characteristics and the organization in which they are making choices (Larsen et al., 2013).

3.3.1. Personal Attributes

The personality traits are described in subsections (Abdolmohammadi & Shanteau, 1992).

3.3.1.1. Knowledge of Information Systems (IS)

Managers will likely make more complex and targeted requests for data if they are aware of the capabilities of computer-based systems. Given their understanding of abilities and expenses, they are in a far better situation to help develop a decent system (Mylopoulos et al., 1990) (Figure 3.3).

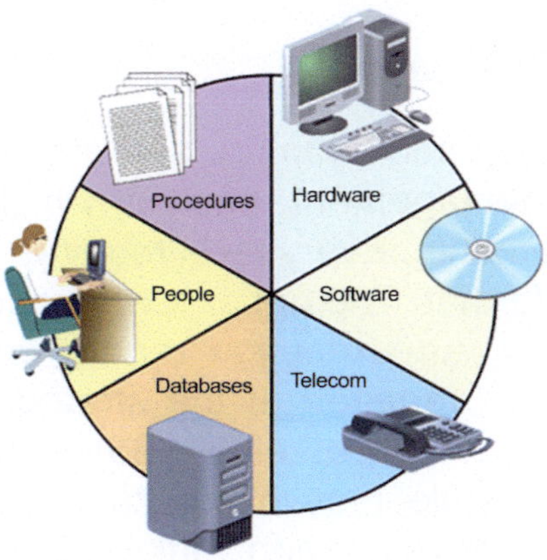

Figure 3.3. Image of components of computer-based system.

Source: E academy, Creative Commons License.

3.3.1.2. Managerial Style

The sort and volume of information needed depend on a manager's style of leadership, judgment skills, and technical expertise. Some people prefer more, while others prefer to make decisions quickly and personally confer with subordinates (Capozza & Seguin, 1998).

3.3.1.3. Manager's Perception of Information Needs

Both "*get me all the facts*" and "*you tell me what I need to know*" illustrate opposing viewpoints on the importance of information. That duality is partially caused by several managers lacking knowledge of the data they require. The vastly divergent perspectives of the top managers and their duty to communicate information to followers and groups from the outside company are another aspect of the problem. A manager unable or unwilling to share responsibility will probably keep information to themselves (Karim & Hussein, 2008).

KEYWORD

Organizational structure defines how activities such as task allocation, coordination, and supervision are directed toward the achievement of organizational aims.

3.3.2. Organizational Environment

The elements of the organizational environment are as in subsections.

3.3.2.1. Nature of the Company

The scale of the corporation and the complexities of its organizational structure appear to be contributing factors to communication, control, and monitoring issues. Even more formal communication systems that larger, more complicated businesses need are vital to their day-to-day operations (Bhattacharya & Sen, 2003).

3.3.2.2. Level of Management

Strategic planning, operation control, and management control are the three levels of management, each of which includes different informational requirements. Every level requires unique information, usually in a distinct format. The upper levels require a single report, overview, and inquiry. An exception report, overview, and range of periodic reports are required at the strategic control levels for ongoing evaluation (Engler et al., 1995). Establish operational control over actions while they occur, the degree of operational control necessitates a formal report with set procedures and a daily update of transactions. Depending on the type and significance of a decision, managers at different levels have varying information demands (Murphy, 2007).

3.3.2.3. Structure of the Organization

It is simpler to identify the information demands the more systematic the company is. The information requirements of managers could be determined more simply when their powers and duties are clearly stated, relationships are known, and decision-making regions are specified (Waterman et al., 1980).

3.4. STAGES IN PROCESS DESIGN

The process of developing IS makes an effort to ascertain the scope of the system that a user desires at its initial phase. Before the system is created and deployed, the following step conducts a detailed inspection and verification of the need above in two parts (Tugnoli et al., 2008).

3.4.1. Requirements Determination

This stage involves gathering user requirements and needs that reflect what users want from the developing system. There are numerous stages to it:

- Problem definition;
- Feasibility study;
- Requirements acquisition;
- Requirements analysis (Davis, 1982).

A basic outline of the intended system is defined during the example of the application and feasibility research stages. The Implementation for the intended *IS* is detailed during the problem definition phase, along with a description of the benefits that will follow from its adoption. The various options that can be used to design the desirable system are assessed during the project inception. An "expression of needs" is the required analysis acquisition phase output. The "requirements specification" is created during the requirements analysis step. The purpose of the requirement analysis is to serve as a structured summary of the system requirements that use the "statement of requirements" as its primary input (Browne & Ramesh, 2002).

KEYWORD

Requirements analysis is the process of determining user expectations for a new or modified product.

3.4.2. Analysis Phase

The objectives from the previous stage are examined inside this stage and transformed into components that are then utilized to create a "specification" of the intended system. For the user to recognize the description, the specification is much more specific than the previous stage and provides more detail while maintaining user semantics. However, the concept operates abstractly and does not include information on how data is represented or how computers are implemented (Garvie & Nicholson, 1972).

3.4.3. Logical Design

This stage results in the intended system's design, which will be the foundation for computer implementation. Logical design entails two main responsibilities. Firstly, the analytical phase's specification is transmitted, and then the human-computer interaction system is developed. The fact that the structure element is now expressed as data marks a considerable change from the previous phase. There are frequently a variety of different representations for relationships. Normalizing may also be used (Teorey et al., 1986). We determine the precise data types needed for data representations, the number of characters needed for every data item, and the architecture of the records, folders, or databases needed to keep the information while considering the kinds of procedures used to manipulate the data. An abstracted programming form, including structural English, action diagrams, or JSP diagrams, is frequently employed here. DFDs can be designed to display other information, such as processes that take place, the data output and input for every process, etc. (Burks et al., 1982).

Remember

A representation of the processors, storage systems, input/output devices, and optionally networking devices needed for the proposed system makes up the hardware design.

Developing human-computer systems would be the second important task in logical design. Usually, two degrees of detail are studied here:

- Design of user processes that include tasks and actions that users will take directly (Wang et al., 1997).
- Computer interface design consists of the specifics of the procedures and the things that these procedures operate. It may also consider interaction style (display and report setups, human-computer conversations), the details of mechanical or manual procedures, and whether processing should be done online or offline (Stucki et al., 1967).

3.4.4. Physical Design

The current phase of design is the final one. Software, hardware, and human-computer systems all be considered three separate parts of the system.

Programs that run mostly on hardware are referred to as software. Since the data type always impacts the programs which process the data, the physical design must be considered. The right applications software categories, including languages and modules, and the software applications needed to support the ultimate system, will need to be chosen (Warnock et al., 2002).

3.4.5. Process Design

There are four possibilities for process design (Figure 3.4):

- We can purchase packaged software for common procedures. Software used in accounting, for instance, is highly standardized;
- Use a language from the fourth generation, like Lotus123, Oracle, VB, etc.;
- Create code applying a CASE tool; and
- Write down our code (Pistikopoulos, 1995).

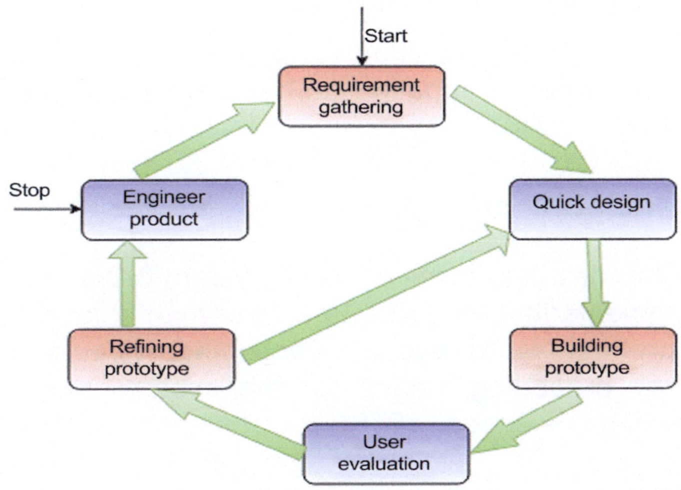

Fig.- Prototype Model

Figure 3.4. Flow diagram of case tool.

Source: career ride, Creative Commons License.

If in-house programming is used, data structures are selected for the applications' data representation and the necessary programming language, such as COBOL, C++, etc. Considerations include program code consistency and execution speed (Hill et al., 2002).

3.4.6. Human-Computer System Design

Some of the program's design details the actions to be taken when interacting with the computer, like the specifics of the operator's conversation with the machine, the steps to begin and end the machine, and the contents of the monitor, including the color or windows, etc. (Bannon, 1995).

3.4.7. Implementation and Testing

Instead of a design, a physical IS serves as the primary product of the installation and evaluation phase. Since it makes up the standard, the physical objects and initial designs will always be available for reference. The main duties include (Bruno & Chaudhuri, 2007):

- Integrate and acquire hardware, create software, produce data for files or databases, and create a human-computer interface (Dolce et al., 2000).
- The system is analyzed, and user remarks are evaluated, perhaps to improve the system.
- During a brief time, the user-implementation organizations of a system's function will be extensively scrutinized (Kouba, 2008).

KEYWORD

Data structure is a data organization, management, and storage format that is usually chosen for efficient access to data.

3.4.8. Maintenance

The maintenance stage involves fixing system flaws or adapting to user requirements that vary due to environmental modifications or individual preferences for system functioning. It could necessitate rebuilding all preceding stages for the system element, which needs updating (Swanson, 1976).

3.5. MODELING A SYSTEM DESIGN

The fundamental information model comprises three pieces, as illustrated below, including a data dictionary. The exterior model describes the system's user perspectives. They are combined into one global conceptual framework, as seen below. A conceptual model makes no assumptions about how the information and processes would be implemented in a system. It is performed using the internal model (represented in Figure 3.5 as 'schemas' and 'programs') (Sander & Jantsch, 2004).

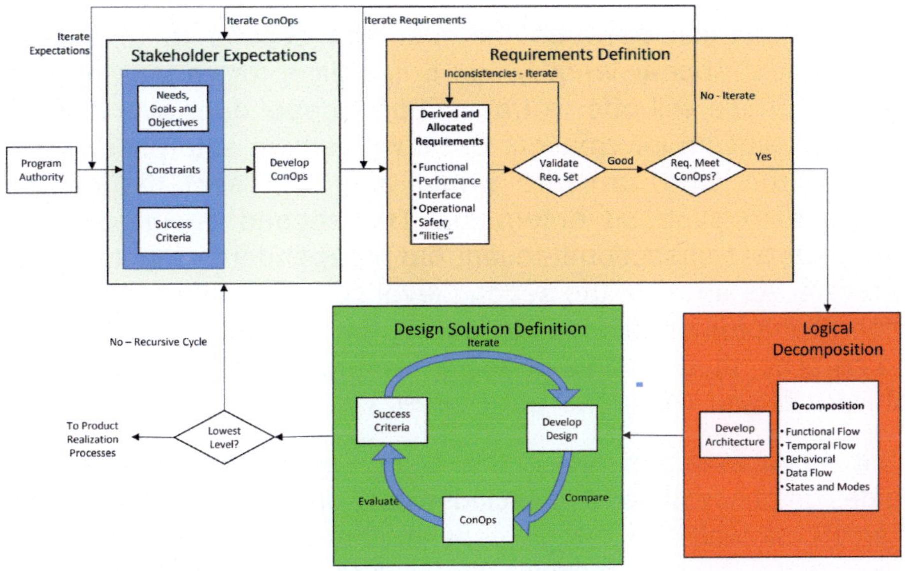

Figure 3.5. Illustration of system design.

Source: Nasa, Creative Common License.

3.6. STAGES IN IS MODELING

As previously said, we need not create the internal representation right away. First, a suggestion for a future model is developed and converted into an internal representation. We must additionally create two conceptual models.

- A conceptual data model; and
- A conceptual process models.

The consistency of these variables is then evaluated, or any required modifications are implemented to get just the data process model. It serves as the basic information structure (the data model, process model, including data processing framework), also known as *first-level design* (Greene et al., 1999).

Second-level design involves customizing a first-level design to a particular processing demand. The initial level design may contain so many links that if applied that way, it might not reach an acceptable degree of performance. As a result, the model may require 'flexing' to satisfy the needs of the operations that information management may provide. As a result, the level two design information model was generated (Farkas et al., 1996).

The *third level design* step is when the design is mapped to internal schemas needed by the software to construct the system.

The transition between the first and second to third phase design could appear lengthy, yet it is critical for various reasons. The first phase will offer a transaction-independent overview of a system's relevant information. But it will remain enterprise-specific because the data structure would only represent the items of relevance to such an enterprise. The second design phase is enterprise or transactional-reliant but independent of software and hardware. As a result, the second level could be utilized to analyze different implementations and aid in the software and hardware choice. The third design phase is enterprise, transactional, and software based (Mhurchu et al., 1997).

It is critical to understand that such a procedure does not imply the design of complete IS. It excludes data on determining the viability of an IS, as well as strategic considerations involved in picking an informational area. Similarly, little is addressed about design for forms, coding, displays, and results, nor is it about strategies for analyzing user demands (Chung et al., 2017) (Figure 3.6).

Figure 3.6. Illustration of stages of information modeling.

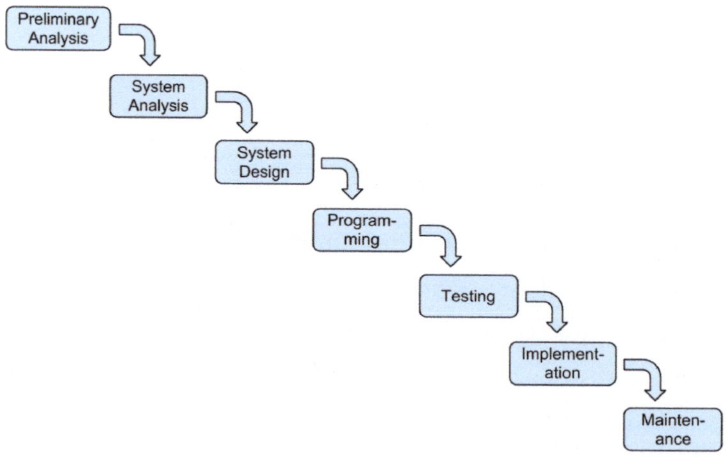

Source: Open Textbook, Creative Commons License.

3.7. SYSTEM DEVELOPMENT METHODS

Developing the system methodologies has evolved gradually. These three stages of advancement of system development approaches are as follows:

- First-generation methods;
- Second-generation methods;
- Third-generation methods (Baskerville, 1993).

3.7.1. First Generation (FG) Methods

Several "structured techniques" created in the late 1960s and early 1970s are among these techniques. Structural strategies break down big issues into smaller, well-defined parts with clear links. 'DIVIDE and RULE'

Components of first-generation methods:

- Structured programming;
- Modular design and structure charts;
- Programming style (Garriott & Nisle, 2018).
  - **Modular Design:** The reusing of groups of instructions is supported by several programming languages; these groups of statements are known as program modules and using them is known as modular programming. Structure diagrams demonstrate the connections between modules in a program (Danthinne & Imperiale, 2000).
  - **Programming Style:** Code could be complicated and difficult to comprehend when using standard techniques, but it was also acknowledged that manageable code needed style requirements (the 1970s).
  - **Data Structures:** Data design techniques were practical for creating data files and structures to assist programs in the 1970s. In the late 1960s, the CODASYL organization pioneered database design.
  - **Structured Design:** Structured programming techniques never provided instructions for how to carry out "design within large," only "design in little" (McKay & Estrella, 2008).

TIPS

When it comes to system development methods, it's important to keep in mind that there is no one-size-fits-all solution. Different projects may require different methods, and it's up to the development team to determine which approach will be most effective. However, one useful tip is to consider using a combination of methods, rather than relying solely on one.

- **Successive Refinement (Top-Down Functional Design):** A necessary system action was divided into a more manageable number of smaller jobs, which could then be merged to complete the function. Every one of them was then divided into more manageable sub-tasks. The procedure was repeated until the sub-task was so easy to code that there was a minimal likelihood of making a mistake (Guttormsen et al., 1987).

Technologies are based on the structural chart's semantics. The following were the main considerations for enhancing program design:

- **Coupling:** Interface complexity is measured; if interactions between modules are straightforward, the design is said to have minimal coupling.
- **Cohesion:** A module's "single-mindedness" as measured. A module is said to have functional coherence if it performs exactly one clearly defined function (Furukawa et al., 2016).

Remember

Data refinement means ensuring the data put into a data analytics platform is relevant, homogenized and categorized so the users can get meaningful results and pinpoint discrepancies.

- **Data Refinement:** All data are treated as "tables" in the relational data paradigm. Design excellence was assessed using refinement criteria. Normalization refers to the method of applying these criteria.
- **Structured Analysis:** The difficulty of identifying and presenting the user need in an unambiguous, intelligible form was addressed by developing the collection of tools and procedures known as "structured analysis." These methods primarily focused on necessary system operations and were "process-oriented."
- **Modeling Tools:** The key request was for modeling tools that would make it easier to break down complex demands into smaller components with clear interrelationships. The modeling software utilized was (Agarwal et al., 2000).
  - The suggested system's division into smaller functional units, or "mini systems," is demonstrated using data flow diagrams;
  - Mini-specs to specify every "mini-system."

A crucial method for obtaining user needs was the usage of review meetings, of which part of the needs were also provided. "*Structure walkthroughs*" were the names given to these evaluation sessions.

Information Modeling: A semantic information modeling method was developed simultaneously with structural analysis techniques. It was based on actual people, places, and things (Noazin et al., 2008).

- **Problems with Top-Down Functional Decomposition (TDFD):** Top-down functioning decomposition was conducted by making an informed judgment on the primary functional area. After that, every functional area was looked at separately and gradually deconstructed until the functionalities were easy to test with the user. It resulted in the second issue, which required TDFD to be enhanced or replaced with procedures of the second generation (Merrill et al., 1990).
  - **Analysis-Paralysis:** The system needed to be understood before it could be properly partitioned and required partitioning. Due to technical issues, creating the best possible expression and arrangement of the user requirements took a lot of time, necessitated extensive model reworking, and resulted in a compromise within the work's quality owing to time constraints (Zhao et al., 2004).
  - **Analyst Bias:** The analyst's perspective or thinking about the system is reflected in TDFD, a creative method. The logical model frequently reflects the analyst's implicit predisposition toward a particular answer (Fulkerson et al., 2007).
  - **Fragmentation of Policy:** It was occasionally discovered that operations broadly distributed in the design required cross-checking, although several rules helped determine the appropriate organization of a user's needs.
  - **Different System Development Philosophies:**
  - Process and data-driven methods.
  - Phase-oriented and model-oriented development (Kurtz et al., 2011).
- **Process-Oriented:** Focusing on how the system works and considering the data as merely there to help the system work (Tedeholm et al., 2013).
- **Data-Driven Methods:** Emphasizing information needs, especially identifying the data housed in databases. Little importance was placed on system functions.

TIPS

information model in software engineering is a representation of concepts and the relationships, constraints, rules, and operations to specify data semantics for a chosen domain of discourse.

- **Phase-Oriented:** The stages of the system development life cycle were viewed as tasks that needed to be completed throughout each phase (Próspero & Vohra, 2007).
- **Model-Oriented:** In this instance, the life cycle was viewed as a series of models for system requirements. Every model had a verifiable predetermined structure (Leucht et al., 2009).

3.7.2. Second Generation Methods

- Developers of first generation (FG) approaches were process- or data-oriented and made informal use of modeling. Building and verifying models are the primary focus of all Second-generation approaches (Kunt et al., 1985).
- Regarding handling each phase of the life cycle of system creation, FG techniques are primarily independent techniques. The transition from needs assessment to later design and execution stages is more seamless using second-generation approaches (Leucht et al., 2015).
- Modeling is not independent; one model grows into the next, considering a new layer of technologies. The FG model serves to capture system needs in terms of the policy. Following models focus on the way the model is projected onto accessible technology.
- FG approaches viewed the systems from a single angle, while other angles' modeling was generally subpar. According to SG techniques, information and system functions are crucial (Reid et al., 1997).

KEYWORD

Accessible technology has been designed in a way that can be accessed by all users.

Second-generation methods were externally oriented. Techniques for analysis are based on two different kinds of real-world needs:

- Respond to real-world events; and
- Store information about real-world entities.
- **Real-World Events:** Time is more specifically described regarding environmental events that affect the system. Only due to such actual events does the system act as it does, necessitating a response strategy.
- **Real World Entities:** The analyst avoids prejudice by gathering information on actual people, places, and things, as well as the connections between them.

- **CASE (Computer-Aided Software Engineering):** While such tools were available around 1975, CASE use did not become widespread until the 1980s. A "draw what you want" approach is used in some instance products, while others have "more well-defined grammar which the diagrams may be tested against."

A diagram is the second-generation technique's primary "diagram oriented" modeling unit. Drawings of diagrams are reviewed (Vasilyev & Bowman, 2000).

3.7.3. Third Generation Methods

The second-generation model view is comparatively simplistic. Instead of addressing the more general questions of how various analytical and design components fit together and interact, it tackles diagrams. A concept that places more emphasis on the entire thing than the pieces will set third-generation methods apart (Conibeer, 2007).

3.7.3.1. Techniques

An IS creation methodology is a group of protocols, methodologies, resources, and documentation aids supporting system developers as they implement new IS. A methodology would be composed of phases, which in turn would be composed of sub-phases. It will help developers create, manage, plan, control, and assess IS projects by guiding users in selecting approaches that may be applicable at each project step (Vittoz, 1994).

KEYWORD

Systems development is the process of defining, designing, testing, and implementing a new software application or program.

3.7.3.2. Tools

There are several tools available for the method of system development, particularly automated tools. All tools categorized (and subsequently defined) into some key groups are given below:

- Project management tools;
- Database management systems;
- Data dictionary systems;
- Systems repositories;
- Drawing tools;
- CASE (computer-aided software engineering) tools (Avison & Fitzgerald, 2003).

Diagrams of data flow, decision tables, decision trees, and structured English are a few of the process-oriented functional decomposition approaches used to develop IS techniques. The most crucial method of data flow diagrams, functional decomposition, lends structure to the activities they depict. This focus on structure provides the first methodology's name. STRADIS (Haux, 2006) (Figure 3.7).

Figure 3.7. Image of project management tools.

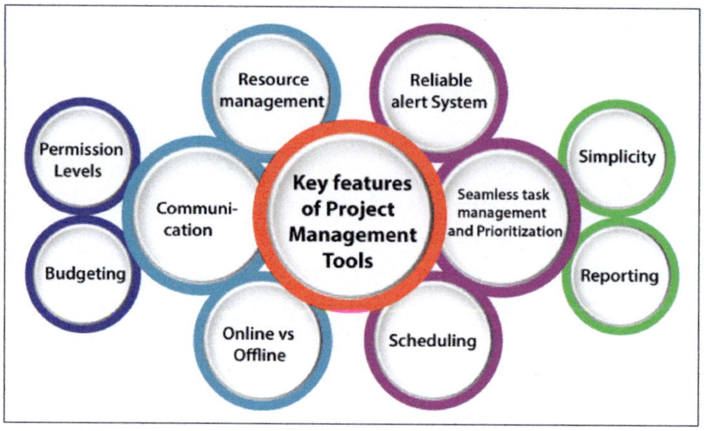

Source: Java Tpoint, Creative Commons License.

3.7.3.3. Methodologies

The following are a few of the several techniques suggested for IS development:

- **Top-Down Technique:** The Top-down technique (functional decomposition) is used by STRADIS (structured analysis and design of information systems) to analyze processes (Hein et al., 2008).
- **Yourdon Systems Method (YSM):** Although initially quite like STRADIS, it now varies in that it uses a middle-up technique—also known as event partitioning—to analyze processes, which is better suited than the top-down approach. We use the YSM in future research and analysis of IS in business due to the aspects above and greater comprehension and clarity of portrayal (Avison & Fitzgerald, 2003).
- **Information Engineering (IE):** Functional structure and data-flow diagrams are the core tools of the first two process-oriented techniques, but the key method of IE

is the data-oriented entity connection method (Ören & Zeigler, 1979).

- **Structured Systems Analysis and Design Methodology (SSADM):** The classic information life cycle of systems development strategy could be considered modernized. It contains entity life histories and data flow modeling methodologies and suggests using workbenches and CASE tools (Gregory & Jackson, 1992).
- **Merise:** Unlike earlier techniques that emphasized procedure or data components, Merise has been built, so both are regarded equally significant and examined and designed simultaneously.
- **Jackson Systems Development (JSD):** It is the evolution of Jackson systems programming (JSP), which has significantly affected the instruction and practice of commercial computer coding. This method focuses on creating efficient and very well software that adheres to specifications and is especially useful where performance is critical, such as in systems for process control (Hauck, 1995).
- **Object-Oriented Analysis:** This method is based on the belief that identifying objects and their basic pieces (attributes) can capture the basic components of information management. It is a unifying method because it may be used for analysis and design (Jennings, 2009).
- **Information Systems Work and Analysis (ISAC):** This methodology tries to discover the core reasons for users' issues while offering solutions (not always involving computer IS) through activity analysis and the inception of change processes. As a result, it is a people-oriented strategy emphasizing change detection and the process of change (*Source:* Information Systems Development: Methodologies, Techniques, and Tools by Avison, Fitzgerald) (Jia et al., 2018).
- **Effective Technical and Human Implementation of Computer-based Systems (ETHICS):** Any people-oriented strategy that includes a socio-technical viewpoint in which effective technology should be tightly aligned with the organizational and social elements within an application domain (Mercer, 2010).
- **Soft Systems Methodology (SSM):** While most previous approaches emphasized scientific investigation, breaking

Remember

Jackson System Development (JSD) is a method of system development that covers the software life cycle either directly or, by providing a framework into which more specialized techniques can fit. Jackson System Development can start from the stage in a project when there is only a general statement of requirements.

a complicated system into constituent elements to allow for analysis, systems thinking may argue that the qualities that make up a system are not wholly explicable of the characteristics of its constituent parts. SSM focuses on 'fuzzy, ill-structured, or soft problem scenarios' that constitute the actual domain of the development of IS approaches rather than basic technical difficulties (Dodgson, 2017).

- **Multiview:** It is a hybrid technique incorporating various methodologies' elements and employing tools and methods as needed. In essence, a contingency approach: approaches and tools are deployed when the problem scenario requires (Keith et al., 2007).
- **Innovation Capability:** It is most closely associated with business process reengineering, informational technology, and data systems. It is the key enabler of the innovation process because it allows for complete process changes (Kharrat et al., 2007).
- **Rapid Application Development (RAD):** It was created in response to the needs of constantly changing business settings. CASE technologies and system repositories are typically used to enable it (Tomiyama et al., 2009).
- **KADS:** This results from a European research initiative to create a complete, commercially feasible methodology for building knowledge-based systems (Wright, 2004).
- **Euro Approach:** Like the outcome of a European project, the Euro approach serves as a structure for acquiring and administrating resources for the study, development, or modification of data systems rather than a methodology (Eshghi et al., 2011).

ACTIVITY 3.1.

Imagine you are working for a software development company and your client has requested the development of a new online shopping platform. As a systems analyst, you are tasked with modeling the information system for this project. What stages of IS modeling will you go through to ensure the successful development of this platform? How will you determine the precise data types needed for data representations, the number of characters needed for every data item, and the architecture of the records, folders, or databases needed to keep the information while considering the kinds of procedures used to manipulate the data? How will you ensure that the human-computer interaction system is developed in a way that meets the needs of the client and the end-users? Finally, how will you communicate your findings and design to the development team to ensure a smooth implementation process?

3.8. SUMMARY

- Developing computer-based systems to handle demands or challenges is covered in the chapter "Modeling and Development of an Information System." The chapter discusses a variety of issues relating to the creation and modeling of IS, such as the value of involving users throughout the process, identifying users' requirements and expectations, identifying the characteristics that define successful overall organizational IS talent, as well as the phases of an IS's design process.
- The chapter also discusses modeling IS, which entails creating a representation of a system under development using a variety of modeling methodologies. Modeling is used to understand systems development better and spot any potential problems or possibilities for development. The chapter examines several modeling approaches and phases involved in IS modeling.
- The chapter offers a thorough overview of the design and modeling of information management, covering the crucial steps and methodologies used in the procedure. It emphasizes how crucial it is to involve users and then use modeling approaches to comprehend better the system is designed, and also how to have a multi-disciplinary team with various skills and knowledge to develop and deploy an IS successfully.

REVIEW QUESTIONS

1. What is the purpose of the analysis stage in developing an information system?
2. Why is it important to involve users in the development of information systems?
3. How can users' requirements be determined for the development of an IS?
4. What are some characteristics of good organizational IS talent?
5. What are the stages of the design process for an IS, and what is the purpose of each stage?
6. What is the purpose of modeming in developing an IS, and what are some common modeming techniques?
7. What are the different stages involved in modeming an IS, and what is the purpose of each stage?

MULTIPLE CHOICE QUESTIONS

1. What is the purpose of the analysis stage in developing an information system?

a. To write the code for the system
b. To create a detailed plan for the system
c. To monitor the system once it has been implemented.

   d. To identify the requirements of the system and understand the business processes that the system will support.

2. **Why is it important to involve users in the development of information systems?**
   a. To ensure the system is secure.
   b. To make updates and improvements to the system
   c. To understand the needs and expectations of the system's intended users
   d. To create representations of the system being developed
3. **What are some common modeming techniques used in the development of information systems?**
   a. Code snippets, logic statements, and database queries
   b. Data flow diagrams, entity-relationship diagrams, and use case modeling.
   c. Software development, project management, and user experience design
   d. Testing, data migration, and technical support
4. **Which of the following is a characteristic of good organizational IS talent?**
   a. Technical expertise only in software development
   b. A focus on completing tasks rather than understanding business processes.
   c. A multi-disciplinary skill set that includes software development, project management, and user experience design.
   d. A narrow perspective that does not consider the needs of end-users.
5. **What is the purpose of modeming in the development of an information system?**
   a. To write the code for the system
   b. To create a detailed plan for the system
   c. To help developers better understand the system being developed and identify any potential issues or areas for improvement.
   d. To monitor the system once it has been implemented.
6. **What are the stages of the design process for an information system?**
   a. Analysis, modeling, Implementation, and maintenance
   b. Data flow diagrams, entity-relationship diagrams, and use case modeling.
   c. Testing, data migration, and technical support
   d. Writing the code, integrating with existing systems, and providing technical support to users

Answers to the Multiple-Choice Questions

1. (d); 2. (c); 3. (b); 4. (c); 5. (c); 6. (a)

REFERENCES

1. Abdolmohammadi, M. J., & Shanteau, J., (1992). Personal attributes of expert auditors. *Organizational Behavior and Human Decision Processes, 53*(2), 158–172.
2. Ackerly, B., & True, J., (2013). Methods and methodologies. *The Oxford Handbook of Gender and Politics*, 135–159.
3. Agarwal, R. C., Aggarwal, C. C., & Prasad, V. V. V., (2000). Depth first generation of long patterns. In: *Proceedings of the Sixth ACM SIGKDD International Conference on Knowledge Discovery and Data Mining* (pp. 108–118).
4. Avison, D. E., & Fitzgerald, G., (2003). Where now for development methodologies? *Communications of the ACM, 46*(1), 78–82.
5. Baby, A., & Kannammal, A., (2020). Network path analysis for developing an enhanced TAM model: A user-centric e-learning perspective. *Computers in Human Behavior, 107*, 106081.
6. Bannon, L. J., (1995). From human factors to human actors: The role of psychology and human-computer interaction studies in system design. In: *Readings in Human–Computer Interaction* (pp. 205–214). Morgan Kaufmann.
7. Baskerville, R., (1993). Information systems security design methods: Implications for information systems development. *ACM Computing Surveys (CSUR), 25*(4), 375–414.
8. Batara, E., Nurmandi, A., Warsito, T., & Pribadi, U., (2017). Are government employees adopting local e-government transformation? The need for having the right attitude, facilitating conditions and performance expectations. *Transforming Government: People, Process and Policy, 11*(4), 612–638.
9. Bhattacharya, C. B., & Sen, S., (2003). Consumer–company identification: A framework for understanding consumers' relationships with companies. *Journal of Marketing, 67*(2), 76–88.
10. Bilgram, V., Brem, A., & Voigt, K. I., (2008). User-centric innovations in new product development—Systematic identification of lead users harnessing interactive and collaborative online-tools. *International Journal of Innovation Management, 12*(03), 419–458.
11. Browne, G. J., & Ramesh, V., (2002). Improving information requirements determination: A cognitive perspective. *Information & Management, 39*(8), 625–645.
12. Bruno, N., & Chaudhuri, S., (2007). An online approach to physical design tuning. In: *2007 IEEE 23rd International Conference on Data Engineering* (pp. 826–835). IEEE.
13. Burks, A. W., Goldstine, H. H., & Von, N. J., (1982). *Preliminary Discussion of the Logical Design of an Electronic Computing Instrument* (pp. 399–413). Springer Berlin Heidelberg.
14. Capozza, D. R., & Seguin, P. J., (1998). Managerial style and firm value. *Real Estate Economics, 26*(1), 131–150.

15. Chung, A. Q., Andreev, P., Benyoucef, M., Duane, A., & O'Reilly, P., (2017). Managing an organization's social media presence: An empirical stages of growth model. *International Journal of Information Management, 37*(1), 1405–1417.
16. Conibeer, G., (2007). Third-generation photovoltaics. *Materials Today, 10*(11), 42–50.
17. Danthinne, X., & Imperiale, M. J., (2000). Production of first generation adenovirus vectors: A review. *Gene Therapy, 7*(20), 1707–1714.
18. Davis, G. B., (1982). Strategies for information requirements determination. *IBM Systems Journal, 21*(1), 4–30.
19. De Castro, V., Marcos, E., & Vara, J. M., (2011). Applying CIM-to-PIM model transformations for the service-oriented development of information systems. *Information and Software Technology, 53*(1), 87–105.
20. Diede, N., McNish, G., & Coose, C., (2000). Performance expectations of the associate degree nurse graduate within the first six months. *Journal of Nursing Education, 39*(7), 302–307.
21. Dodgson, J. E., (2017). About research: Qualitative methodologies. *Journal of Human Lactation, 33*(2), 355–358.
22. Dolce, M., Cardone, D., & Marnetto, R., (2000). Implementation and testing of passive control devices based on shape memory alloys. *Earthquake Engineering & Structural Dynamics, 29*(7), 945–968.
23. Engler, D. R., Kaashoek, M. F., & O'Toole, Jr. J., (1995). Exokernel: An operating system architecture for application-level resource management. *ACM SIGOPS Operating Systems Review, 29*(5), 251–266.
24. Eshghi, A., Haughton, D., Legrand, P., Skaletsky, M., & Woolford, S., (2011). Identifying groups: A comparison of methodologies. *Journal of Data Science, 9*(2), 271–291.
25. Faraj, S., & Sambamurthy, V., (2006). Leadership of information systems development projects. *IEEE Transactions on Engineering Management, 53*(2), 238–249.
26. Farkas, A. J., Pierce, J. P., Zhu, S. H., Rosbrook, B., Gilpin, E. A., Berry, C., & Kaplan, R. M., (1996). Addiction versus stages of change models in predicting smoking cessation. *Addiction, 91*(9), 1271–1280.
27. Fulkerson, E., Tejwani, N., Stuchin, S., & Egol, K., (2007). Management of periprosthetic femur fractures with a first generation locking plate. *Injury, 38*(8), 965–972.
28. Furukawa, T. A., Salanti, G., Atkinson, L. Z., Leucht, S., Ruhe, H. G., Turner, E. H., & Cipriani, A., (2016). Comparative efficacy and acceptability of first-generation and second-generation antidepressants in the acute treatment of major depression: Protocol for a network meta-analysis. *BMJ Open, 6*(7), e010919.
29. Garriott, P. O., & Nisle, S., (2018). Stress, coping, and perceived academic goal progress in first-generation college students: The role of institutional supports. *Journal of Diversity in Higher Education, 11*(4), 436.
30. Garvie, R. C., & Nicholson, P. S., (1972). Phase analysis in zirconia systems. *Journal of the American Ceramic Society, 55*(6), 303–305.

31. Greene, G., Rossi, S. R., Rossi, J. S., Velicer, W. F., Fava, J. L., & Prochaska, J. O., (1999). Dietary applications of the stages of change model. *Journal of the American Dietetic Association, 99*(6), 673–679.
32. Gregory, A. J., & Jackson, M. C., (1992). Evaluation methodologies: A system for use. *Journal of the Operational Research Society, 43*(1), 19–28.
33. Guttormsen, M., Ramsøy, T., & Rekstad, J., (1987). The first generation of γ-rays from hot nuclei. *Nuclear Instruments and Methods in Physics Research Section A: Accelerators, Spectrometers, Detectors and Associated Equipment, 255*(3), 518–523.
34. Haag, S., Cummings, M., & Dawkins, J., (1998). Management information systems. *Multimedia Systems, 279*, 280–297.
35. Hauck, S., & Borriello, G., (1997). An evaluation of bipartitioning techniques. *IEEE Transactions on Computer-Aided Design of Integrated Circuits and Systems, 16*(8), 849–866.
36. Hauck, S., (1995). Asynchronous design methodologies: An overview. *Proceedings of the IEEE, 83*(1), 69–93.
37. Haux, R., (2006). Health information systems–past, present, future. *International Journal of Medical Informatics, 75*(3, 4), 268–281.
38. Hein, J. R., Evans, J., & Jones, P., (2008). Mobile methodologies: Theory, technology and practice. *Geography Compass, 2*(5), 1266–1285.
39. Hill, A. V., Collier, D. A., Froehle, C. M., Goodale, J. C., Metters, R. D., & Verma, R., (2002). Research opportunities in service process design. *Journal of Operations Management, 20*(2), 189–202.
40. Jennings, G. R., (2009). Methodologies and methods. *Handbook of Tourism Studies,* 672–692.
41. Jia, X., Huang, B., Feng, J., Cai, H., & Lee, J., (2018). A review of PHM data competitions from 2008 to 2017: Methodologies and analytics. In: *Proceedings of the Annual Conference of the Prognostics and Health Management Society* (pp. 1–10).
42. Karim, N. S. A., & Hussein, R., (2008). Managers' perception of information management and the role of information and knowledge managers: The Malaysian perspectives. *International Journal of Information Management, 28*(2), 114–127.
43. Keith, L. H., Gron, L. U., & Young, J. L., (2007). Green analytical methodologies. *Chemical Reviews, 107*(6), 2695–2708.
44. Khan, G. F., Moon, J. H., Rhee, C., & Rho, J. J., (2010). E-government skills identification and development: Toward a staged-based user-centric approach for developing countries. *Asia Pacific Journal of Information Systems, 20*(1), 1–31.
45. Kharrat, A. M., Zacharia, J., Cherian, V. J., & Anyatonwu, A., (2007). Issues with comparing SARA methodologies. *Energy & Fuels, 21*(6), 3618–3621.
46. Kouba, J., (2008). Implementation and testing of the gridded Vienna mapping function 1 (VMF1). *Journal of Geodesy, 82*, 193–205.

47. Kunt, M., Ikonomopoulos, A., & Kocher, M., (1985). Second-generation image-coding techniques. *Proceedings of the IEEE, 73*(4), 549–574.

48. Kurtz, S. M., Gawel, H. A., & Patel, J. D., (2011). History and systematic review of wear and osteolysis outcomes for first-generation highly crosslinked polyethylene. *Clinical Orthopaedics and Related Research®, 469*, 2262–2277.

49. Larsen, C. H., Alfermann, D., Henriksen, K., & Christensen, M. K., (2013). Successful talent development in soccer: The characteristics of the environment. *Sport, Exercise, and Performance Psychology, 2*(3), 190.

50. Leucht, S., Corves, C., Arbter, D., Engel, R. R., Li, C., & Davis, J. M., (2009). Second-generation versus first-generation antipsychotic drugs for schizophrenia: A meta-analysis. *The Lancet, 373*(9657), 31–41.

51. Leucht, S., Samara, M., Heres, S., Patel, M. X., Furukawa, T., Cipriani, A., & Davis, J. M., (2015). Dose equivalents for second-generation antipsychotic drugs: The classical mean dose method. *Schizophrenia Bulletin, 41*(6), 1397–1402.

52. McKay, V. C., & Estrella, J., (2008). First-generation student success: The role of faculty interaction in service learning courses. *Communication Education, 57*(3), 356–372.

53. Mercer, N., (2010). The analysis of classroom talk: Methods and methodologies. *British Journal of Educational Psychology, 80*(1), 1–14.

54. Merrill, M. D., Li, Z., & Jones, M. K., (1990). Limitations of first generation instructional design. *Educational Technology, 30*(1), 7–11.

55. Mhurchu, C. N., Margetts, B. M., & Speller, V. M., (1997). Applying the stages-of-change model to dietary change. *Nutrition Reviews, 55*(1), 10–16.

56. Murphy, B. L., (2007). Locating social capital in resilient community-level emergency management. *Natural Hazards, 41*, 297–315.

57. Mylopoulos, J., Borgida, A., Jarke, M., & Koubarakis, M., (1990). Telos: Representing knowledge about information systems. *ACM Transactions on Information Systems (TOIS), 8*(4), 325–362.

58. Noazin, S., Modabber, F., Khamesipour, A., Smith, P. G., Moulton, L. H., Nasseri, K., & Tanner, M., (2008). First generation leishmaniasis vaccines: A review of field efficacy trials. *Vaccine, 26*(52), 6759–6767.

59. Ören, T. I., & Zeigler, B. P., (1979). Concepts for advanced simulation methodologies. *Simulation, 32*(3), 69–82.

60. Pistikopoulos, E. N., (1995). Uncertainty in process design and operations. *Computers & Chemical Engineering, 19*, 553–563.

61. Próspero, M., & Vohra-Gupta, S., (2007). First generation college students: Motivation, integration, and academic achievement. *Community College Journal of Research and Practice, 31*(12), 963–975.

62. Reid, M. M., Millar, R. J., & Black, N. D., (1997). Second-generation image coding: An overview. *ACM Computing Surveys (CSUR), 29*(1), 3–29.

63. Robey, D., Smith, L. A., & Vijayasarathy, L. R., (1993). Perceptions of conflict and success in information systems development projects. *Journal of Management Information Systems, 10*(1), 123–140.
64. Sander, I., & Jantsch, A., (2004). System modeling and transformational design refinement in ForSyDe [formal system design]. *IEEE Transactions on Computer-Aided Design of Integrated Circuits and Systems, 23*(1), 17–32
65. Siau, K., Long, Y., & Ling, M., (2010). Toward a unified model of information systems development success. *Journal of Database Management (JDM), 21*(1), 80–101.
66. Stucki, M. J., Ornstein, S. M., & Clark, W. A., (1967). Logical design of macromodules. In: *Proceedings of the April 18–20, 1967, Spring Joint Computer Conference* (pp. 357–364).
67. Swanson, E. B., (1976). The dimensions of maintenance. In: *Proceedings of the 2nd International Conference on Software Engineering* (pp. 492–497).
68. Tedeholm, H., Lycke, J., Skoog, B., Lisovskaja, V., Hillert, J., Dahle, C., & Andersen, O., (2013). Time to secondary progression in patients with multiple sclerosis who were treated with first generation immunomodulating drugs. *Multiple Sclerosis Journal, 19*(6), 765–774.
69. Teorey, T. J., Yang, D., & Fry, J. P., (1986). A logical design methodology for relational databases using the extended entity-relationship model. *ACM Computing Surveys (CSUR), 18*(2), 197–222.
70. Tomiyama, T., Gu, P., Jin, Y., Lutters, D., Kind, C., & Kimura, F., (2009). Design methodologies: Industrial and educational applications. *CIRP Annals, 58*(2), 543–565.
71. Tugnoli, A., Santarelli, F., & Cozzani, V., (2008). An approach to quantitative sustainability assessment in the early stages of process design. *Environmental Science & Technology, 42*(12), 4555–4562.
72. Vasilyev, O. V., & Bowman, C., (2000). Second-generation wavelet collocation method for the solution of partial differential equations. *Journal of Computational Physics, 165*(2), 660–693.
73. Vetter, J. S., & Worley, P. H., (2002). Asserting performance expectations. In: *SC'02: Proceedings of the 2002 ACM/IEEE Conference on Supercomputing* (pp. 33–33). IEEE.
74. Vittoz, E. A., (1994). Micropower techniques. *Design of VLSI Circuits for Telecommunication and Signal Processing*, 53–97.
75. Voss, G. B., Parasuraman, A., & Grewal, D., (1998). The roles of price, performance, and expectations in determining satisfaction in service exchanges. *Journal of Marketing, 62*(4), 46–61.
76. Wang, X. S., Bettini, C., Brodsky, A., & Jajodia, S., (1997). Logical design for temporal databases with multiple granularities. *ACM Transactions on Database Systems (TODS), 22*(2), 115–170.

77. Warnock, J. D., Keaty, J. M., Petrovick, J., Clabes, J. G., Kircher, C. J., Krauter, B. L., & Anderson, C. J., (2002). The circuit and physical design of the POWER4 microprocessor. *IBM Journal of Research and Development, 46*(1), 27–51.
78. Waterman, Jr. R. H., Peters, T. J., & Phillips, J. R., (1980). Structure is not organization. *Business Horizons, 23*(3), 14–26.
79. Webster, Jr. M., & Rashotte, L. S., (2010). Behavior, expectations and status. *Social Forces, 88*(3), 1021–1049.
80. Whitman, M. E., (1996). IT divergence in reengineering support: Performance expectations vs. perceptions. *Information & Management, 30*(5), 239–250.
81. Wright, J., (2004). Post-structural methodologies. *Body Knowledge and Control: Studies in the Sociology of Physical Education and Health*, 19–30.
82. Zhao, Y., Pu, J., Lynch, B. J., & Truhlar, D. G., (2004). Tests of second-generation and third-generation density functionals for thermochemical kinetics. *Physical Chemistry Chemical Physics, 6*(4), 673–676.

CHAPTER 4

DATABASE MANAGEMENT SYSTEM

UNIT INTRODUCTION

An ordered collection of data is called a database. A database should aid an organization in achieving its objectives, much like other elements of an information system (IS). A database may contribute to the success of an organization by providing decision-makers and managers with relevant, timely, and accurate data-based information. For instance, Comic Relief in England and London organizes comedy shows to raise money for the underprivileged. This organization employs a database to keep tabs on which segments from its televised fundraiser are the most well-received emotionally by viewers (McHugh et al., 1997).

Databases assist businesses in producing information to lower costs, boost profitability, monitor previous company operations, and uncover new market prospects. In some instances, businesses work together to develop and use global databases. Six organizations use a database to keep track of the world's oil supply, such as the United Nations, the IEA (International Energy Agency), and the OPEC (Organization of Petroleum Exporting Countries) (McCarthy & Dayal, 1989).

The term "database management system" (DBMS) refers to a collection of programs that runs in the background to manage databases and provide an interface for other applications. DBMS, which can be purchased from specialized database vendors, provide streamlined administration of all data-related resources, which is crucial for maintaining data privacy and integrity. The management system, the database, and the applications that access the data make up what is known as a database environment (Stonebraker & Kemnitz, 1991) (Figure 4.1).

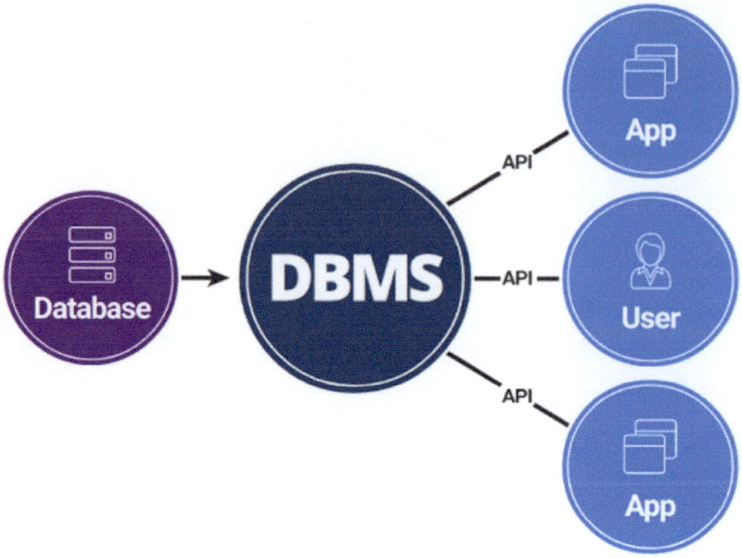

Figure 4.1. Difference between database and DBMS.

Source: Shehan PW, Creative Commons License.

A database administrator (DBA) is a qualified and experienced IT specialist that oversees all operations involving a company's database, including ensuring protection against attackers. For a variety of reasons, people break into databases. For example, consider the Latvian computer specialist who, by breaking into a government database, uncovered the salaries of government employees. He wanted to demonstrate to the populace that government employees continued to be paid well despite the country's serious economic issues (Huang et al., 2009). In 2010, 3.3 million students' names, dates of birth, and Social Security numbers were taken from a database that belonged to a student loan company. Since many databases may now be accessed online, these data breaches have become frequent for corporations. Data accuracy and quality continue to be crucial challenges for DBAs. For instance, a land registry error caused Pauline Grant's and her farm's government records in Uckfield, England, to become jumbled. Due to the error, Blossom, the pig on Grant's farm, received mail urging her to cast a ballot in the next election (Taylor & Frank, 1976).

Businesses have been relying increasingly on databases and DBMS as they deal with growing volumes of digital data. According to a report by International Data Corporation (IDC) titled "The Digital Universe Decade – Are researchers ready?" the digital universe will grow to 1.2 zettabytes (or 1.2 trillion gigabytes) by the end of the decade. Data that is one zettabyte in size would be the size of a million Earths if each tennis ball represented a byte. Also, between 2009 and 2020, storage capacity would rise by 30%, while the amount of information humans produce would increase by a factor of 44. Yet only 1.4 more will be spent on database infrastructure and management. IDC urges businesses to create the standards, resources, and guidelines necessary to manage the impending deluge of digital data and information (Batoory et al., 1988).

Learning Objectives

At the end of this chapter, readers will be able to learn the following:

- Data management and its various concepts, including data entities, attributes, and keys;
- Overview of the database types, including flat file, single users, and multiple users;
- A view of the user, including data gathering, manipulating, and using the data with software;
- Selection of database system for particular data sets;
- Various applications of the database, including data warehouse, data marts, and data mining;
- Concepts of object-oriented database management;
- Visual, audio, and other database systems.

Key Terms

- Business intelligence
- Data
- Data management
- Data marts
- Data mining
- Data warehouse
- Database
- Database system
- Entity
- Flat file

4.1. DATA MANAGEMENT

If an organization cannot access data and the resources to process it, it could struggle to function. It could not handle administrative tasks like deciding policies, sending invoices, paying workers, placing orders, or providing data. As researchers may remember, data comprises unprocessed facts like the number of employees and sales information. Data should first be meaningfully organized to be translated into valuable information (Schadt et al., 2010) (Figure 4.2).

Did you get it?

The worldwide data volume is projected to grow to 175 zettabytes by 2025, driving the adoption of data management technologies such as data warehousing, mining, and analytics in information systems.

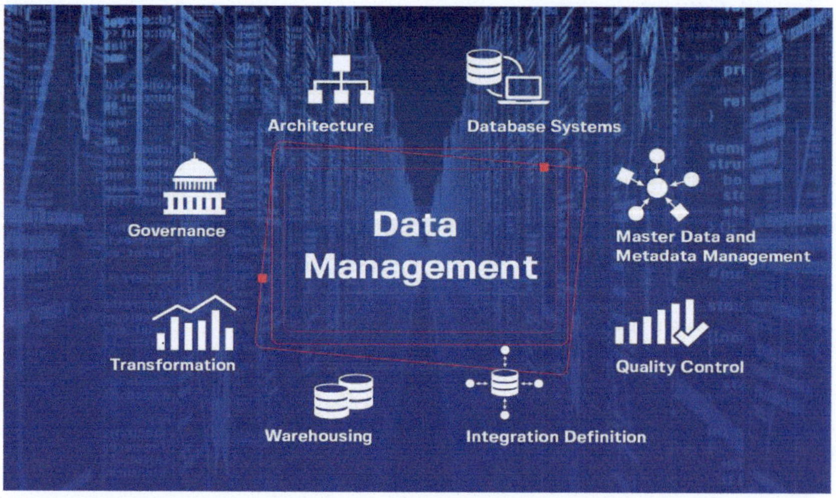

Figure 4.2. Data management roadmap.

Source: Divectors, Creative Commons License.

4.1.1. Data Entities, Attributes, and Keys

The key database concepts are attributes, entities, and keys. An entity is a broad category of individuals, locations, or things (objects) about which data is gathered, kept, and updated. Customers, inventory, and staff are a few instances of entities. Most businesses use entities to store and organize data (Efthymiou et al., 2015).

An entity's attribute is one of its properties. Department number, hire date, first name, last name, and employee number are employee characteristics (*see* Figure 4.3). Items in inventory have features such as their inventory number, description, quantity on hand, and location within the warehouse. Customers have the following characteristics: customer number, address, name, credit rating, phone number, and contact person. Attributes are often picked to represent important characteristics of entities like workers or customers accurately. The fields in the record describing the entity have the precise value of each attribute (also known as a data item) (Hur & Noh, 2010).

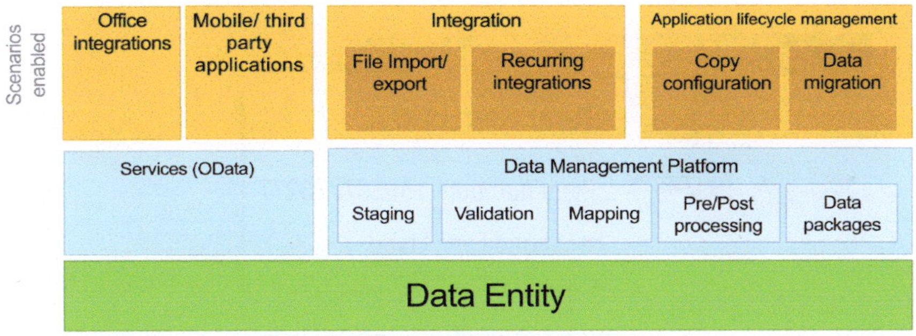

Figure 4.3. An example of a data entity.

Source: Priyanka Agarwal, Creative Commons License.

Attributes and data items are commonly used in companies. Various governments employ characteristics and data points to aid in homicide investigations. The FBI (Federal Bureau of Investigation) in the United States is compiling a sizable database of people's biometrics. The next generation identity DBMS, which would cost $1 billion, will store digital photographs of visitors' and citizens' fingerprints, faces, and palm prints. Each biometric class is an attribute, every human is an entity, and every image is a piece of data in the database. This data will be used as a forensics resource to strengthen national security (Dinu et al., 2006).

A record, as was previously stated, is a set of fields associated with a single item. A record's key is the field (or set of fields) that serves as its identifying information. A record can be identified by its primary key, a field, or a group of combined fields. The primary key can't be shared with any other records. The main key for an employee record would be the employee number. Records are differentiated using the primary key to be retrieved, arranged, and modified. Primary keys provide every record in a database with its distinct identifier. eBay uses an "item number" as its primary key to ensure that bids are attached to the correct item shown in Figure 4.4 (Hur, 2011).

Figure 4.4. eBay assigns an "item number" as a primary key to keep track of each item in its database.

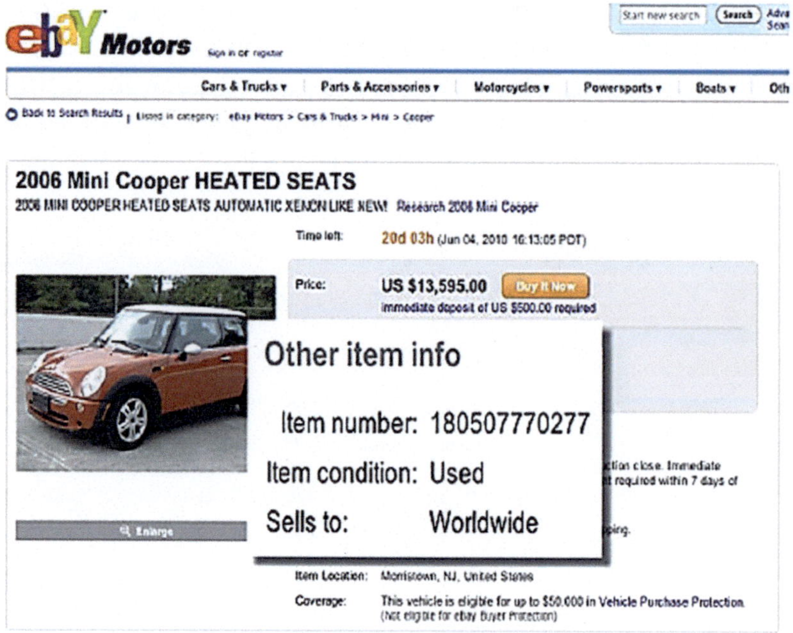

Source: eBay Motors, Creative Commons License.

Using a mix of secondary keys may make finding a specific record that fits certain requirements simpler and quicker. For instance, a customer could phone a mail-order business to order clothing. If the client does not remember the correct primary key, they can use a secondary key, including a last name, to access their account (Braganholo, 2018). Upon entering the primary key, typically a customer number, the order clerk can access the customer's billing and shipping details. The order clerk, like Adams, enters the last name in this instance. If several customers share the same surname, the clerk may need to use other information, such as the customer's first name or address, to locate the relevant customer file. After locating the appropriate client record, the order can be processed, and the purchased apparel may be shipped (Duftschmid et al., 2010).

4.1.2. The Database Approach

Information systems (IS) are used to reference particular files containing pertinent data. A payroll file might be used, for instance, by a payroll system. Each unique operational system used specific data files. The term "conventional approach to data management" refers to this method of handling data.

Data management via a database entails a centralized repository of information from which multiple systems can draw. Databases make it possible for groups to pool their information and data. DNA test results, for instance, are often included as a defining feature of convicted criminals in federal databases. It can be distributed to law enforcement authorities around the country (Plattner, 2009).

Extra software, known as a DBMS, is required for the database method to work. A DBMS, as was said before, comprises a suite of programs that act as a bridge between a database and its end user. Typically, this program acts as a buffer between the database and the apps. Figure 4.5 depicts the database plan.

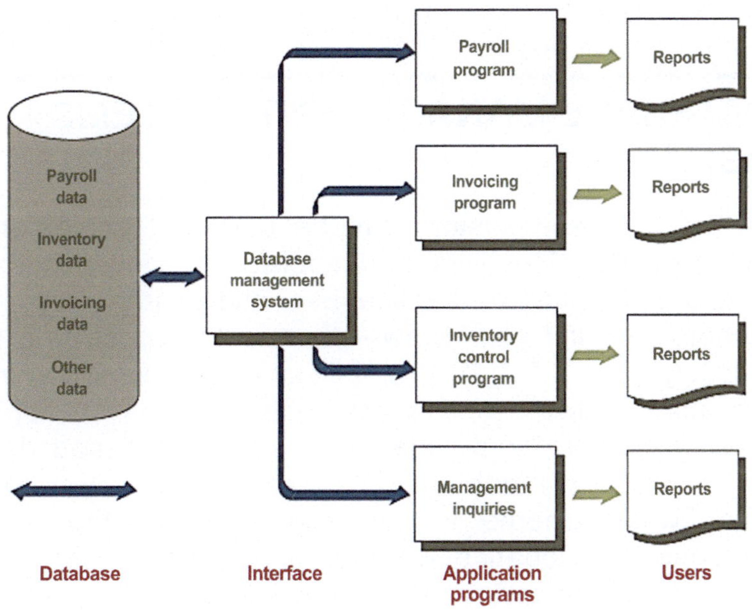

Figure 4.5. The database approach to data management.

Source: Ralph Stair, Creative Commons License.

Several contemporary databases include most of the data in the organization and service entire businesses. Enterprise-wide databases are frequently linked to other unique but connected databases. For instance, several Wal-Mart locations provide customer-accessible on-site medical clinics. Wal-Mart stores patients' medical records in one central electronic health records database. Customers' store and clinic histories can be traced to the main Walmart database (Császár et al., 2007) (Table 4.1).

Table 4.1. Comparison of Data and OLAP

Disadvantages	Explanation
More complexity	DBMSs can be challenging to install and run. For the DBMS to function correctly, several decisions should be made appropriately. Users must also master new processes to utilize DBMSs to their full potential.
More difficult to recover from a failure	A failure of a file while using the conventional method of managing files only impacts one program. A DBMS failure might cause the entire database to go down.
More expensive	DBMSs may cost more to buy and maintain than conventional file management. The cost covers the price of the database and the cost of specialist staff, like a database administrator, who is required to create and manage the database. Perhaps even more hardware is needed.

Source: Ralph, Creative Commons License.

4.2. DATABASE MANAGEMENT SYSTEMS (DBMS)

The correct database system can be built and implemented to support corporate objectives and operations. However, how do researchers build, put into practice, use, and upgrade a database? Researchers can find your answer there with access to a DBMS. As previously said, a DBMS is a suite of applications that mediate between other software and a database, such as an application or a user. Yet, there is a wide range of features and database systems available (Stonebraker & Kemnitz, 1991). For example, Brightkite, Twitter, Google, and other Internet firms that offer GPS location apps are debating whether or not to create a “Unified Database of Locations.” Instead of each company maintaining separate databases for company and attraction sites, they will want to pool resources to develop one massive database of places that contains information on each site on earth, fueling apps such as Google Street View. DBMS manage many kinds of information for many purposes (McCarthy & Dayal, 1989).

4.3. OVERVIEW OF DATABASE TYPES

DBMS can be as simple as inexpensive software or as complex as expensive. The parts that follow go through a few well-liked substitutes. Figure 4.6 provides one illustration.

4.3.1. Flat File

A flat file is a straightforward database software with no connections between the records. Flat file databases, which don't employ previously covered database models, like the relational model, are frequently used to store and modify a single table or file. Flat files are supported by many spreadsheet and word-processing programs. These computer programs could do simple calculations, comparisons, and table sorting. With Microsoft OneNote, anyone may make a flat file to store their ideas, thoughts, and notes. OneNote allows researchers to place each note anywhere on a page or in a box or container on a page. Sections and subsections are arranged on pages as colored tabs (Myers et al., 2011). The researcher may access, copy, and paste a note after researchers have entered it into another program, like a word processor or spreadsheet. OneNote is used by ResMed, a medical company that creates solutions to help patients with respiratory disorders, to document the status of new ideas for product enhancements through evaluation and deployment. OneNote supports the business in boosting engagement in cost-cutting and efficiency improvements (Drake et al., 2004).

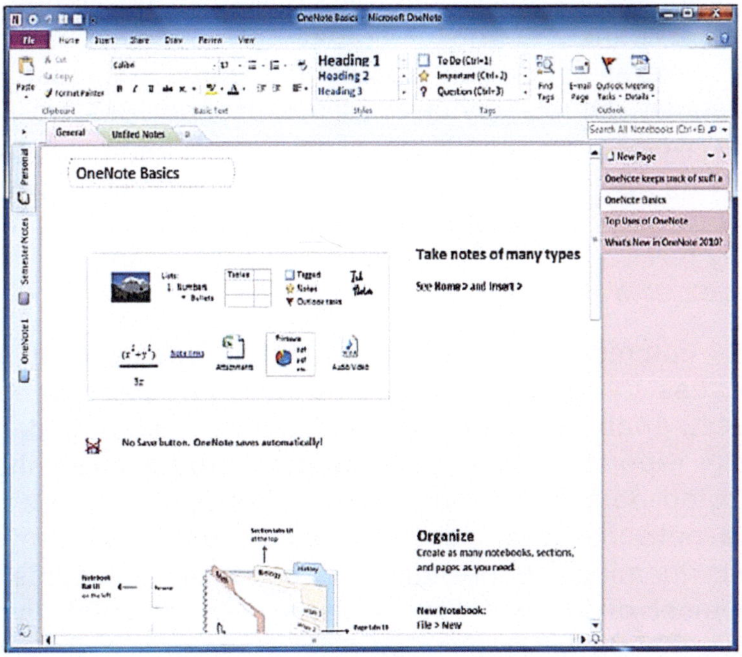

Figure 4.6. *Schematic of the Microsoft OneNote.*

Source: Microsoft Corporation, Creative Commons License.

EverNote is a complimentary online database service where a researcher may store notes and other information, similar to OneNote. Databases that can manage unstructured data will continue to increase in popularity due to the vast volumes of data that today's high-capacity hard discs can hold (Orwat et al., 2008).

4.3.2. Single User

A personal computer's installed database is normally made for a single user. Both FileMaker Pro and Microsoft Office Access are built to enable single-user setups. Another illustration of a database application that supports one user is Microsoft InfoPath. This program, a component of the Microsoft Office package, assists users in gathering and organizing data from many sources. The built-in forms in InfoPath may be utilized to enter timesheet data, expenditure data, and various other types of data (Ekins et al., 2006).

4.3.3. Multiple Users

Multiuser DBMSs are necessary for small, medium-sized, and large enterprises to share information across the company over a network. Thanks to these increasingly sophisticated, pricey devices, several users can access the same database system simultaneously. Oracle, Sybase, Microsoft, and IBM are some of the more well-known providers of multiuser database systems. Several single-user databases, such as Microsoft Access, may be set up to handle multiple users over a network. However, they frequently have a cap on how many users they can accommodate (Fernández et al., 2017).

TIPS

When storing and retrieving data, consider the organization and structure to ensure easy searching, retrieval, and analysis. Develop a data management strategy that includes storage, backup, and recovery for efficient and effective access and utilization of data.

Some common tasks performed by all DBMSs include giving users access to data, retrieving data and physically storing from databases, enabling database modification, altering data, and producing reports. These DBMSs can handle even the most sophisticated data processing activities since they are accessed across a network, meaning that a single database can service numerous locations worldwide. For instance, the Linde Group controls most of the world's hydrogen and industrial gas sales. They have 50,000 workers in 100 different countries, yet everyone can access the same data center in Munich, Germany (Md. Nor et al., 2020).

4.4. PROVIDING A USER VIEW

Since the DBMS regulates access to a database, "teaching" the DBMS the logical and physical structure of the data and the links among the data for each user is one of the first jobs in installing and utilizing a large database. A schema is used to describe this (as in the schematic diagram). Schemas are frequently used in large database systems like Oracle to specify the tables and other database characteristics connected to a certain user or person. Either the database itself or a separate schema file may contain a schema. The DBMS may use a schema to determine how to retrieve the information requested in connection to other data (Luo et al., 2009).

4.4.1. Storing and Retrieving Data

One of the roles of a DBMS is to act as a bridge between an application and the database. Whenever software needs information, it queries the DBMS. For example, the cost of a brand-new car may depend on a pricing scheme that requires data on the additional cost of a six-cylinder engine in addition to the standard four. This information is requested from the DBMS by the application program. The application program adopts a logical access path (LAP) to achieving this. The DBMS then communicates with the other programs on the system to get the data from a storage medium like a disc drive. The physical access path (PAP) (physical location) in which the pricing of this option is kept is followed by the DBMS when it accesses this storage device to get the data (Baden et al., 2009).

The DBMS may read the six-cylinder engine pricing information from a disc. Such a correlation is seen in Figure 4.7.

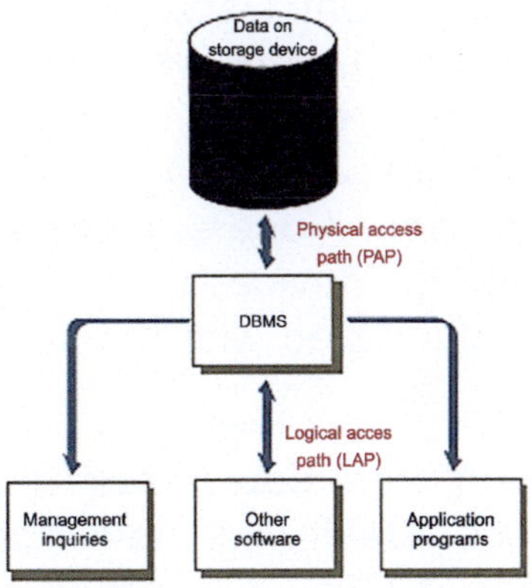

Figure 4.7. Logical and physical access.

Source: Ralph Stair, Creative Commons License.

The same procedure is followed when a user requests information from the database. The user must request the DBMS. For instance, the user could use the query to display all available options that cost more than $200 (Li et al., 2010). What researchers have here is the LAP. The DBMS can retrieve the user's data by reading the disc's options price section. To be specific, the PAP (Li et al., 2010).

4.4.2. Manipulating Data and Generating Reports

Employees, supervisors, and customers can utilize a DBMS to analyze reports and get crucial information after deployment. For instance, the Food Allergen and Consumer Protection Act, which went into force in 2006, mandates that companies that manufacture food produce reports on the components, recipes, and food preparation methods for the general public. A business can handle this demand by using a DBMS (Koyama, 2011).

KEYWORD

data manipulation language is a computer programming language used for adding, deleting, and modifying data in a database.

QBE (query by example), a visual approach for constructing database requests or inquiries, is used by many databases. By opening windows and choosing the features or data the researcher needs, a researcher may run queries and carry out other database tasks, such as Windows and other GUI operating systems (OSs) (Bernstein & Melnik, 2007).

In other circumstances, programming language commands for databases can be utilized. For instance, simple applications that access or alter particular pieces of data in the database can be written using C++ commands. Here's another illustration of a DBMS: SELECT * FROM EMPLOYEE WHERE JOB_CLASSIFICATION = "C2." All columns from the EMPLOYEE table will be included in the query if the asterisk (*) is present. Data manipulation language (DML) often includes commands to work with the database. Accessing and modifying data, running queries, and creating reports can all be done in the DBMS's native language, making it convenient for managers and other database users. Once again, data on a disc or other persistent storage device cannot be accessed until the applications have communicated with the schemas and the DBMS (Paton et al., 2011).

D. D. Chamberlain and coworkers at the IBM Research Laboratory in San Jose, California, developed Structured Query Language (SQL) in the 1970s. It is pronounced similarly to the word sequel. Before, researchers saw a SQL version of the EMPLOYEE query. The American National Standards Institute

(ANSI) officially recognized SQL as the standard query language for relational databases in 1986 (ANSI). After its ratification by ANSI, interest in using SQL in relational databases on PCs and mainframes increased. The average (AVG), maximum value (MAX), and minimum value (MIN) are only a few of the built-in functions available in SQL (Tang et al., 2016) (Figure 4.8).

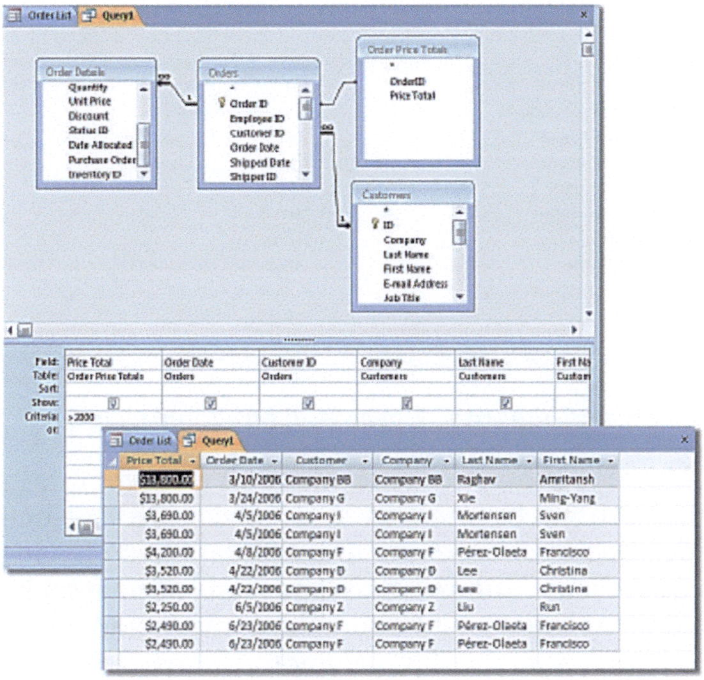

Figure 4.8. Query by example (QBE) is a method several databases use to produce information and reports.

Source: George Reynolds, Creative Commons License.

As a result, programmers need to master one powerful query language to use SQL on everything from personal computers to massive mainframes. Database users and developers benefit from SQL's portability; SQL statements may be written in various languages, including the increasingly popular Java, C++, and COBOL. Popular database query language SQL may be simple to learn and use because it uses standardized and efficient data collection, storage, and modification methods (Chock et al., 1981).

A database can generate the needed reports, documents, and other outputs once it has been set up and filled with data. These outputs typically take the form of printed hard copies or screen displays. A database program's output-control features let the researcher choose which records and fields should be included in reports. The researcher can even do computations by changing database fields, particularly for the report. The researcher can personalize reports and build versatile, practical, and effective information-handling tools using formatting controls and organizing options (like report headings) (Sutton et al., 1997) (Figure 4.9).

Figure 4.9. A database application provides complex formatting and organization options to output the correct information in style.

Monthly Sales Report

Monthly Sales Report

Sunday, July 29, 2007 5:38:07 PM

June, 2006

Product	Sales
Northwind Traders Boysenberry Spread	$2,250.00
Northwind Traders Dried Apples	$1,590.00
Northwind Traders Fruit Cocktail	$1,560.00
Northwind Traders Chocolate	$1,020.00
Northwind Traders Dried Pears	$900.00
Northwind Traders Cajun Seasoning	$660.00
Northwind Traders Coffee	$230.00
Northwind Traders Clam Chowder	$96.50
June Sales Total	$8,306.50

Source: Ralph and George, Creative Commons License.

A DBMS may provide a wide range of files, reports, and other outputs that can aid businesses in achieving their objectives. The most typical reports choose and arrange data to summarize certain business operations. For instance, financial information like current and past-due accounts is frequently summarized in accounting reports (Larson et al., 2005). Numerous businesses base their everyday operational choices on frequent status updates that track the progress of particular orders toward fulfillment and delivery.

4.4.3. Popular Database Management Systems (DBMS)

FileMaker Pro and Microsoft Access are two common DBMSs for lone users. The DBMS industry encompasses software professional programmers use and run on midrange servers, mainframes, and supercomputers. Companies like Oracle, IBM, and Microsoft bring in billions of dollars annually from the overall market (McHugh et al., 1997).

Several open-source database systems are offered, including PostgreSQL and MySQL, just as other software products. The availability of many conventional database programs on open-source OSs has also increased. Linux is compatible with numerous relational databases, including IBM's well-known DB2 database. The Linux OS also supports various databases and the Sybase IQ database.

Database-as-a-service (DaaS) is a novel cloud-based platform. Data-as-a-service (DaaS) is analogous to SaaS, or "software-as-a-service (SaaS)." Remember that a SaaS model is one in which the end user organization (e.g., client company) gains access to the software via the service provider's servers. In the case of DaaS, the client connects to a service provider's servers via a network, often the Internet, to access the database. The service provider offers database administration in a SaaS model. DaaS and SaaS are a component of the broader cloud computing trend (Cahill et al., 2009). High-performance applications are performed on a massive cluster of machines in the cloud computing environment. For cloud computing to work, all necessary hardware, software, and data must be stored and managed by a third party, with access granted via the Internet. There is no obligation for businesses or individuals to set up, maintain, upgrade, or safeguard their infrastructure (Dolk & Konsynski, 1984).

More than a dozen businesses are adopting DaaS at the moment. Examples include Oracle, MyOwnDB, Google, Intuit, Amazon, and TrackVia. Oracle's DaaS integrates grid computing, cloud computing, and virtualization to deliver reliable, scalable, and cost-effective database solutions. Oracle provides customers with its dedicated cloud infrastructure. Razorfish, a digital advertising agency, uses Amazon's Elastic Cloud service to gather and analyze anonymous, aggregated data from users' browser sessions. Procter & Gamble centralized hundreds of projects into one cloud database to cut costs and reduce wasted time previously spent in meetings and data entry (Kovalskyi et al., 2014).

KEYWORD

Database administrator is responsible for maintaining, securing, and operating databases and also ensures that data is correctly stored and retrieved.

4.4.4. Special-Purpose Database Systems

Along with the widely used DBMS we've been discussing; several specialized database packages are also used for niche purposes or by certain sectors. For example, the Urbanspoon RexBook iPad app stores and manages dinner reservations in a specially designed online database. Morphbank (www.morphbank.net) is another specialized DBMS for biologists that enables researchers and students worldwide to contribute to and manage an image library of more than 96,000 biological specimens. iTunes uses a database that stores information about songs, including titles, ratings, genres, download sizes, release dates, artists, and albums. When an iTunes user searches for an artist in the iTunes store, they are essentially making a query against the main iTunes database (*see* Figure 4.10) (Kutvonen & Kutvonen, 1996).

Figure 4.10. Apple's iTunes software uses a database to access and catalog music.

Source: Apple, Creative Commons License.

4.4.5. Selecting a Database Management System (DBMS)

DBAs are often in charge of selecting the most suitable database management solution for a company. Analyzing database requirements and characteristics is the first step in the process. The data gathered and the DBMS employed depends on the organization's information requirements. The following are significant database properties (Stonebraker et al., 1983):

- **Database Size:** The total amount of data stored in a database.
- **Concurrent Users:** The necessary minimum number of users to access the database in real-time.
- **Database Cost:** The cost of buying or leasing the database.
- **Performance:** How quickly can database records be updated.
- **Vendor:** Reputation and economic stability of the database vendor.

- **Integration:** The capacity to effortlessly integrate with other programs and databases.

4.5. DATABASE APPLICATIONS

Today's database applications alter database content to generate informative results. Common data manipulations include searching, filtering, synthesizing, and assimilation using several database programs. Online processing and open connectivity standards, object-oriented database development, and the discovery and use of unstructured data like videos, images, audio, and more are all facilitated by such tools, allowing businesses to better leverage the Internet for a wide range of business processes (Chays et al., 2000).

Remember

Linking the company database to the internet enables real-time data sharing, but security and restricted access must be ensured. Consider risks and benefits and implement appropriate controls and safeguards. Comply with relevant laws and regulations regarding data privacy and security.

4.5.1. Linking the Company Database to the Internet

One of the reasons the Internet is so widely used is its capability to connect databases. A common Web browser can access most corporate databases via the Internet. Users benefit from easy internet access to a wide range of information, including financial records, educational histories, credit card statements, and product catalogs. It aids in making businesses and organizations more productive and efficient. Companies like Amazon, eHarmony, and eBay have generated billions in revenue by fusing databases, the Web, and astute business practices (Veugelers et al., 2010).

Several companies, including Google, Apple, Microsoft, and others, have created PHR systems to centralize patients' and doctors' medical data in one place that may be accessed from any Internet-connected device. "Patient-centered" health records like those offered by Google Health and Microsoft HealthVault make it simpler for patients to manage their health actively. President Obama has allocated $17 billion to e-health initiatives and programs to implement universal access to electronic health information (e-health records) by 2015. Companies specializing in databases will devote many resources to creating online medical and health records (Heinen, 1996).

Certain privacy advocates are concerned about public Web access to confidential medical information. Nonetheless, most in the sector favor the switch to a centralized system due to its convenience by drastically lowering the number of paper forms to complete and keep and reducing clerical errors via simplified data management methods. The systems shall be as safe as possible using encryption and authentication methods.

A process known as "creating a semantic web" is required to link databases to the Internet. A semantic Web, made possible by the resource description framework (RDF), annotates all online material with metadata. The end effect is a Web that is more like a unified database and easier to navigate. World Wide Web Consortium (W3C) standards for a semantic Web include the RDF, which aims to enlist the support of content creators (RDF) (Mercier & Hembree, 1998).

KEYWORD

Resource Description Framework (RDF) is an infrastructure that enables the encoding, exchange and reuse of structured metadata.

4.5.2. Data Marts, Data Warehouses, and Data Mining

The raw data required to make sound business judgments are stored in various locations and file types. This information was originally stored, collected, and managed by the company's transaction processing systems (TPSs), which were developed to aid in the smooth running of daily operations. Online transaction processing (OLTP) systems have been used by businesses for many years to collect operational, sales, and financial data. Data warehouses, mining, and marts may leverage the data to help decision-making (Manjunath et al., 2012).

4.5.2.1. Data Warehouses

Information about a company's products and services and its clients can be stored in a data warehouse, a huge database that pulls data from many internal and external sources. A dimensional view of the data necessary for analyzing market trends and performance is available to business users via the data warehouse. Managers can roll up detailed data to produce aggregate or summary reports or drill down to obtain more specific information using data warehouses. Yet, a data warehouse's primary function is to support administrative decision-making rather than TPSs' needs. The data warehouse stores information from many OSs and external sources (Figure 4.11). Take a look! When operational and external data are "cleaned up" and combined, it creates a new information database better suited for business analysis (Ghezzi, 2001).

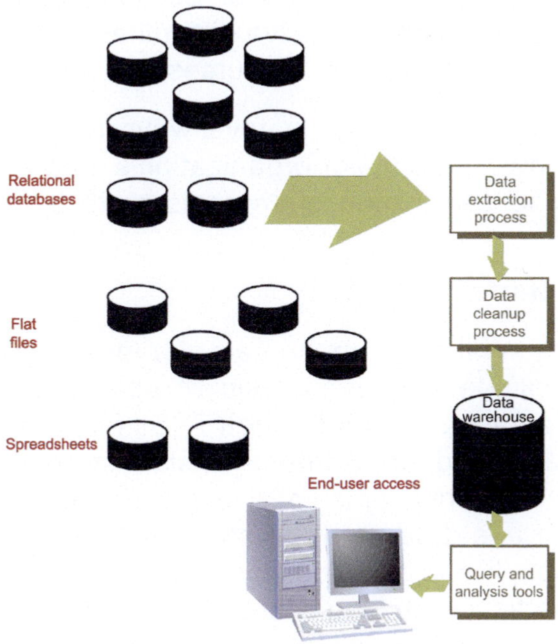

Figure 4.11. Elements of a data warehouse.

Source: George, Creative Commons License.

The foundation of most data warehouses is a huge database with tens of millions of records. When this data is gathered from the various production systems, business analysts can look back on the company's past and look ahead to the future using the resulting historical database. The data warehouse is updated frequently to maintain its current and accuracy. The data warehouse is cleaned of outdated data that is no longer required (Martinez et al., 2008). The data warehouse's ultimate usefulness must not be compromised by slow, ineffective, or manual updating. A data warehouse typically has three to 10 years of recent and old data. Data-cleansing systems can verify and collect data automatically, eliminate redundant data, store data in a DBMS, and merge data from several sources into a single database (Lyman et al., 2008).

Data warehouses can get their information from unusual sources. For instance, radio frequency identification (RFID) technology may receive information from Oracle's Warehouse Management software to tag things as they have been moved or shipped from the first location to the second. Honda Italia, the industry leader in powered two-wheel vehicle manufacture, employs RFID to send production data into its data warehouse. Each part of the vehicle is equipped with an RFID chip to enable tracking throughout the whole manufacturing process. As a result of the detailed information provided by the RFID-based system, production managers can make adjustments to production to resolve difficulties and improve supply with minimal downtime and lost resources (Mazón & Trujillo, 2008).

The capability to relate data in novel ways is data warehousing's main benefit. However, a major organization's data warehouse may be challenging to set up and often costs more than $2 million.

4.5.2.2. Data Marts

A data mart is a smaller database part of a larger data warehouse. Data marts facilitate online analysis of sales, stock, and other critical business data acquired through TPSs for small and medium-sized businesses and departments inside larger firms. Instead of keeping all enterprise data in a single, humongous database, businesses can use data marts to store data relevant to a single business function, like accounting, inventory management, or human resources. A particular section of the data mart may provide more technical information than the data warehouse (Ghezzi, 2001).

> **KEYWORD**
>
> **Data warehouse** is a type of data management system that is designed to enable and support business intelligence (BI) activities, especially analytics.

The best application of data marts is for smaller organizations requiring extensive data access. A warehouse has summarized data that the entire business can use. Since data marts often only hold tens of gigabytes, as opposed to the hundreds of gigabytes seen in data warehouses, they can be installed on less powerful hardware with smaller secondary storage devices, resulting in significant cost savings for an organization. A data mart may be created using any database software; however, some manufacturers also offer specialist software that is priced and priced exclusively for data marts. These streamlined data warehouses may be deployed more easily and affordably thanks to products and services from businesses like Sybase, Microsoft, Software AG, and others (Chenoweth et al., 2003). The selling argument is that data marts give more decision-makers access to specific business information. For instance, the Defense Health Services Systems' clinical data mart (CDM) was created by the United States Department of Defense to serve as a hub for medical data for the military's global population of more than 9 million people. The system was established after President Obama requested ways to "increase health care quality at decreased costs" (Ha et al., 1998).

4.5.2.3. Data Mining

Information analysis via data mining can be considered the automated process of discovering links and patterns inside a data warehouse. Data mining, like gold mining, involves sorting through large amounts of information to find the nuggets of value within the data. Being the oldest apparel company in the United States, Brooks Brothers uses data mining to provide insights to store managers that increase productivity and customer satisfaction (Romero & Ventura, 2013).

Data mining evaluates proposed business strategies by identifying trends, extracting patterns and rules from data warehouses, and scoring them. It will ultimately lead to an improvement in competitiveness, an increase in profitability, and a transformation of corporate processes. In marketing, it is used extensively to improve cross-selling opportunities, client retention, channels, market, campaign management, price analysis, and customer segmentation analysis (specifically one-to-one marketing). Data mining techniques, in a nutshell, make it possible for users to find solutions to problems for which they had not previously explored any options (Witten et al., 2005) (Figure 4.12).

Figure 4.12. Amazon uses data mining to suggest products attracting site visitors.

Source: Amazon, Creative Commons License.

E-commerce gives an additional significant possibility for successful data mining. Getting clients to websites is difficult; retaining and assuring their return is even more difficult. For instance, when retail websites have significant discount sales, it is difficult to predict how many first-time clients are likely to return. They also lack a method for determining whether clients obtained during the sale are more likely to participate in future transactions. As a result, businesses are collecting and storing information regarding website visitors in databases. Data mining strategies are then used to examine this data to customize the website and create sales promotions for particular clients. Users have expressed their displeasure with Facebook for disclosing member data to business partners who subsequently mine it to support targeted advertising efforts. Several members believe that the practice violates their right to privacy (Zhang et al., 2003).

KEYWORD

Predictive analytics is a form of business analytics applying machine learning to generate a predictive model for certain business applications.

The purpose of predictive analysis, which is a subset of data mining, is to forecast the outcomes of events based on the combination of historical data and assumptions about the conditions that will exist in the future. It could include predicting future product sales or the likelihood of a customer defaulting on a loan. By forecasting which things customers will buy if given the right incentive, retailers may convert infrequent buyers into loyal customers. Magnify, Genalytics, SAS Institute, NCR Teradata, SPSS, Sightward, and Quadstone have created predictive analytic tools. A company's client list and a year's worth of sales data may be analyzed using predictive analytic software to identify new market categories that may be lucrative (Rajakumari & Nalini, 2014).

Predictive analysis is used by American Airlines' Consumer Research Department to inform business decisions. American Airlines asks passengers on around 100 of the 3,300 daily flights they operate to complete a quick survey. The information is processed by predictive analytics software in a data warehouse to produce useful statistics. The statistics are examined to determine flight schedules, crewing levels, in-flight amenities like food and Wi-Fi, and other airline-related factors.

The huge potential of data mining is well-known to traditional DBMS providers. As a result, businesses like oracle, tandem, Sybase, and red brick systems all include data-mining technology in their products (Thuraisingham, 2000).

4.5.3. Business Intelligence (BI)

Data mining and utilizing databases for business information are closely related ideas. Business intelligence (BI) is the process of compiling sufficient quantities of the appropriate data in a timely and usable form, then analyzing it to make it useful for corporate operations, strategy, or tactics. In the pharmaceutical industry, for instance, IMS Health provides a BI solution to aid in the targeted marketing of products to pharmacists, physicians, customers, nurses, government agencies, and non-profit healthcare organizations. BI processes data to produce actionable intelligence shared across a company. When put into practice, it can enhance business processes and give insight into the root causes of issues. For instance, Puma North America, a producer of sports footwear, employs SPSS software to give its sales advisors BI. The data that Puma's 70 independent sales consultants rely on to make choices about shipments, orders, and product availability is provided by SPSS (Chaudhuri et al., 2011).

A subset of BI known as competitive intelligence focuses only on competitor information and how it influences strategy, operations, and tactics. Competitive intelligence is crucial in a company's capacity to recognize market changes and react swiftly and effectively. Competitive intelligence does not involve using shady methods to obtain information, which is espionage. In fact, by reviewing published data resources, conducting interviews, and utilizing additional morally and legally acceptable methods, a competitive intelligence specialist may gather practically all the required information. An experienced competitive intelligence professional may fill in the gaps in the material acquired by deduction using various analytical tools (Jourdan et al., 2008).

KEYWORD

Data Loss Prevention (DLP) is the practice of detecting and preventing data breaches, exfiltration, or unwanted destruction of sensitive data.

An organization's actions to safeguard information "hostile" intelligence operatives seek are called counterintelligence. Defining "trade secret" information pertinent to the organization and managing its release are two of the most efficient counterintelligence strategies.

Data loss prevention (DLP) refers to programs created to secure data inside a company. DLP software is made by companies like Symantec, RSA, Safend, Code Green, Sophos, Trend Micro, and others, and it may be used to find, monitor, and safeguard data on any system. It includes information transmitted via a network, stored on a disc, in databases, e-mail, files, and elsewhere. DLP is an effective counterintelligence weapon and is essential for firms to use to abide by government requirements requiring them to protect sensitive consumer data (Negash, 2004).

4.5.4. Online Analytical Processing (OLAP)

For nearly two decades, multidimensional databases and associated analytical data display technologies have enabled the development of captivating sales presentations and competitive demonstrations. Inquire, "Where is this product selling particularly well?" The screen transitions to an esthetically appealing table showing sales performance by product category, region, and time. Today, data warehouses rely on these programs, also referred to as online analytical processing (OLAP), to efficiently store and transfer data. Cognos, Microsoft, Business Objects, SAP, MicroStrategy, Infor, Applix, and Oracle are some of the top OLAP software providers. The largest mountain resort in Ontario, Blue Mountain, employs OLAP to enable its executives, managers, and analysts to analyze and comprehend huge volumes of complex data quickly. The resort has 13 business sectors: restaurants, lift tickets, tourist information centers, and lodging. The OLAP system allows decision-makers to examine their data from several angles and narrow in on specifics (Alkharouf et al., 2005).

KEYWORD

Data mining is the process by which organizations detect patterns in data for insights relevant to their business needs.

Data is just as useful as the conclusions that may be drawn from it. Implementing potent information-analysis tools like OLAP and data mining into a data warehousing architecture helps organizations better understand market conditions and create a competitive advantage. Regarding data analysis, OLAP is query-driven and top-down, while data mining is discovery-driven and bottom-up. Data mining discovers facts and discoveries according to determined patterns, while OLAP relies on the iterative testing of user-generated hypotheses. OLAP, or multidimensional analysis, requires substantial human intelligence and database interaction to extract relevant data. The researcher can say, "Give me the data; tell me what intriguing patterns arise," and a data-mining program will handle the rest. Data-mining technology used in a credit card company's client database might infer fraudulent activity from the past. Next, the profile can be applied to all incoming transaction data to detect and prevent fraudulent activities.

Similar to the general concept of object-oriented programming, an object-oriented database follows this methodology. In this method, the database serves as both a repository for data and a set of rules for how that data should be processed. A monthly budget, for instance, could be recorded in an object-oriented database, along with the calculations required to generate that budget. Monthly costs might be the only data stored by a conventional DBMS. Skype, a well-known Internet phone service, is satisfied with PostgreSQL's object-oriented database. Because of its object-oriented design, Skype's database has been able to adapt to the company's changing needs. An object-oriented database is a good option whenever a database needs to process complex data fast and efficiently (Yu et al., 2019).

4.5.5. Object-Relational Database Management Systems (ORDBMS)

A "method" is a sequence of operations in an object-oriented database. For instance, one method for calculating sales tax would be to multiply the total price of an order by 7.5% (or whatever the applicable sales tax rate happens to be in a given area). A message is an instruction to perform some action. For instance, a salesperson could communicate with the object-oriented database to determine the appropriate amount of tax to add to a customer's order. Object-oriented databases typically use a query language known as object query language (OQL), similar to SQL (Türker & Gertz, 2001).

When implemented in an object-oriented DBMS, an object-oriented database provides a user interface and integration with other applications (OODBMS). Versant and Objectivity are two computer companies that offer OODBMSs for purchase or rent. Because of their processing power, object-oriented databases are popular among businesses. Versant's OODBMS is utilized by various industries, not just the government. It includes the telecommunications sector, the defense sector, the online gambling sector, and the healthcare sector. The Object Database Management Group created the Object Data Standard as a collection of rules for developing object-oriented databases (www.odmg.org).

In addition to offering the full set of relational database features, an object-relational database management system (ORDBMS) also allows for the addition of new data types and processes by third parties. These novel data formats, which need additional optimization, indexing, and retrieval characteristics, may be audio, pictures, unstructured text, geographical, or time series data. Each provider of ORDBMS services offers a collection of application programming interfaces that let users connect external data definitions and operations to the database system. Essentially, they provide a standard socket into which consumers may plug individual instructions. Oracle and IBM refer to their products' add-ons as Cartridges, Data Blades, and Extenders. Some plugins act as web service interfaces (D'Andrea & Janus, 1996).

KEYWORD

Object Query Language (OQL) is a version of the Structured Query Language (SQL) that has been designed for use in Network Manager.

4.5.6. Audio, Visual, and Other Database Systems

Corporations are learning to also store and handle vast amounts of audio and video data alongside traditional data. Credit card companies commonly use scanners to store digital photographs of charge slips. Photos of clients could be stored in the database under their respective names, printed, and sent out with monthly invoices. Radiographs are archived in image databases and sent to satellite clinics outside the main hospital. Image databases are being used by financial services, insurance providers, and government agencies to keep important records and do away with traditional paperwork. Drug companies frequently need to examine many visual pictures from labs. Certain object-relational databases and specialized database systems may hold visual databases. Images may be stored in several relational databases (Marcus & Subrahmanian, 1996).

The challenge of combining and evaluating data from many databases is becoming increasingly significant. Multinational businesses, for instance, occasionally need to examine sales and accounting data kept in various database systems worldwide. Organizations like IBM have created virtual database systems to enable the collaboration of various databases into a single database system. A federated database system is a term sometimes used to describe the combining of different databases into one. Lloyds of London, one of the world's most well-known insurance providers, merged its informational resources with the International Underwriting Association (IUA) to better serve its clients at cheaper costs.

In addition to audio, visual, and virtual databases, several specialized systems are available to meet the unique requirements of various businesses. The ability to store and retrieve data based on the areas it describes is made possible by spatial data technology, facilitating geographic inquiries and analysis. Businesses like Home Depot, CVS Corporation, Sonic Restaurants, and Chico's can use MapInfo software from Pitney Bowes to determine the best site for new stores and restaurants based on geographic demographics. It could also aid emergency response teams and law enforcement in providing better community safety. The software predicts a business's success in a certain area based on factors including the number of residents, nearby businesses, and accessibility of public transit. Construction companies and insurers use spatial data to assess the likelihood of natural disasters and make informed decisions. With data organized by investment kind, interest rates, currency type, and time, spatial data may enhance financial risk management. Geographic information systems (GIS) utilize spatial data technology as a potent tool to map information (Noroozi et al., 2017).

ACTIVITY 4.1.

A retail company that operates multiple stores across different locations needs to manage its inventory and sales data efficiently. The company decides to implement a database management system (DBMS) to store and manage the data in a central location, which can be accessed by authorized users across different departments and locations. The DBMS allows the company to track inventory levels, sales trends, and customer preferences in real-time, and generate reports and analytics to support decision-making. The company also implements appropriate security controls and backups to ensure the data is secure and recoverable in the event of a system failure or cyberattack. As a result, the company is able to streamline its operations, improve customer satisfaction, and drive growth and profitability.

4.6. SUMMARY

An introduction to the ideas, varieties, and uses of DBMS are given in the chapter "Database Management System." The first learning objective covers a variety of concepts, including data entities, attributes, and keys, and it focuses on data administration. A description of several database types, including single users, flat files, and multiple users, is given in the second learning objective.

The third goal examines how users interact with software to obtain, manipulate, and use data. The fourth goal emphasizes choosing the right database system for a specific data set.

The fifth goal discusses the different database uses, such as data marts, data warehouses, and data mining. The fundamentals of object-oriented database management, a more recent method of managing data that makes use of object-oriented programming principles, are introduced in the sixth aim. The eighth aim briefly discusses customized audio, visual, and other media database systems.

The chapter aims to give readers a thorough understanding of DBMS foundations, including their many types, uses, and factors to consider when choosing the best system for a particular data collection.

REVIEW QUESTIONS

1. What exactly is an attribute? What is its relationship to an entity?
2. Explain what the researcher means by the phrase "database." When compared to a database management system, how is it different?
3. What is the data hierarchy in a database?
4. What is a relation, and what role does it play in relational databases?
5. What function does a primary key serve? How can it help in reducing data redundancy?
6. What is the objective of data cleaning?
7. What benefits does the database method provide over the conventional database management strategy?
8. What is a data warehouse, and how does it vary from a conventional database used to support OLTP operations?

MULTIPLE CHOICE QUESTIONS

1. **A(n) _______________ is the name of a collection of programs that interact with databases and serve as an interface between them, their users, and other application programs.**
   a. Operating system
   b. GUI
   c. Productivity software
   d. DBMS
2. **A(n) _______________ is a field or group of fields that identifies a database record uniquely.**
   a. Data item
   b. Attribute
   c. Primary key
   d. Key
3. **What database model uses two-dimensional tables to store data?**
   a. Network
   b. Relational
   c. Normalized
   d. Hierarchical
4. **_______________ involves combining two or more database tables.**
   a. Projecting
   b. Joining
   c. Selecting
   d. Data cleanup
5. **The _______________ contains the commands utilized to access and report data from the database.**
   a. Data manipulation language
   b. Data definition language
   c. Data normalization language
   d. Schema
6. **Access is a common database management system for _______________.**
   a. Graphics workstations
   b. Personal computers
   c. Supercomputers
   d. Mainframe computers

Answers to Multiple Choice Questions

1. (d); 2. (c); 3. (b); 4. (b); 5. (a); 6. (b)

REFERENCES

1. Adjeroh, D. A., & Nwosu, K. C., (1997). Multimedia database management-requirements and issues. *IEEE Multimedia, 4*(3), 24–33.
2. Alkharouf, N. W., Jamison, D. C., & Matthews, B. F., (2005). Online analytical processing (OLAP): A fast and effective data mining tool for gene expression databases. *Journal of Biomedicine and Biotechnology, 2005*(2), 181.
3. Baden, R., Bender, A., Spring, N., Bhattacharjee, B., & Starin, D., (2009). Persona: An online social network with user-defined privacy. In: *Proceedings of the ACM SIGCOMM 2009 Conference on Data Communication*, 135–146.
4. Batoory, D. S., Barnett, J. R., Garza, J. F., Smith, K. P., Tsukuda, K., Twichell, B. C., & Wise, T. E., (1988). GENESIS: An extensible database management system. *IEEE Transactions on Software Engineering, 14*(11), 1711–1730.
5. Bernstein, P. A., & Melnik, S., (2007). Model management 2.0: Manipulating richer mappings. In: *Proceedings of the 2007 ACM SIGMOD International Conference on Management of Data* (Vol. 1, pp. 1–12).
6. Braganholo, V., (2018). Versioned-PROV: A PROV extension to support mutable data entities. In: *Provenance and Annotation of Data and Processes: 7th International Provenance and Annotation Workshop, IPAW 2018, London, UK, July 9–10, 2018, Proceedings* (Vol. 11017, p. 87).
7. Cahill, M. J., Röhm, U., & Fekete, A. D., (2009). Serializable isolation for snapshot databases. *ACM Transactions on Database Systems (TODS), 34*(4), 1–42.
8. Chaudhuri, S., Dayal, U., & Narasayya, V., (2011). An overview of business intelligence technology. *Communications of the ACM, 54*(8), 88–98.
9. Chays, D., Dan, S., Frankl, P. G., Vokolos, F. I., & Weyuker, E. J., (2000). A framework for testing database applications. In: *Proceedings of the 2000 ACM SIGSOFT International Symposium on Software Testing and Analysis* (Vil. 1, pp. 147–157).
10. Chen, S. C., & Kashyap, R. L., (2001). A spatio-temporal semantic model for multimedia database systems and multimedia information systems. *IEEE Transactions on Knowledge and Data Engineering, 13*(4), 607–622.
11. Chen, S. C., Shyu, M. L., Peeta, S., & Zhang, C., (2003). Learning-based spatio-temporal vehicle tracking and indexing for transportation multimedia database systems. *IEEE Transactions on Intelligent Transportation Systems, 4*(3), 154–167.
12. Chen, S. C., Shyu, M. L., Zhang, C., & Kashyap, R. L., (2001). Identifying overlapped objects for video indexing and modeling in multimedia database systems. *International Journal on Artificial Intelligence Tools, 10*(04), 715–734.

13. Chenoweth, T., Schuff, D., & St. Louis, R., (2003). A method for developing dimensional data marts. *Communications of the ACM, 46*(12), 93–98.
14. Chock, M., Cardenas, A. F., & Klinger, A., (1981). Manipulating data structures in pictorial information systems. *Computer, 14*(11), 43–50.
15. Császár, A. G., Czakó, G., Furtenbacher, T., & Mátyus, E., (2007). An active database approach to complete rotational–vibrational spectra of small molecules. *Annual Reports in Computational Chemistry, 3*, 155–176.
16. D'Andrea, A., & Janus, P., (1996). UniSQL's next-generation object-relational database management system. *ACM SIGMOD Record, 25*(3), 70–76.
17. Dinu, V., Nadkarni, P., & Brandt, C., (2006). Pivoting approaches for bulk extraction of entity–attribute–value data. *Computer Methods and Programs in Biomedicine, 82*(1), 38–43.
18. Dolk, D. R., & Konsynski, B. R., (1984). Knowledge representation for model management systems. *IEEE Transactions on Software Engineering*, (6), 619–628.
19. Döller, M., & Kosch, H., (2008). The MPEG-7 multimedia database system (MPEG-7 MMDB). *Journal of Systems and Software, 81*(9), 1559–1580.
20. Drake, D. B., Steckler, N. A., & Koch, M. J., (2004). Information sharing in and across government agencies: The role and influence of scientist, politician, and bureaucrat subcultures. *Social Science Computer Review, 22*(1), 67–84.
21. Duftschmid, G., Wrba, T., & Rinner, C., (2010). Extraction of standardized archetyped data from electronic health record systems based on the entity-attribute-value model. *International Journal of Medical Informatics, 79*(8), 585–597.
22. Efthymiou, V., Stefanidis, K., & Christophides, V., (2015). Big data entity resolution: From highly to somehow similar entity descriptions in the web. In: *2015 IEEE International Conference on Big Data (Big Data)* (Vol. 1, pp. 401–410).
23. Ekins, S., Nikolsky, Y., Bugrim, A., Kirillov, E., & Nikolskaya, T., (2006). Pathway mapping tools for analysis of high content data. *High Content Screening: A Powerful Approach to Systems Cell Biology and Drug Discovery, 1*, 319–350).
24. Esposito, M., Coulthard, P., Thomsen, P., & Worthington, H. V., (2005). The role of implant surface modifications, shape and material on the success of Osseo integrated dental implants. A Cochrane systematic review. *The European Journal of Prosthodontics and Restorative Dentistry, 13*(1), 15–31.
25. Fernández, A., Del, R. S., Bawakid, A., & Herrera, F., (2017). Fuzzy rule based classification systems for big data with MapReduce: Granularity analysis. *Advances in Data Analysis and Classification, 11*, 711–730.
26. Ghezzi, C., (2001). Designing data marts for data warehouses. *ACM Transactions on Software Engineering and Methodology (TOSEM), 10*(4), 452–483.
27. Golfarelli, M., Maio, D., & Rizzi, S., (1998). The dimensional fact model: A conceptual model for data warehouses. *International Journal of Cooperative Information Systems, 7*(02n03), 215–247.

28. Ha, S. H., & Park, S. C., (1998). Application of data mining tools to hotel data mart on the intranet for database marketing. *Expert Systems with Applications, 15*(1), 1–31.
29. Heinen, J., (1996). Internet marketing practices. *Information Management & Computer Security, 4*(5), 7–14.
30. Hillman, C. H., Rosengren, K. S., & Smith, D. P., (2004). Emotion and motivated behavior: Postural adjustments to affective picture viewing. *Biological Psychology, 66*(1), 51–62.
31. Huang, J., Antova, L., Koch, C., & Olteanu, D., (2009). MayBMS: A probabilistic database management system. In: *Proceedings of the 2009 ACM SIGMOD International Conference on Management of Data* (Vol. 1, pp. 1071–1074).
32. Hur, J., & Noh, D. K., (2010). Attribute-based access control with efficient revocation in data outsourcing systems. *IEEE Transactions on Parallel and Distributed Systems, 22*(7), 1214–1221.
33. Hur, J., (2011). Improving security and efficiency in attribute-based data sharing. *IEEE Transactions on Knowledge and Data Engineering, 25*(10), 2271–2282.
34. Jain, R., & Hampapur, A., (1994). Metadata in video databases. *ACM SIGMOD Record, 23*(4), 27–33.
35. Jourdan, Z., Rainer, R. K., & Marshall, T. E., (2008). Business intelligence: An analysis of the literature. *Information Systems Management, 25*(2), 121–131.
36. Kossaifi, J., Walecki, R., Panagakis, Y., Shen, J., Schmitt, M., Ringeval, F., & Pantic, M., (2019). Sewa DB: A rich database for audio-visual emotion and sentiment research in the wild. *IEEE Transactions on Pattern Analysis and Machine Intelligence, 43*(3), 1022–1040.
37. Kotidis, Y., & Roussopoulos, N., (1999). Dynamat: A dynamic view management system for data warehouses. *ACM SIGMOD Record, 28*(2), 371–382.
38. Kovalskyi, D., Sfiligoi, I., Wuerthwein, F., & Yagil, A., (2014). Performance of popular open source databases for HEP related computing problems. In: *Journal of Physics: Conference Series,* (Vol. 513, No. 4, p. 042027).
39. Koyama, J. P., (2011). Generating, comparing, manipulating, categorizing: Reporting, and sometimes fabricating data to comply with no child left behind mandates. *Journal of Education Policy, 26*(5), 701–720.
40. Kutvonen, P., & Kutvonen, L., (1996). Measured performance of a special-purpose database engine for distributed system software. *Computer Communications, 19*(1), 22–29.
41. Kwok, Y. K., Karlapalem, K., Ahmad, I., & Pun, N. M., (1996). Design and evaluation of data allocation algorithms for distributed multimedia database systems. *IEEE Journal on Selected Areas in Communications, 14*(7), 1332–1348.
42. Larson, C. L., Ruffalo, D., Nietert, J. Y., & Davidson, R. J., (2005). Stability of emotion-modulated startle during short and long picture presentation. *Psychophysiology, 42*(5), 604–610.

43. Li, C., Donizelli, M., Rodriguez, N., Dharuri, H., Endler, L., Chelliah, V., & Laibe, C., (2010). BioModels database: An enhanced, curated and annotated resource for published quantitative kinetic models. *BMC Systems Biology, 4*(1), 1–14.

44. Luo, W., Xie, Q., & Hengartner, U., (2009). Facecloak: An architecture for user privacy on social networking sites. In: *2009 International Conference on Computational Science and Engineering* (Vol. 3, pp. 26–33).

45. Lyman, J. A., Scully, K., & Harrison, Jr. J. H., (2008). The development of health care data warehouses to support data mining. *Clinics in Laboratory Medicine, 28*(1), 55–71.

46. Manjunath, T. N., Hegadi, R. S., Umesh, I. M., & Ravikumar, G. K., (2012). Realistic analysis of data warehousing and data mining application in education domain. *International Journal of Machine Learning and Computing, 2*(4), 419.

47. Marcus, S., & Subrahmanian, V. S., (1996). Foundations of multimedia database systems. *Journal of the ACM (JACM), 43*(3), 474–523.

48. Martinez, J. M. P., Berlanga, R., Aramburu, M. J., & Pedersen, T. B., (2008). Integrating data warehouses with web data: A survey. *IEEE Transactions on Knowledge and Data Engineering, 20*(7), 940–955.

49. Mazón, J. N., & Trujillo, J., (2008). An MDA approach for the development of data warehouses. *Decision Support Systems, 45*(1), 41–58.

50. McCarthy, D., & Dayal, U., (1989). The architecture of an active database management system. *ACM SIGMOD Record, 18*(2), 215–224.

51. McHugh, J., Abiteboul, S., Goldman, R., Quass, D., & Widom, J., (1997). Lore: A database management system for semistructured data. *ACM SIGMOD Record, 26*(3), 54–66.

52. Md Nor, N., Che, H. C. R., & Hussain, M. A., (2020). A review of data-driven fault detection and diagnosis methods: Applications in chemical process systems. *Reviews in Chemical Engineering, 36*(4), 513–553.

53. Mercier, C. D., & Hembree, S. D., (1998). What the Internet can do for you. *IEEE Industry Applications Magazine, 4*(6), 8–15.

54. Myers, R. B., Jones, S. L., & Sittig, D. F., (2011). Review of reported clinical information system adverse events in US Food and Drug Administration databases. *Applied Clinical Informatics, 2*(01), 63–74.

55. Negash, S., (2004). Business intelligence. *Communications of the Association for Information Systems, 13*(1), 15.

56. Noroozi, F., Marjanovic, M., Njegus, A., Escalera, S., & Anbarjafari, G., (2017). Audio-visual emotion recognition in video clips. *IEEE Transactions on Affective Computing, 10*(1), 60–75.

57. Orwat, C., Graefe, A., & Faulwasser, T., (2008). Towards pervasive computing in health care–A literature review. *BMC Medical Informatics and Decision Making, 8*(1), 1–18.

58. Paton, C., Hellstrom, J., Paul, B., Woodhead, J., & Hergt, J., (2011). Iolite: Freeware for the visualization and processing of mass spectrometric data. *Journal of Analytical Atomic Spectrometry, 26*(12), 2508–2518.
59. Plattner, H., (2009). A common database approach for OLTP and OLAP using an in-memory column database. In: *Proceedings of the 2009 ACM SIGMOD International Conference on Management of Data* (Vol. 1, pp. 1, 2).
60. Rajakumari, S. B., & Nalini, C., (2014). An efficient data mining dataset preparation using aggregation in relational database. *Indian Journal of Science and Technology, 7*, 44.
61. Romero, C., & Ventura, S., (2013). Data mining in education. *Wiley Interdisciplinary Reviews: Data Mining and Knowledge Discovery, 3*(1), 12–27.
62. Schadt, E. E., Linderman, M. D., Sorenson, J., Lee, L., & Nolan, G. P., (2010). Computational solutions to large-scale data management and analysis. *Nature Reviews Genetics, 11*(9), 647–657.
63. Stonebraker, M., & Kemnitz, G., (1991). The POSTGRES next generation database management system. *Communications of the ACM, 34*(10), 78–92.
64. Stonebraker, M., Woodfill, J., Ranstrom, J., Murphy, M., Meyer, M., & Allman, E., (1983). Performance enhancements to a relational database system. *ACM Transactions on Database Systems (TODS), 8*(2), 167–185.
65. Sutton, S. K., Davidson, R. J., Donzella, B., Irwin, W. I., & Dottl, D. A., (1997). Manipulating affective state using extended picture presentations. *Psychophysiology, 34*(2), 217–226.
66. Tang, F., Eller, C. K., & Wier, B., (2016). Reporting frequency and presentation format: Detecting real activities manipulation. *Journal of Information Systems, 30*(3), 63–77.
67. Taylor, R. W., & Frank, R. L., (1976). CODASYL data-base management systems. *ACM Computing Surveys (CSUR), 8*(1), 67–103.
68. Thuraisingham, B., (2000). A primer for understanding and applying data mining. *IT Professional, 2*(1), 28–31.
69. Türker, C., & Gertz, M., (2001). Semantic integrity support in SQL: 1999 and commercial (object-) relational database management systems. *The VLDB Journal, 10*, 241–269.
70. Van, A. D., Pavlo, A., Gordon, G. J., & Zhang, B., (2017). Automatic database management system tuning through large-scale machine learning. In: *Proceedings of the 2017 ACM International Conference on Management of Data* (Vol. 1, pp. 1009–1024).
71. Veugelers, M., Bury, J., & Viaene, S., (2010). Linking technology intelligence to open innovation. *Technological Forecasting and Social Change, 77*(2), 335–343.
72. Witten, I. H., Frank, E., Hall, M. A., Pal, C. J., & DATA, M., (2005). Practical machine learning tools and techniques. In: *Data Mining* (Vol. 2, No. 4, pp. 3–12).

73. Yoshitaka, A., & Ichikawa, T., (1999). A survey on content-based retrieval for multimedia databases. *IEEE Transactions on Knowledge and Data Engineering, 11*(1), 81–93.
74. Yu, D., Xu, D., Wang, D., & Ni, Z., (2019). Hierarchical topic modeling of Twitter data for online analytical processing. *IEEE Access, 7*, 12373–12385.
75. Zhang, L. M., Xu, Y., & Jia, J. S., (2009). Analysis of earth dam failures: A database approach. *Georisk, 3*(3), 184–189.
76. Zhang, S., Zhang, C., & Yang, Q., (2003). Data preparation for data mining. *Applied Artificial Intelligence, 17*(5, 6), 375–381.

CHAPTER 5

ROLE OF TELECOMMUNICATION AND NETWORKS IN INFORMATION SYSTEMS

UNIT INTRODUCTION

Telecommunication and networks are essential components of modern information systems (IS) that enable people and organizations to communicate and share information over long distances. Telecommunication refers to the transmission of information and data through different types of communication channels, including wired, wireless, and satellite networks. Networks, on the other hand, are collections of interconnected devices that can communicate and share resources such as data, applications, and services (Dewett & Jones, 2001).

In today's world, telecommunication and networks have become increasingly important due to the rise of globalization, mobile devices, and the internet. They play a critical role in enabling people and organizations to communicate and collaborate across different locations, making the world a smaller and more connected place. For businesses, telecommunication and networks are essential for enabling remote work, conducting online transactions, and providing customer support. They also play a vital role in the delivery of essential services such as healthcare, education, and emergency response (Grover et al., 1996).

Overall, telecommunication and networks have become a fundamental aspect of modern society, shaping the way people interact and conduct business on a global scale. Their importance is likely to continue growing as technology continues to evolve and new innovations emerge, leading to new possibilities for communication, collaboration, and data sharing (Subba, 2004).

Learning Objectives

At the end of this chapter, readers will be able to learn:

- Define and explain the concept of telecommunication and networks in information systems.
- Identify the different types of telecommunication and networks, as well as their components and protocols.
- Understand the advantages and examples of using telecommunication and networks in information systems, including e-mail, video conferencing, and cloud computing.
- Recognize the challenges and risks associated with telecommunication and networks in information systems, such as security, reliability, and cost, as well as the potential risks of hacking, data breaches, and cyber-attacks.
- Explore the future trends of telecommunication and networks in information systems, such as 5G, IoT, and AI, and their implications on society and information systems development.
- Emphasize the importance of telecommunication and networks in information systems for future development and progress, and their role in modern society.

Key Terms

- Cloud computing
- Data breaches
- Networks
- Protocols
- Satellite communication
- Telecommunication
- Transmission media
- Video conferencing
- Wired communication
- Wireless communication

5.1. A FOUNDATION FOR TELECOMMUNICATION AND NETWORK MANAGEMENT

In the late 1980s, the International Telecommunications Union (ITU) and the International Organization for Standardization (ISO) collaborated to release network and system management standards known as the OSI reference model. The telecommunication management network (TMN) was established as a framework based on this model and has since become a popular reference framework for network and system management (Gupta et al., 1999).

The ISO model introduced fundamental concepts in network management, defining a network management system as an application with the aim of analyzing, controlling, and managing network and service infrastructure. The model differentiates between management entities and agent entities, with agents representing network resources or end systems and providing management information to the network managers, who monitor the agents and make management and control decisions accordingly (Raman, 1998).

While the ISO model still serves as a foundation for network management, the role of managers and agents has become less distinct with advancements in distributed system architectures and peer-to-peer based systems, and more intelligence is being distributed into networks. However, the terms manager and agent are still used conceptually to describe the roles entities play in given operations or functions.

The OSI reference model also emphasizes the distinction between managed entities, which are physical resources or end systems being managed, and managed objects, which refer to the informational view of the entity and provide relevant management information and capacities. A common information model is necessary to present such information in a consistent manner, and a common communication medium is needed for conveying management information to the managers.

The OSI reference model defines a management system based on functional, communicational, and informational aspects, with five functional areas of management: configuration, fault, performance, accounting, and security (FCAPS). These areas have helped structure network management research efforts (Schwartz, 1995).

Telecommunication networks are complex infrastructures spanning over networks, services, users, and business entities. Effective

Remember

TMN provides a framework for achieving interconnectivity and communication across heterogeneous operations system and telecommunication networks. To achieve this, TMN defines a set of interface points for elements which perform the actual communications processing (such as a call processing switch) to be accessed by elements, such as management workstations, to monitor and control them.

management of these networks involves various functions such as configuration, fault detection and recovery, performance monitoring, accounting, and security. The open systems interconnection (OSI) model defines these management functions, while the TMN framework adds layers for element management, network management, service management, and business management (Haggerty & Seetharaman, 1998) (Figure 5.1).

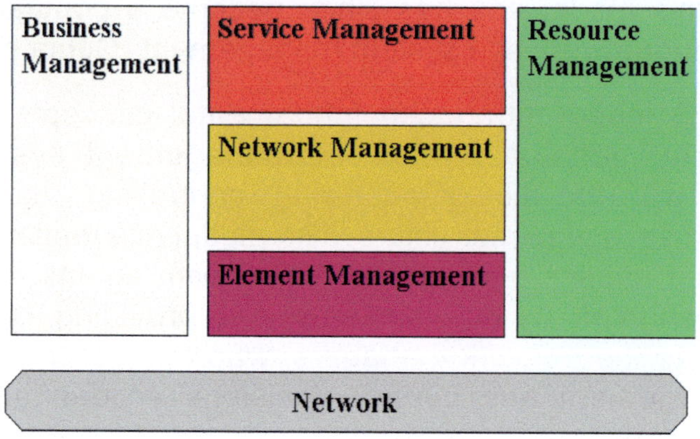

Figure 5.1. Illustration of telecommunications network – network management architecture.

Source: Martin John Baker, Creative Commons License.

The element management layer provides a view of the collection of network elements and mediates data between the network element and the network manager. It is device and network technology specific. The network management layer provides an end-to-end network view of the managed resources and devices, and it is device neutral. The service management layer provides contacts with customers and service providers, quality of service assurances, service orders, billing information, and trouble ticketing. The business management layer focuses on product and human resource planning and provides a business-level view of the services and financial concerns.

However, as the telecommunication infrastructures have evolved over the past 15 years, the community's view of the upper layers of management has changed substantially. There is no representation of customers in the TMN model, but as service differentiation and customization have grown, customers have become increasingly important in management. There is also an increasing need for user profiling for location and context tracking. The service layer has grown more complex as well, with a mix of multimedia services, personalized user services, and third-party applications (Hunt, 1997).

The constant evolution of telecommunication networks has brought about new challenges and opened new issues in old problems. This has led to changes in network management research and a need to address new challenges in configuration, fault management, performance monitoring, accounting, and security.

5.2. TELECOMMUNICATION

Telecommunication refers to the process of transmitting and receiving information over a distance through the use of different types of communication channels, such as wired, wireless, and satellite networks. The information being transmitted can include voice, data, images, and video (Al-Mamary et al., 2014).

5.2.1. Types of Telecommunications

There are several types of telecommunications, including (Grover et al., 1994):

- **Wired Telecommunication:** This type of telecommunication uses physical cables, such as copper or fiber optic cables, to transmit information. Examples of wired telecommunications include traditional telephone systems and wired internet connections.
- **Wireless Telecommunication:** This type of telecommunication uses radio waves to transmit information wirelessly over the air. Examples of wireless telecommunications include mobile phones, Wi-Fi, and Bluetooth (Figure 5.2).

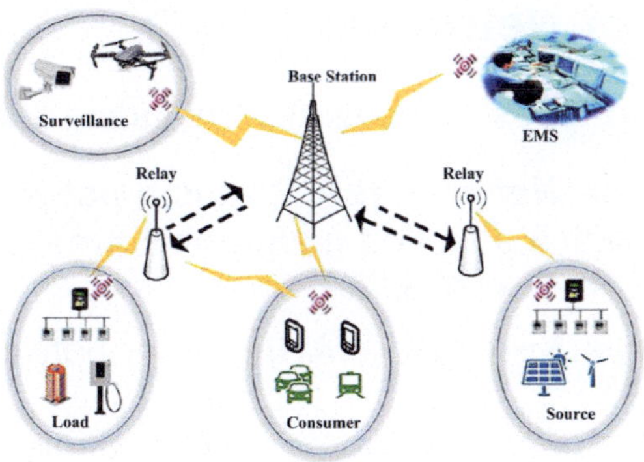

Figure 5.2. Schematic of the wireless communication networks.

Source: Xiurong Zhang, Creative Commons License.

Did you get it?

According to the International Telecommunication Union (ITU), as of 2021, there are over 5.27 billion mobile phone users worldwide, with mobile broadband penetration reaching 79% globally.

- **Satellite Telecommunication:** This type of telecommunication uses satellites in space to transmit information over long distances. Examples of satellite telecommunications include satellite TV and satellite-based internet connections.

5.2.2. Components of Telecommunication

The components of telecommunication include (Kim et al., 2011):

- **Transmission Media:** This refers to the physical channels used to transmit information. Examples of transmission media include cables, radio waves, and satellite signals.
- **Equipment:** This refers to the physical devices used to transmit and receive information. Examples of equipment include telephones, modems, routers, and antennas.
- **Protocols:** This refers to the set of rules and procedures used to transmit and receive information. Protocols ensure that the information being transmitted is delivered accurately and efficiently. Examples of protocols include TCP/IP, HTTP, and SMTP.

Remember

Networks are a crucial component of information systems as they facilitate communication and data transfer between devices and users. It is important to design and maintain secure, efficient, and reliable networks to ensure the smooth operation of information systems and prevent potential security breaches.

5.3. NETWORK

A network refers to a collection of interconnected devices, such as computers, servers, printers, and storage devices, which can communicate and share resources with each other. Networks can be used for various purposes, such as sharing information, accessing resources, and collaborating on projects (Ben-Akiva et al., 1991).

5.3.1. Types of Networks

There are several types of networks, including (Zachman, 1987):

- **Local Area Network (LAN):** It is a network that connects devices within a limited geographic area, such as a home, school, or office building.
- **Wide Area Network (WAN):** It is a network that spans a larger geographic area, such as a city, state, or country. WANs are often used to connect multiple LANs or remote offices.
- **Metropolitan Area Network (MAN):** It is a network that connects devices within a city or metropolitan area. MANs

are often used by organizations that have multiple locations within a city (Figure 5.3).

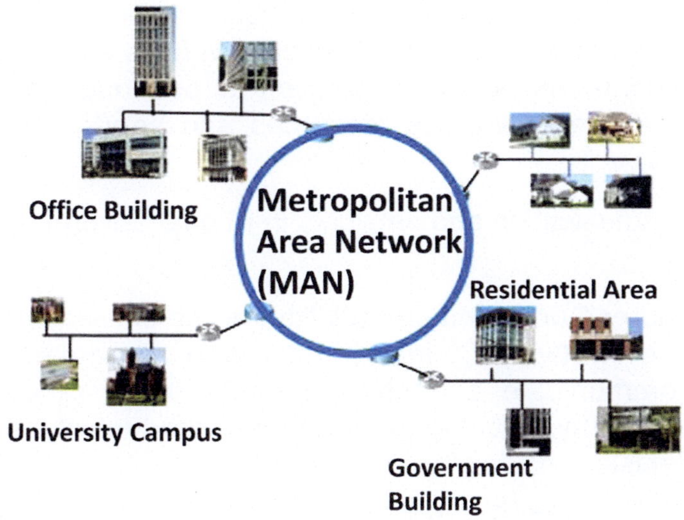

Figure 5.3. Diagram representing metropolitan area network (MAN).

Source: Eric Conrad, Creative Commons License.

5.3.2. Components of Networks

The components of networks include (Mahmassani & Peeta, 1993):

- **Nodes:** These are the devices that are connected to a network, such as computers, servers, printers, and storage devices.
- **Links:** These are the communication channels used to connect nodes in a network. Examples of links include Ethernet cables, wireless signals, and satellite connections.
- **Protocols:** These are the rules and procedures used to transmit data between nodes in a network. Examples of protocols include TCP/IP, HTTP, and FTP.

Overall, networks are essential for enabling communication and resource sharing among devices and users. They play a critical role in facilitating business operations, enhancing collaboration, and enabling access to information and resources. Different types of networks and their associated components are used in various contexts, depending on the scale and requirements of the organization (Hanseth et al., 2004).

5.4. TELECOMMUNICATION AND NETWORKS IN INFORMATION SYSTEMS (IS)

TIPS

Stay up to date with the latest trends in telecommunication and networks such as 5G, IoT, and AI to remain competitive and take advantage of new opportunities in information systems development.

Telecommunication and networks are crucial components of modern information systems (IS). They enable individuals and organizations to communicate and share information across long distances and facilitate the use of various resources and services (Al-Mamary et al., 2014).

Telecommunication and networks in IS offer several advantages, including:

- **Faster Communication:** With the use of telecommunication and networks, individuals and organizations can communicate and share information more quickly and efficiently, leading to improved productivity and faster decision-making.
- **Wider Reach:** Telecommunication and networks allow individuals and organizations to connect with people and resources from different geographic locations, leading to a wider reach and greater access to information and resources.
- **Better Collaboration:** Telecommunication and networks enable individuals and organizations to collaborate and work together in real-time, regardless of their physical location. This leads to better teamwork, improved innovation, and greater creativity.

Examples of telecommunication and networks in IS include:

- **E-mail:** It is a form of telecommunication that enables individuals and organizations to send and receive messages, documents, and other information electronically over the internet.
- **Video Conferencing:** It is a type of telecommunication that enables individuals and organizations to conduct meetings and conferences in real-time, regardless of their physical location. This is made possible through the use of video and audio communication tools.
- **Cloud Computing:** It is a type of network-based computing that allows individuals and organizations to store and access data and applications over the internet. This enables them to access their resources from any location, leading to improved collaboration and greater efficiency.

Overall, the use of telecommunication and networks in IS plays a vital role in enabling communication, collaboration, and access to resources and services. The advantages offered by these technologies are increasingly important in today's world, where remote work, globalization, and the internet have made it essential for individuals and organizations to be connected and efficient (Sheldon, 1993).

Networks are essential in IS because they enable the sharing and transfer of data and information between different devices, systems, and locations. Here are some of the reasons why networks are necessary in IS:

- **Data and Information Sharing:** Networks enable the sharing of data and information between different devices and systems. This allows individuals and organizations to access and use data from different locations, leading to improved collaboration and productivity.
- **Resource Sharing:** Networks also enable the sharing of resources such as printers, storage devices, and servers. This means that multiple users can access the same resources, leading to cost savings and increased efficiency.
- **Communication:** Networks enable communication between devices, systems, and individuals. This means that individuals can communicate and collaborate with each other regardless of their location, leading to improved collaboration and productivity.
- **Centralized Management:** Networks allow for centralized management of devices and systems. This means that IT professionals can manage and monitor multiple devices and systems from a single location, leading to improved efficiency and security.
- **Scalability:** Networks are scalable, meaning they can easily accommodate additional devices and systems as needed. This means that organizations can easily expand their IS as their needs grow and change.

Overall, networks are necessary in IS because they enable data and information sharing, resource sharing, communication, centralized management, and scalability. These benefits lead to improved collaboration, productivity, and efficiency for individuals and organizations (Kim et al., 2011).

KEYWORD

Remote work is the practice of working from one's home or another space rather than from an office.

5.5. CHALLENGES AND RISKS IN TELECOMMUNICATION AND NETWORKS

While telecommunication and networks play a crucial role in modern IS, they also come with their own set of challenges and risks which are discussed in subsections.

5.5.1. Challenges

Following are the challenges:

- **Security:** Telecommunication and networks are vulnerable to security threats such as unauthorized access, malware, and data breaches. Organizations need to implement robust security measures to protect against these threats (Atay & Masera, 2011).
- **Reliability:** The reliability of telecommunication and networks is critical for the smooth operation of IS. Network downtime, slow internet speeds, and other issues can lead to reduced productivity and lost revenue.
- **Cost:** Building and maintaining a network can be expensive, particularly for small businesses or organizations with limited resources. The cost of hardware, software, and network maintenance can be a significant challenge.

KEYWORD

Denial-of-Service (DoS) attack is an attack meant to shut down a machine or network, making it inaccessible to its intended users.

5.5.2. Risks

Following are the risks:

- **Hacking:** Hackers can gain unauthorized access to networks and IS, leading to data theft, system disruption, and other issues.
- **Data Breaches:** These can occur when sensitive information is stolen or accessed without authorization. This can lead to loss of revenue, legal liability, and damage to the reputation of the organization.
- **Cyber Attacks:** These can take many forms, including malware, phishing, and denial-of-service attacks. These attacks can cause significant damage to networks and IS, leading to data loss, system disruption, and other issues (Figure 5.4).

Figure 5.4. Various cybersecurity attacks in information systems.

Source: Reciprocity, Creative Commons License.

In summary, while telecommunication and networks offer many benefits to IS, they also pose significant challenges and risks. Organizations need to take proactive steps to address these issues, including implementing robust security measures, maintaining network reliability, and managing costs. By doing so, they can ensure that their networks and IS remain secure, efficient, and productive (Smith et al., 2011).

The future of telecommunication and networks in IS is promising and full of exciting possibilities. Some of the significant trends that are expected to shape the future of IS include:

- **5G Technology:** It is the latest wireless technology that offers significantly faster speeds, lower latency, and improved capacity compared to the previous 4G technology. This will enable the development of new and innovative applications that rely on fast and reliable networks, such as augmented reality (AR) and virtual reality (VR).
- **Internet of Things (IoT):** It refers to the interconnectedness of everyday objects and devices through the internet. The use of IoT is expected to grow rapidly, with devices such as smart home appliances, medical devices, and industrial sensors becoming more prevalent (Figure 5.5).

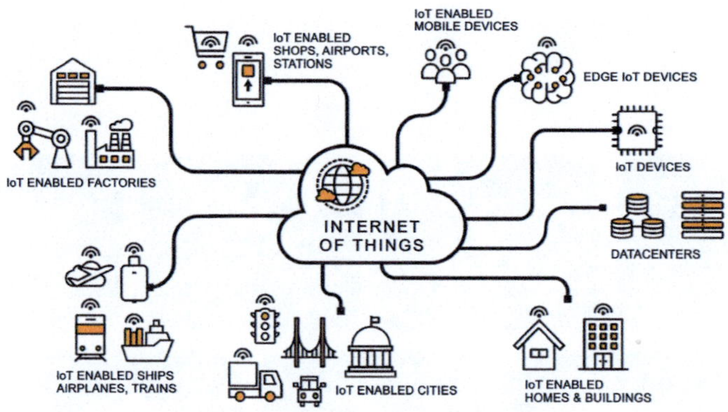

Figure 5.5. Illustration of internet of things (IoT).

Source: TIBCO, Creative Commons License.

- **Artificial Intelligence (AI):** It is expected to play a significant role in the future of IS. AI technologies such as machine learning and natural language processing are already being used in various applications, including virtual assistants, autonomous vehicles, and intelligent decision-making systems.

ACTIVITY 5.1.

How will the widespread adoption of 5G, IoT, and AI impact the future of transportation and logistics systems, and what challenges and opportunities will arise for information systems development in these industries?

The implications of these future trends on IS and society are numerous. Some of the key implications include (Hawilo et al., 2014):

- **Greater Efficiency:** The use of advanced networks and technologies will lead to greater efficiency and productivity in IS, with tasks being completed faster and with fewer errors.
- **New Business Opportunities:** The emergence of new technologies and applications will create new business opportunities and revenue streams for organizations that can take advantage of them.
- **Improved Quality of Life:** The use of IoT and AI technologies is expected to improve the quality of life for individuals, with smart homes, healthcare devices, and other applications leading to greater convenience, safety, and comfort.

However, there are also potential risks associated with these future trends, including privacy and security concerns, as well as the displacement of jobs and changes to the way people live and work. It will be essential for organizations and individuals to take proactive steps to address these risks and ensure that the benefits of these future trends are realized while minimizing the potential negative impacts (Ravi et al., 2004).

5.6. SUMMARY

In conclusion, telecommunication and networks play a critical role in IS. They enable the transmission of information and data between devices, systems, and networks, leading to faster communication, wider reach, better collaboration, cost savings, and improved productivity and efficiency.

Telecommunication and networks are necessary in IS because they enable data and information sharing, resource sharing, communication, centralized management, and scalability. They also provide a platform for future developments and progress, such as the integration of emerging technologies like 5G, IoT, and AI, which will further enhance the capabilities and potential of IS.

As technology continues to advance and organizations increasingly rely on digital infrastructure, the importance of telecommunication and networks in IS will only continue to grow. It is therefore essential that individuals and organizations understand the benefits and challenges of these technologies and take steps to ensure their proper implementation and management in order to achieve optimal results.

REVIEW QUESTIONS

1. What is telecommunication, and why is it important in modern society?
2. What are the different types of telecommunications, and what are some examples of each type?
3. What are the components of a network, and how do they work together to facilitate communication and data transfer?
4. How are telecommunication and networks used in information systems, and what are some advantages of using these technologies?
5. What are some challenges and risks associated with telecommunication and networks in information systems, and how can they be mitigated?

MULTIPLE CHOICE QUESTIONS

1. What is the main advantage of using telecommunication and networks in information systems?

a. Slower communication
b. Limited reach
c. Better collaboration
d. Higher cost

2. Which type of network covers the largest geographic area?

a. LAN

b. WAN
c. MAN
d. WLAN

3. **Which of the following is an example of wired telecommunication?**
   a. Wi-Fi
   b. Bluetooth
   c. Ethernet
   d. Infrared
4. **What is one of the main challenges of telecommunication and networks in information systems?**
   a. Low cost
   b. High reliability
   c. Low security
   d. High speed
5. **Which of the following is a future trend in telecommunication and networks in information systems?**
   a. 6G
   b. 5G
   c. 4G
   d. 2G

Answers to Multiple Choice Questions

1. (c); 2. (b); 3. (c); 4. (c); 5. (b)

REFERENCES

1. Ahn, J. H., & Skudlark, A. E., (1997). Resolving conflict of interests in the process of an information system implementation for advanced telecommunication services. *Journal of Information Technology, 12*(1), 3–13.
2. Al-Mamary, Y. H., Shamsuddin, A., & Aziati, N., (2014). The meaning of management information systems and its role in telecommunication companies in Yemen. *American Journal of Software Engineering, 2*(2), 22–25.
3. Assegie, T. A., & Nair, P. S., (2019). A review on software defined network security risks and challenges. *TELKOMNIKA (Telecommunication Computing Electronics and Control), 17*(6), 3168–3174.
4. Atay, S., & Masera, M., (2011). Challenges for the security analysis of next generation networks. *Information Security Technical Report, 16*(1), 3–11.

5. Batalla, J. M., Andrukiewicz, E., Gomez, G. P., Sapiecha, P., Mavromoustakis, C. X., Mastorakis, G., & Imran, M., (2020). Security risk assessment for 5G networks: National perspective. *IEEE Wireless Communications, 27*(4), 16–22.
6. Ben-Akiva, M., De Palma, A., & Isam, K., (1991). Dynamic network models and driver information systems. *Transportation Research Part A: General, 25*(5), 251–266.
7. Benzaid, C., & Taleb, T., (2020). AI-driven zero touch network and service management in 5G and beyond: Challenges and research directions. *IEEE Network, 34*(2), 186–194.
8. Chen, A. J., Boudreau, M. C., & Watson, R. T., (2008). Information systems and ecological sustainability. *Journal of Systems and Information Technology, 10*(3), 186–201.
9. Dewett, T., & Jones, G. R., (2001). The role of information technology in the organization: A review, model, and assessment. *Journal of Management, 27*(3), 313–346.
10. Grover, V., Cheon, M. J., & Teng, J. T., (1994). A descriptive study on the outsourcing of information systems functions. *Information & Management, 27*(1), 33–44.
11. Grover, V., Cheon, M. J., & Teng, J. T., (1996). The effect of service quality and partnership on the outsourcing of information systems functions. *Journal of Management Information Systems, 12*(4), 89–116.
12. Gupta, A., Stahl, D. O., & Whinston, A. B., (1999). The economics of network management. *Communications of the ACM, 42*(9), 57–63.
13. Haggerty, P., & Seetharaman, K., (1998). The benefits of CORBA-based network management. *Communications of the ACM, 41*(10), 73–79.
14. Hanseth, O., Aanestad, M., & Berg, M., (2004). Guest editors' introduction: Actor-network theory and information systems. What's so special? *Information Technology & People, 17*(2), 116–123.
15. Hawilo, H., Shami, A., Mirahmadi, M., & Asal, R., (2014). NFV: State of the art, challenges, and implementation in next generation mobile networks (vEPC). *IEEE Network, 28*(6), 18–26.
16. Hellström, T., (2003). Systemic innovation and risk: Technology assessment and the challenge of responsible innovation. *Technology in Society, 25*(3), 369–384.
17. Hunt, R., (1997). SNMP, SNMPv2 and CMIP—The technologies for multivendor network management. *Computer Communications, 20*(2), 73–88.
18. Kim, K. K., Ryoo, S. Y., & Jung, M. D., (2011). Inter-organizational information systems visibility in buyer–supplier relationships: The case of telecommunication equipment component manufacturing industry. *Omega, 39*(6), 667–676.
19. Mahmassani, H. S., & Peeta, S., (1993). Network performance under system optimal and user equilibrium dynamic assignments: Implications for advanced traveler information systems. *Transportation Research Record, 1408*, 83.
20. Raman, L., (1998). OSI systems and network management. *IEEE Communications Magazine, 36*(3), 46–53.

21. Ravi, S., Raghunathan, A., Kocher, P., & Hattangady, S., (2004). Security in embedded systems: Design challenges. *ACM Transactions on Embedded Computing Systems (TECS), 3*(3), 461–491.

22. Schwartz, M., (1995). Network management and control issues in multimedia wireless networks. *IEEE Personal Communications, 2*(3), 8–16.

23. Sheldon, P. J., (1993). Destination information systems. *Annals of Tourism Research, 20*(4), 633–649.

24. Smith, P., Hutchison, D., Sterbenz, J. P., Schöller, M., Fessi, A., Karaliopoulos, M., & Plattner, B., (2011). Network resilience: A systematic approach. *IEEE Communications Magazine, 49*(7), 88–97.

25. Subba, R. S., (2004). Role of ICTs in India's rural community information systems. *INFO, 6*(4), 261–269.

26. Watson, R. T., Kelly, G. G., Galliers, R. D., & Brancheau, J. C., (1997). Key issues in information systems management: An international perspective. *Journal of Management Information Systems, 13*(4), 91–115.

27. Zachman, J. A., (1987). A framework for information systems architecture. *IBM Systems Journal, 26*(3), 276–292.

28. Zio, E., & Aven, T., (2011). Uncertainties in smart grids behavior and modeling: What are the risks and vulnerabilities? How to analyze them? *Energy Policy, 39*(10), 6308–6320.

CHAPTER 6

INFORMATION SYSTEMS IN BUSINESS AND SOCIETY

UNIT INTRODUCTION

Information systems (IS) are an assembled mix of hardware, software, people, telecommunications networks, data resources, and rules and regulations that are used by an organization to reserve, recover, transform, and distribute information. People depend on contemporary technology to interact with one another through different physical devices (referred to as hardware), information processing commands and methods (referred to as software), communications channels (referred to as networks), and data resources (referred to as data resources). In order to facilitate tasks like forecasting, designing, monitoring, decision-making, and operational support, an organization needs an IS, which according to Patterson is a collection of interlinked elements that collaborate in order to carry out input, processing, storage, output, and control operations to transform data into information. This information is used to back activities such as prediction, planning, decision-making, and operational activities (Legner et al., 2017). Every corporate firm today requires some kind of IS to control all of its operations, starting with business planning and continuing through product delivery, which includes the production and quality control cycles. Technically, the word "information system" refers to a network of interlinked components used to gather, process, store, and transfer data to facilitate the organization's decision-making, coordination, and control processes. IS may assist the staff in problem analysis, the visualization of difficult topics, and the development of new products, along with assisting in decision-making, collaboration, and control (Lawrence et al., 2010). The information that is stored in an organization's IS typically pertains to notable people, locations, and things either within the firm itself or in its surroundings. When we talk about information, we're referring to raw data that has been organized in a manner that is related and helpful to others. While data are a collection of unprocessed facts representing events that are taking place in organizations before they have been structured and sorted into a format that is easy to comprehend. An IS is a digital system that processes data and generates information, as stated by Shim. A cycle in the processing of information is what this process is known as (IPC). Four different operations make up the information processing cycle. These are referred to as input, processing, output, and storage, respectively (Hedberg & Jönsson, 1978).

IS play an important role in the modern business landscape and society as a whole. ISs are computer-based tools that are used to store, process, and communicate information. In a business context, ISs are used to assist the business in daily operations and decision-making. ISs have become essential tools for communication, collaboration, and entertainment in society (Fountain, 2000).

ISs support several business activities, including auditing, finance, marketing, and supply chain management (SCM). IS can help businesses to manage inventory, track sales, analyze market trends, and identify areas for cost savings. With the rise of e-commerce, ISs have become even more important, as they allow businesses to sell products and services online and to manage transactions and customer data (Goss, 2015).

ISs are also critical in society, as they have transformed how we communicate and interact. Social media platforms, messaging apps, and online forums have become essential tools for staying connected with friends and family and sharing information and ideas. Online education, remote work, and telehealth services have all become more prevalent due to the availability of ISs (Gordon & Miller, 1976).

Nonetheless, the utilization of information technologies brings up questions regarding confidentiality, security, and morality. There is an increased potential for unauthorized individuals or organizations to get access to personally identifiable information that is kept and shared online due to the growing volume of such information. Threats to cybersecurity, including malware, phishing attempts, and data leaks, are ongoing worries for individuals and corporations. There are also ethical considerations associated with utilizing ISs, such as the influence on employment, the possibility for bias in decision-making algorithms, and the part that ISs play in perpetuating inequality (Argyris, 1977).

Overall, the impact of ISs on business and society has been profound. ISs have transformed how we work, communicate, and access information, but they also present significant challenges that must be addressed to ensure these powerful tools' responsible and ethical use (MacGuire, 1968).

Learning Objectives

At the end of this chapter, readers will be able to learn:

- Various types of IS in businesses and society;
- Information systems' function in business;

- Transaction processing systems and enterprise collaboration systems;
- Management and decision systems;
- Professional and expert information systems;
- Knowledge and strategic information systems;
- Functional business systems and sales information systems;
- Production information systems;
- Finance, accounting, and human resources information systems;
- Information systems' role in society in communication, education, entertainment, health, and security.

Key Terms

- Accounting information systems
- Business
- Communication
- Decision support systems
- Enterprise collaboration system
- Executive information systems
- Expert systems
- Finance information systems
- Human resources information systems
- Information systems
- Knowledge systems
- Management systems
- Production information systems
- Society
- Transaction processing systems

6.1. TYPES OF INFORMATION SYSTEMS (ISS) IN BUSINESSES

There are numerous methods to classify the IS applications that are employed in contemporary business settings. For example, some types of IS can be referred to as operations (support of business operations) or (Support of managerial decision making). Transaction processing systems (TPSs), operation control systems, and enterprise collaboration systems are examples of business support systems. Management information systems (MIS), decision support systems (DSS), and executive information systems (EIS) support managers in making decisions (Stine et al., 2008) (Figure 6.1).

Figure 6.1. Illustration of the different types of information systems in businesses.

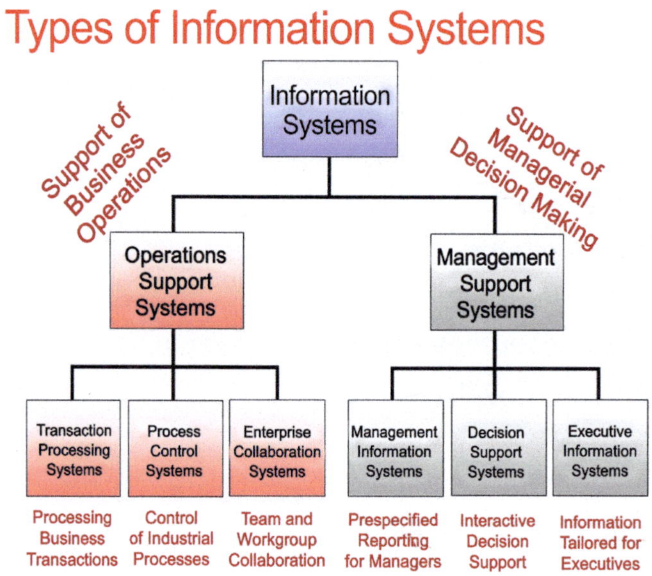

Source: Oleh Anonim, Creative Commons License.

6.2. THE FUNCTIONS OF SEVERAL IS TYPES IN CORPORATE GROUPS

6.2.1. Transaction Processing Systems (TPSs)

TPS are the systems that assist a firm at the operational level. It is an electronic system that carries out and keeps track of the transactions required for a business' operation (Kemme et al., 2003).

6.2.2. Process Control Systems

Process control systems track as well as supervise physical or commercial processes. Steel, power, and petroleum refining systems are a few examples.

A petroleum refinery, for example, uses digital electronic equipment to observe chemical processes and make immediate changes that govern the refinery process. A process control system incorporates all of the required hardware, software, and operational processes (Leveson et al., 1994).

6.2.3. Enterprise Collaboration Systems

Enterprise Collaboration System is among the most prevalent IS that managers use to monitor the information flow in their firms. These systems are increasing team and workgroup productivity and interaction.

They back a wide range of users and are not specific to any individual level of the firm. IT is utilized to make routine office work easier via these systems. Voicemail, multimedia systems, e-mail, video conferencing, file sharing, and even collective decision-making are all possible with the help of office information systems (IS) (Prakash et al., 2020).

Remember

MIS provide real-time information for managers to make informed decisions. Design MIS that align with organizational goals and needs, and ensure they are secure, reliable, and scalable.

6.2.4. Management Information Systems (MIS)

Management information systems (MIS) are a particular type of computer IS that can gather and analyze information from diverse sources to aid in management-level decisions. Information management systems deliver data in the form of predefined statements and exhibit them to support business decision-making.

The next level of the organizational hierarchy is occupied by low-level managers and supervisors, who use computer systems designed to aid operational management in tracking and supervising clerical-level transaction processing processes. MIS uses data from TPS to create related control reports for supervisors. MIS are ISs that extract internal data from a system and converts it into relevant and useful schemes, such as management reports, to support management operations (Mason & Mitroff, 1973) (Figure 6.2).

Figure 6.2. Schematic of management information systems.

Source: Al Yamamah University, Creative Commons License.

6.2.5. Decision Support Systems (DSS)

When managers at any level of an organization face semi-structured decision-making options, a decision support system can be a useful tool. These are a sort of computerized organizational ISs that aid executives in opting choices that require simulation, computation, comparison, opting the best alternative, or scenario prediction. Decision-support systems are developed explicitly to aid management in making decisions in situations where there is uncertainty about the potential effects of those decisions. It is a computer based IS that aids executives in making challenging decisions (Liu et al., 2010).

6.2.6. Executive Information Systems (EIS)

The fully established organizational ISs offer quick access to internal as well as external information and possess the capability to report detailed micro-level data if necessary. EIS gives managers and executives quick access to important information from internal and external resources. Patterson states that an EIS grants the executives with a procedure that assists in making deliberate decisions. An executive IS is created to provide information that is conceptual enough to convey the entire firm function in a condensed form to appease the executives (Leidner & Elam, 1993).

6.2.7. Expert Systems

Expert systems are the class of AI used most productively in establishing business applications. These are knowledgeable computers that offer consumers guidelines and act as advisors. An expert system is a computer software that seeks to simulate human analysis.

An expert system is a collection of computer programs that can complete a job as effectively as a human expert (Durkin, 1996).

TIPS

To build an effective knowledge management system, focus on fostering a culture of knowledge sharing and collaboration among all stakeholders, including management, employees, and customers.

6.2.8. Knowledge Management (KM) Systems

Knowledge-based ISs or knowledge management (KM) systems assist in the manufacturing, structuring, and circulating business knowledge to all the members of an organization.

KM is the proper implementation of the whole system to expand a firm's knowledge (Alavi & Leidner, 2001).

6.2.9. Strategic Information Systems (IS)

In order to give a company a competitive edge over rivals, strategic ISs integrate information technology (IT) into its operations, services, or business processes. Strategic ISs are a crucial distinct kind of organizational IS that is utilized to secure a market edge (Peppard & Ward, 2004) (Figure 6.3).

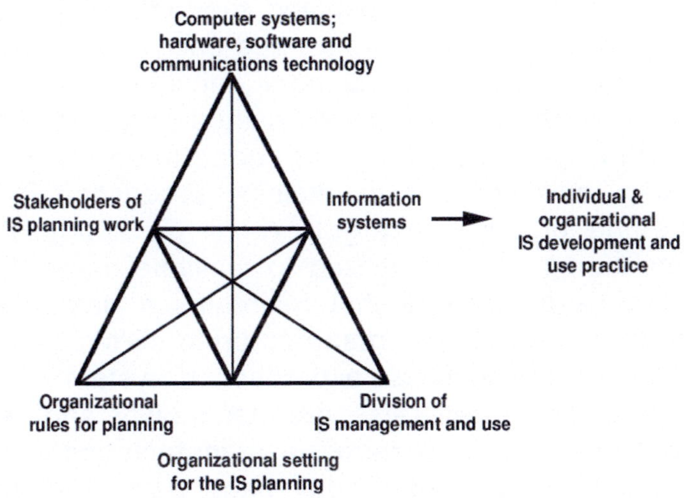

Figure 6.3. The structure of strategic information systems planning in organizations.

Source: Mikko J. Ruohonen, Creative Commons License.

6.2.10. Functional Business Systems

ISs that emphasize the executive and operational applications to back basic business operations are known as functional business systems. ISs backing applications in auditing, marketing, operations management, and HRM are a few examples. ISs can be classified into four categories.

6.2.11. Sales and Marketing Information Systems (IS)

Marketing and sales system include the selling of the firm's goods and services. Recognizing the clients of a company, determination of their needs, establishing plans to fulfill those needs by creating required goods or services, and then marketing and advertisement of those goods or services comes under the jurisdiction of 'marketing.' Similarly, 'sales' include building contacts with the customers, offering the goods and services, receiving orders, and recording sales. These efforts are supported by sales and marketing ISs. Shim is of the opinion, that a marketing MIS supports executive activities in the product creation sections, allocation, pricing choices, promotional efficacy, and sales forecasting (Chonko et al., 1991).

KEYWORD

Sales forecasting is the process of estimating future revenue by predicting the amount of product or services a sales unit (which can be an individual salesperson, a sales team, or a company) will sell in the next week, month, quarter, or year.

6.2.12. Manufacturing and Production Information Systems (IS)

The manufacturing and production department is accountable for creating the company's services and products. This department oversees the procurement, storage, and accessibility of materials, and plans the necessary machinery, facilities, resources, and workforce required to manufacture finished products. Additionally, the production and manufacturing department is responsible for designing, building, and maintaining production facilities, as well as setting production targets (Li & Li, 2000). Production and manufacturing ISs are utilized to facilitate these duties. The production IS is a software that maintains a database of data pertaining to fabrication. A manufacturing IS's goal is to use computer technology to boost a production system's productivity and efficiency, which will raise product quality and reduce the production budget. In other terms, a manufacturing system uses management, ISs technology, equipment, data, and material as inputs and manufacturing and information processes as outputs to give final products (Bharadwaj et al., 2007).

6.2.13. Finance and Accounting Information Systems (IS)

The finance department handles the company's economic resources, including cash, stocks, bonds, and other investments. The accounting function handles and preserves the company's monetary records, including wages, depreciation, and receipts. Asserts that accounting software's primary function is to computerize the tedious process of inputting and reporting accounting transactions. In order to create financial statements, this information is grouped in an electronic manner that can be quickly accessible to help with business management. A financial MIS gives all financial managers within a firm access to financial information. Generally, accounting system information is used to make financial decisions (Ezzamel & Bourn, 1990).

TIPS

Human resources information system (HRIS) helps companies manage and automate core HR processes. These HR software systems support benefits administration, time and attendance, payroll, and other workflows, as well as the storage of employee data, such as personal, demographic, and compensation information.

6.2.14. Human Resource Information Systems (HRIS)

Human resource information systems (HRIS) enable organizations to generate, organize, store, and distribute human resource data, aiding decision-making at all levels of administration. Almost all successful companies utilize HRIS for the day-to-day management of their human resources. The HR department is in charge of attracting, nurturing, and retaining the organization's workforce. HR ISs back various tasks, such as recognizing potential candidates, maintaining comprehensive records of current employees, and building programs to improve employees' skills (Hendrickson, 2003).

6.3. ROLE OF IS IN SOCIETY

ISs have become a necessary component of contemporary society, and they have an impact on all facets of our everyday life. In this chapter, we'll talk about how information technologies have changed communication, education, the workplace, amusement, health and wellness, confidentiality, and security (Sambamurthy et al., 2003).

6.3.1. Communication

Communication has changed dramatically as a result of ISs. People can now connect and collaborate more easily across distances thanks to social media platforms, messaging apps, and online forums. We now have access to innovative communication methods like virtual reality (VR) and video conferencing, allowing us to have immersive and interactive experiences (Lee et al., 2015) (Figure 6.4).

Figure 6.4. Schematic of the evolution of the communication.

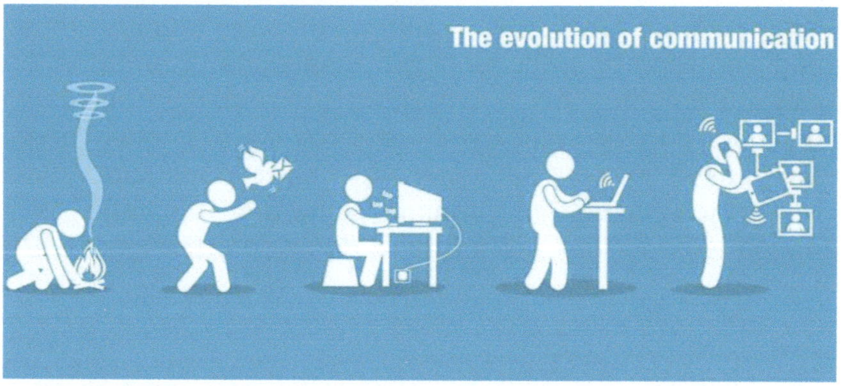

Source: Vandan Mehta, Creative Commons License.

6.3.2. Education

The development of ISs has altered our approach to education. Online education and e-learning have increased access to and affordability of education, while digital textbooks and tools have made learning more interesting and participatory. Virtual classrooms and collaborative tools have also been enabled by IT, making education more versatile and individualized (Chiang et al., 2012).

Did you get it?

The global market size for enterprise software, including information systems, was estimated to be around 426 billion U.S. dollars in 2021, with projected growth to over 600 billion U.S. dollars by 2025, reflecting the increasing adoption and impact of these technologies in business and society.

6.3.3. Work

The workplace has been revolutionized by ISs. Telecommuting and remote work have become more common, allowing people to work from anywhere in the world. Digital collaboration and project management tools have made it easier for teams to collaborate, while cloud-based software and services have enabled firms to operate and compete in new ways (Suh et al., 2017).

6.3.4. Entertainment

ISs have had a big influence on the entertainment industry as well. New kinds of entertainment and media consumption have emerged as a result of streaming media platforms, internet gaming, and VR. Consumers now have greater flexibility over what they listen to and when they listen to it, thanks to digital music and podcasts (Hew et al., 2016).

6.3.5. Health and Wellness

Health and wellness have also been influenced by ISs. Telehealth and remote patient monitoring have made it easier for patients to access medical treatment, particularly in rural and disadvantaged areas. People have more control over their health thanks to wearable technologies and health-tracking applications, while online fitness programs and tools have made it easier for people to exercise and stay healthy (Shim & Jo, 2020).

6.3.6. Privacy and Security

The increased usage of IT has prompted privacy and security concerns. Personal information is at risk online, and cybersecurity threats are becoming increasingly sophisticated. Individuals and organizations must take precautions to secure themselves, and their data as regulatory and ethical considerations become more significant (Turn & Ware, 1976).

Finally, ISs have had a significant impact on society. As we progress towards a more digital society, we must continue to investigate the benefits and drawbacks of information technologies and ensure that they are used responsibly and ethically (Lawler & Molluzzo, 2010).

ACTIVITY 6.1.

How can the implementation of Information Systems in supply chain management enhance the transparency and efficiency of global supply chains, and what ethical and social implications should be considered when implementing these technologies in business and society?

6.4. SUMMARY

Commercial organizations utilize different types of ISs, each with specific purposes. Transaction processing systems (TPSs) record the routine day-to-day transactions necessary for a company's operation. Office automation systems are designed to aid with office tasks, while process control systems are utilized to monitor and regulate physical or industrial processes. MIS focus on transforming internal data into useful information, which is then communicated to managers at all levels and functions to enable accurate and efficient decision-making for planning, directing, and overseeing operations. DSS are designed to assist managers with complex decisions involving modeling, formulation, calculation, comparison, selection, or scenario prediction. Executive information systems (EIS) provide a tool for senior managers to make strategic and tactical choices. Expert system software simulates human reasoning. This research aims to describe the role of each IS type in business organizations.

REVIEW QUESTIONS

1. What are the different types of information systems commonly used in business? Provide an example of each and explain its purpose.
2. What is the difference between transaction processing systems and enterprise collaboration systems? How do they support different aspects of business operations?
3. How do management and decision support systems assist organizations in making informed and strategic decisions? Provide an example of a scenario where such a system would be useful.
4. What are expert information systems, and how are they different from executive information systems? What types of problems might an expert system be particularly helpful in solving?
5. In what ways do information systems play a role in society beyond their use in businesses? Provide examples of how information systems are used in fields such as communication, education, and health.

MULTIPLE CHOICE QUESTIONS

1. What type of information system is typically used to support daily, routine business transactions such as processing orders or managing inventory?

a. Executive information system

b. Decision support system

c. Transaction processing system

d. Enterprise collaboration system

2. Which of the following is not an example of a functional business system?

a. Marketing automation software

b. Supply chain management system

c. Enterprise resource planning software

d. Virtual reality headset

3. What is the purpose of an expert information system?

a. To provide summary information for executives and managers

b. To process routine transactions and maintain records

c. To support collaborative work across different teams and departments

d. To provide specialized, expert knowledge to support decision-making

4. Which of the following is a way that information systems are used in society beyond their application in businesses?

a. To support supply chain management and logistics

b. To provide customer relationship management tools

c. To support virtual reality gaming experiences

d. To provide telehealth services and remote patient monitoring

5. What is the primary role of a decision support system?

a. To support routine, daily transactions

b. To provide high-level, executive summaries of business activity

c. To help managers and employees make informed, data-driven decisions

d. To automate manufacturing and production processes

Answers to the Multiple-Choice Questions

1. (c); 2. (d); 3. (d); 4. (d); 5. (c)

REFERENCES

1. Aithal, P. S., (2016). Study on ABCD analysis technique for business models, business strategies, operating concepts & business systems. *International Journal in Management and Social Science, 4*(1), 95–115.
2. Alavi, M., & Leidner, D. E., (2001). Knowledge management and knowledge management systems: Conceptual foundations and research issues. *MIS Quarterly*, 107–136.
3. Argyris, C., (1977). Organizational learning and management information systems. *Accounting, Organizations and Society, 2*(2), 113–123.

4. Bharadwaj, S., Bharadwaj, A., & Bendoly, E., (2007). The performance effects of complementarities between information systems, marketing, manufacturing, and supply chain processes. *Information Systems Research, 18*(4), 437–453.
5. Chiang, R. H., Goes, P., & Stohr, E. A., (2012). Business intelligence and analytics education, and program development: A unique opportunity for the information systems discipline. *ACM Transactions on Management Information Systems (TMIS), 3*(3), 1–13.
6. Chonko, L. B., Tanner, Jr. J. F., & Smith, E. R., (1991). Selling and sales management in action: The sales force's role in international marketing research and marketing information systems. *Journal of Personal Selling & Sales Management, 11*(1), 69–80.
7. Durkin, J., (1996). Expert systems: A view of the field. *IEEE Intelligent Systems, 11*(02), 56–63.
8. Ezzamel, M., & Bourn, M., (1990). The roles of accounting information systems in an organization experiencing financial crisis. *Accounting, Organizations and Society, 15*(5), 399–424.
9. Fountain, J. E., (2000). Constructing the information society: Women, information technology, and design. *Technology in Society, 22*(1), 45–62.
10. Gordon, L. A., & Miller, D., (1976). A contingency framework for the design of accounting information systems. *Accounting, Organizations and Society, 1*(1), 59–69.
11. Goss, D., (2015). *Small Business and Society* (Vol. 1, pp. 1–5). Routledge.
12. Hedberg, B., & Jönsson, S., (1978). Designing semi-confusing information systems for organizations in changing environments. *Accounting, Organizations and Society, 3*(1), 47–64.
13. Hendrickson, A. R., (2003). Human resource information systems: Backbone technology of contemporary human resources. *Journal of Labor Research, 24*(3), 381.
14. Hew, T. S., Leong, L. Y., Ooi, K. B., & Chong, A. Y. L., (2016). Predicting drivers of mobile entertainment adoption: A two-stage SEM-artificial-neural-network analysis. *Journal of Computer Information Systems, 56*(4), 352–370.
15. Kemme, B., Pedone, F., Alonso, G., Schiper, A., & Wiesmann, M., (2003). Using optimistic atomic broadcast in transaction processing systems. *IEEE Transactions on Knowledge and Data Engineering, 15*(4), 1018–1032.
16. Lawler, J. P., & Molluzzo, J. C., (2010). A study of the perceptions of students on privacy and security on social networking sites (SNS) on the internet. *Journal of Information Systems Applied Research, 3*(12), 3–18.
17. Lawrence, A., Weber, J., & Post, J., (2010). *Business and Society* (Vol. 1, pp. 1–21). McGraw-Hill Publishing.
18. Lee, J., Park, J. G., & Lee, S., (2015). Raising team social capital with knowledge and communication in information systems development projects. *International Journal of Project Management, 33*(4), 797–807.

19. Legner, C., Eymann, T., Hess, T., Matt, C., Böhmann, T., Drews, P., & Ahlemann, F., (2017). Digitalization: Opportunity and challenge for the business and information systems engineering community. *Business & Information Systems Engineering, 59*, 301–308.

20. Leidner, D. E., & Elam, J. J., (1993). Executive information systems: Their impact on executive decision making. *Journal of Management Information Systems, 10*(3), 139–155.

21. Leveson, N. G., Heimdahl, M. P. E., Hildreth, H., & Reese, J. D., (1994). Requirements specification for process-control systems. *IEEE Transactions on Software Engineering, 20*(9), 684–707.

22. Li, H., & Li, L. X., (2000). Integrating systems concepts into manufacturing information systems. *Systems Research and Behavioral Science: The Official Journal of the International Federation for Systems Research, 17*(2), 135–147.

23. Liu, S., Duffy, A. H., Whitfield, R. I., & Boyle, I. M., (2010). Integration of decision support systems to improve decision support performance. *Knowledge and Information Systems, 22*, 261–286.

24. MacGuire, J. W., (1968). *Business and Society* (Vol. 1, pp. 1–10). Ardent Media.

25. Mason, R. O., & Mitroff, I. I., (1973). A program for research on management information systems. *Management Science, 19*(5), 475–487.

26. Peppard, J., & Ward, J., (2004). Beyond strategic information systems: Towards an IS capability. *The Journal of Strategic Information Systems, 13*(2), 167–194.

27. Prakash, S., Joshi, S., Bhatia, T., Sharma, S., Samadhiya, D., Shah, R. R., & Prasad, M., (2020). Characteristic of enterprise collaboration system and its implementation issues in business management. *International Journal of Business Intelligence and Data Mining, 16*(1), 49–65.

28. Sambamurthy, V., Bharadwaj, A., & Grover, V., (2003). Shaping agility through digital options: Reconceptualizing the role of information technology in contemporary firms. *MIS Quarterly,* 237–263.

29. Shim, M., & Jo, H. S., (2020). What quality factors matter in enhancing the perceived benefits of online health information sites? Application of the updated DeLone and McLean information systems success model. *International Journal of Medical Informatics, 137*, 104093.

30. Stine, K., Kissel, R., Barker, W., Lee, A., & Fahlsing, J., (2008). *Guide for Mapping Types of Information and Information Systems to Security Categories: Appendices* (No. NIST Special Publication (SP) 800–60 Vol. 2 Rev. 1). National Institute of Standards and Technology.

31. Suh, A., Cheung, C. M., Ahuja, M., & Wagner, C., (2017). Gamification in the workplace: The central role of the aesthetic experience. *Journal of Management Information Systems, 34*(1), 268–305.

32. Turn, R., & Ware, W. H., (1976). Privacy and security issues in information systems. *IEEE Transactions on Computers, 25*(12), 1353–1361.

CHAPTER 7

ETHICAL AND SECURITY ISSUES OF INFORMATIVE SYSTEM

UNIT INTRODUCTION

Today's modern digital age has significantly benefited individuals and organizations through the growing usage of information technology (IT), which has enhanced efficiency, communication, and decision-making. Yet, to guarantee that using information security does not result in harm or exploitation, these advantages come with ethical and security concerns that need to be addressed (Dhillon & Backhouse, 2000).

Information systems' (IS) ethical ramifications for confidentiality, reliability, accessibility, and copyrighted material are covered here. When ISs are created to prevent specific demographics, such as people with impairments, from accessing the information, accessibility concerns can occur. Intellectual property issues occur when material protected by copyright or a trademark is used without authorization (Bansal et al., 2021).

Phishing, botnets, malware, and denial-of-service attacks are a few security challenges affecting ISs. These dangers have the potential to jeopardize the confidentiality, integrity, and accessibility of data and systems, resulting in monetary loss, damage to one's reputation, as well as legal and regulatory repercussions. Addressing these ethical and security challenges becomes more critical as our reliance on IT increases (Siponen & Oinas-Kukkonen, 2007).

This chapter will delve deeper into the ethical and security concerns pertaining to ISs in this chapter. The author will talk about how these problems affect people and organizations (Figure 7.1).

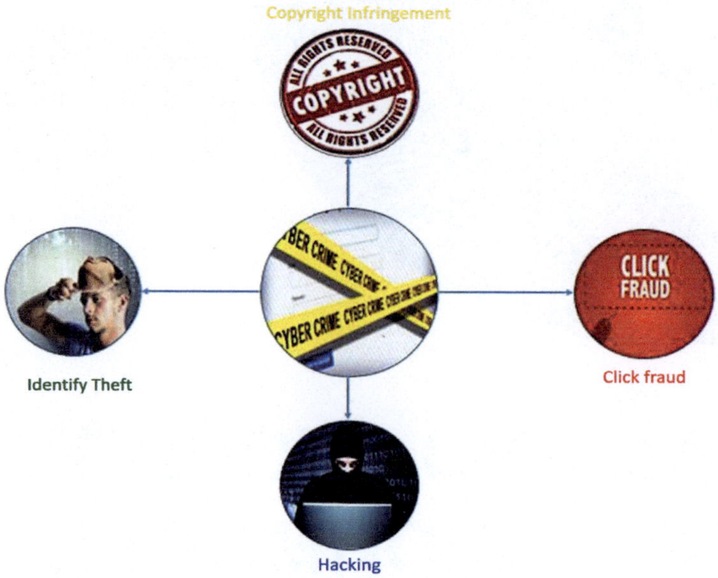

Figure 7.1. Illustration of ethical and security issue of informative system.

Source: Guru99, Creative Commons License.

Learning Objectives

At the end of this chapter, the reader will be able to understand:

- The ethical and security issues of the informative system;
- The importance and issues about the privacy of information system;
- The concept of intellectual property;
- The issues of viruses and malicious programs;
- The concept of phishing.

Key Terms

- Botnets
- Denial of service
- Drive-by download attacks
- Malicious programs
- Malvertising
- Phishing
- Ransomware
- Zero-day exploits

7.1. ETHICAL ISSUES OF INFORMATION SYSTEMS (IS)

Information systems (IS) are now essential for enabling efficient leadership, data analysis, and decision-making in the digital age. However, several ethical issues that have emerged due to the increasing use of computer systems must be addressed to assure their ethical and responsible usage (Rogerson et al., 2019).

ISs' primary ethical problems about privacy, accuracy, accessibility, and intellectual property. When personal data is collected and utilized without the subject's consent, privacy issues arise. Inaccurate or altered information might cause accuracy problems. When ISs are created in a way that prevents particular groups of individuals from accessing the information, accessibility issues may occur. Intellectual property issues occur when material protected by copyright, or a trademark is used without authorization. To prevent harm or exploitation from occurring due to the usage of ISs, businesses, and organizations must be knowledgeable of these ethical challenges and take action to solve them (Paradice et al., 2018).

Remember

Accuracy problems can develop when data is falsified or altered, while privacy concerns can arise when personal data is gathered and utilized without the individual's agreement.

7.2. PRIVACY IN INFORMATION SYSTEMS (IS)

Several novel approaches to data processing seemed unthinkable just a few years ago. Nowadays, few people are shocked by technology like profiling, banner advertisements, or personalized services. When creating client data-based online services and information technology (IT) solutions, merely adhering to legal requirements and privacy rules is no longer acceptable. The security of personal data could be threatened by these technologies. Consider national healthcare applications as an illustration. Computer systems gather much personal information about inherited disorders, age, race, health information, and lifestyle (such as bad habits and mobility) (Bélanger & Crossler, 2011).

Another illustration would be financial software and services like internet banking, tax preparation, or digital wallets. The consequences of a confidentiality breach can be severe and frequently permanent.

First employed by casinos to identify cheaters, it now helps law enforcement. Yet, it also compromises people's right to privacy (Kalloniatis & Mouratidis, 2014) (Figure 7.2).

Figure 7.2. Flow diagram of NORA (non-obvious relationship awareness).

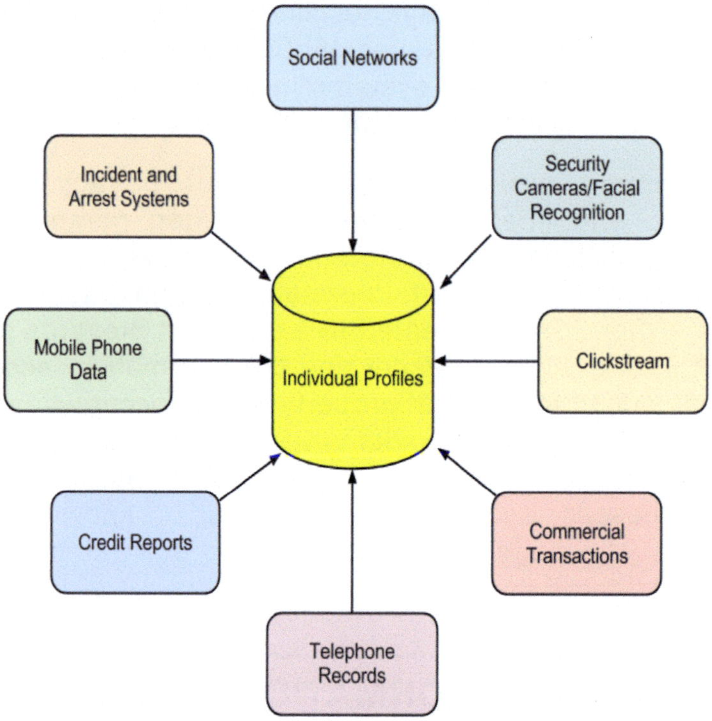

Source: Opentext Books, Creative Commons License.

TIPS

NORA (non-obvious relationship awareness) technology should be used by private and public institutions to gather massive amounts of data and integrate it into profiles.

Tech corporations are eager to offer any product or service they provide for free to collect personal data continuously. In turn, this causes "privacy inflation." The user must give access to an ever-increasing variety of identifiable data to receive any new or enhanced service. These dishonest actions come in many forms and get more complex every time. Deloitte defines conduct risk as a collection of unethical tactics businesses use to get more personal information about their clients, such as fine print, unclear contract terms, the imposition of unneeded services, or customer misinformation (Smith et al., 2011).

Due to concerns with confidentiality in IT, the Privacy by Design framework was developed and put into practice. This framework is based on the usage of information through seven core principles:

- Respect for user privacy—keep it user-centric;
- Privacy as the default setting;

- Whole lifecycle protection and end-to-end security;
- Embedded into the design;
- Full functionality—positive-sum, not zero-sum;
- Proactive rather than reactive; preventative rather than corrective;
- Visibility and transparency—keep it open.

A site was developed by the NCSA (National Cyber Security Alliance) to track privacy preferences and data security. It contains links to well-known social media platforms, e-mail, and phone services, google searches, and e-commerce websites. The NCSA advises updating its privacy controls on well-known online services and gadgets by clicking these links (Onsrud et al., 1994) (Figure 7.3).

Figure 7.3. Image of NCSA (National Cyber Security Alliance).

Source: Stat Safe Online, Creative Commons License.

7.3. INTELLECTUAL PROPERTY

Intellectual property protection is the next touchy subject concerning ethical dilemmas in information technologies. The collective phrase "intellectual property" denotes the sole ownership of the outcomes of creative effort and means of individualization (Stock & Stock, 2006).

- It's simple to get unauthorized access to content. Few people consider the ethical implications and factors.
- Free streaming, downloading, and sharing practices on the Internet have an impact on how people comprehend the idea of intellectual property. Piracy of software and content is frequently accepted as the standard.
- In the context of digital media, people frequently lack empathy for those who are impacted by their decisions.
- Confusion increases with easy access to a lot of content.

Proprietary information, franchises, patents, and copyrights safeguard intellectual property. Businesses employ trade secrets to safeguard sensitive information that is strategically valuable but that they are unwilling to share. When non-tangible landowners disclose information that needs to be protected, legal professionals utilize the other three terms (Lavenue, 1997).

7.4. ACCESSIBILITY

The term "accessibility" describes how ISs are created and put into use so that people with disabilities may use and access them. To prevent disability prejudice and exclusion, companies must face this ethical dilemma (Culnan, 1985) (Figure 7.4).

Figure 7.4. Picture of web accessibility.

Source: Search Engine Journal, Creative Commons License.

7.4.1. Lack of Accessibility in Information Systems (IS)

When businesses fail to give accessibility top priority throughout the development and creation of their systems, the ethical problem of accessibility in ISs may arise. As a result, people with disabilities may be unable to use certain technologies because they are inaccessible.

7.4.2. Failure to Ensure Accessibility

When businesses do not take the necessary steps to make sure that their computer networks are usable by people with impairments, the ethical problem of accessibility might also come up. Even if availability is a top priority for the company, this could lead to technology that is not entirely accessible (Culnan, 1984).

7.4.3. Consequences of Inaccessibility

The negative effects of having inaccessible ISs are severe because they can prevent people with disabilities from participating fully in society, limit their prospects, and have legal and regulatory repercussions. Furthermore, it may prevent organizations from realizing their full potential while excluding a sizable population segment (Kovach & Cathcart, 1999).

7.5. ACCURACY

Ensuring that the information and data are accurate and error-free is a crucial ethical concern in ISs. Inaccurate information can influence decisions that are harmful to people and society.

KEYWORD

Computer network is defined as a system that connects two or more computing devices for transmitting and sharing information.

7.5.1. Causes of Inaccurate Information

Human mistake is one of the main reasons why information is wrong. Any phase of the computer network, from data entry through analysis and reporting, is susceptible to this. Nevertheless, misinformation might be supplied due to falsified or biased data. This might happen either on purpose or accidentally (Thapa & Bossler, 1992).

7.5.2. Consequences of Inaccurate Information

Inaccurate data can have serious repercussions on people as well as society at large. For instance, inaccurate medical information may lead to the patient receiving the wrong diagnosis and treatment, which is harmful. Financial losses and poor investment choices can be caused by inaccurate financial knowledge. The dissemination of false information that causes public alarm or harm is one example of how inaccurate information can have negative effects on society (Peabody et al., 2004).

7.6. SECURITY ISSUES OF INFORMATION SYSTEM (IS)

ISs are susceptible to security risks that could endanger data availability, confidentiality, and integrity. Since the scale and variety of security risks continue to rise in the modern digital era, security has elevated to the top priority list for businesses and organizations.

Attacks on ISs using malware, phishing scams, denial-of-service assaults, and malicious advertising are among the top security concerns. Malicious software can degrade IS security or compromise it through malware assaults. Social control methods like phishing trick people into disclosing sensitive information. Malvertising is disseminating harmful software through internet advertising, whereas denial-of-service assaults target the disruption of ISs' regular operations. To safeguard their ISs from these dangers, businesses, and organizations must implement strong security measures, such as routers, cryptography, systems for detecting and preventing intrusions, and staff training on best security practices (Bosch-Capblanch et al., 2009) (Figure 7.5).

Figure 7.5. Illustration of malvertising.

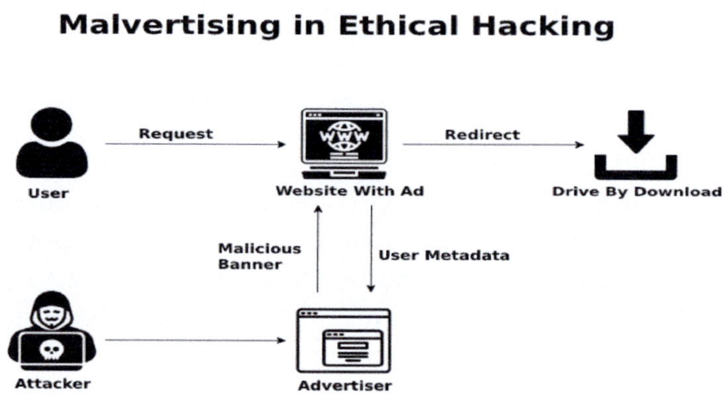

Source: Vaibhav Rawal, Creative Commons License.

7.7. VIRUSES AND MALICIOUS PROGRAMS

As Internet usage develops, the likelihood of malicious software, such as viruses, entering a firm's computer network increases. Malware is an aspect of software material that is inserted to another application and remains dormant until it is activated by an unknowing user. This could be as easy as downloading a file from a webpage or opening an attachment. Viruses can be comical, displaying an amusing image on the user's computer, or extreme, deleting data files permanently. Even the most modern anti-virus technologies cannot keep up with an international surge in viruses and malicious programs. Viruses can be created for a variety of purposes, including financial gain, the aim to express a political agenda, personal entertainment, to demonstrate the existence of a software vulnerability, deceit, and service rejection, or just because hackers are interested in cyber-security concerns. These viruses and malicious software can have disastrous repercussions, destroying a company's network and electronic data (McGraw & Morrisett, 2000).

7.8. PHISHING

A phishing scam is one of the most common cyberattacks. Hacking is when a con artist sends them phony e-mails, texts, or websites to trick them into divulging sensitive personal data, including bank details, numbers for Social Security, or login credentials. Fraudsters utilize the information they provide to steal their cash, identity, or both. Scammers also utilize phishing e-mails to access their network or computer and install malicious software that can prevent them from accessing critical data on their computer (Wright & Marett, 2010).

Remember

Phishing is a type of online scam that targets consumers by sending them an e-mail that appears to be from a well-known source – an internet service provider, a bank, or a mortgage company, for example.

Scammers use phishing to trick their victims into thinking they are safe to do this by creating fake versions of well-known and reliable company logos that belong to established and respected companies. Alternatively, they can pretend to be a friend or member of the family. Phishing is a sort of online fraud in which the perpetrators make it appear as though the victim or another person's personal information is required immediately, or else terrible things will occur. They can say that their bank account will be closed, that they won't get a tax refund, that their manager will become angry, that a member of their family might get wounded, or that they might even get arrested. They intentionally mislead individuals in order to elicit information from those individuals (Sharma et al., 2022).

7.9. DENIAL OF SERVICE

When a hostile cyber threat actor prevents authorized users from accessing data management, gadgets, or other network resources, it is said to be a denial-of-service (DoS) attack. Services that rely on the impacted computer or network, such as e-mail, internet, online accounts, or other services, may also be impacted. By overwhelming the targeted host or system with traffic until it becomes unresponsive or fails, a denial-of-service attack blocks access for authorized users. DoS attacks can cost companies money and time while their services and resources are unavailable. Not one, but two, but a staggering six U.S. institutions were the targets of a series of denial-of-service attacks in 2012. The victims comprised Bank of America, JP Morgan Chase, U.S. Bancorp, Citigroup, and PNC Bank, none of which were small-town banks (Paulson & Weber, 2006).

These are but a handful of security concerns related to ISs. In the interest of safeguarding computer systems from theft, damage to their hardware, software, or electronic data, and interruption or diversions of the services they offer, these dangers highlight the need for increased cybersecurity. Due to the expanding use of computer systems, the Internet, wireless networks like Bluetooth and Wi-Fi, and the proliferation of "smart" gadgets like smartphones, televisions, and the numerous items that make up the Internet of Things, the field is becoming more and more important (Zlomislić et al., 2017) (Figure 7.6).

Figure 7.6. Schematic of denial-of-service attack.

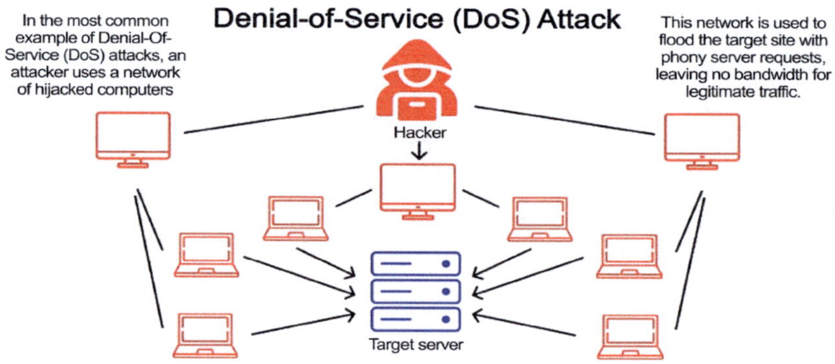

Source: Wallarm, Creative Commons License.

7.10. BOTNETS

A group of Internet-connected devices, such as PCs, smartphones, servers, and IoT devices that have been infected and are being controlled remotely by a common form of malware is known as a botnet. The botnet software typically scours the internet for susceptible devices. The threat actor who builds a botnet wants to infiltrate as many smart devices as possible, taking advantage of their computational power and resources for automated actions that are typically hidden from the owners of the devices. These botnets are controlled by threat actors, who are frequently cybercriminals.

They are used to send spam e-mails, run click-fraud operations, and produce malicious traffic for widespread denial-of-service assaults (Frank et al., 2018).

7.10.1. Drive-by Download Attacks

Drive-by download attacks are a security problem when a person visits a website infiltrated by hackers and unintentionally installs malicious software onto their desktop or smartphone. Unlike classic malware attacks, drive-by download attacks can occur just by visiting a hacked website, where another user must click on a phishing e-mail or install an infected file (Akiyama et al., 2010). Some crucial specifics regarding drive-by download attacks are discussed in subsections.

Did you get it?

According to a report by Radware, the number of DDoS attacks increased by 20% in the first quarter of 2020 compared to the same period in 2019.

7.10.2. Working on Drive-by Download Attacks

Hackers frequently compromise by taking advantage of software flaws or inserting malicious code into legitimate websites. When a user accesses the infected website, the infected code is executed and secretly downloads ransomware onto the user's device. After that, the virus may perform several tasks, including stealing confidential information, installing other malware, or taking control of the user's device (Sood & Zeadally, 2016).

7.10.3. Types of Drive-by Download Attacks

Drive-by download assaults come in a variety of forms which are discussed in subsections.

7.10.3.1. Malvertising

By inserting harmful code into trustworthy ad networks or by making false advertising that links visitors to malicious websites, hackers exploit adverts to spread malware.

7.10.3.2. Watering Hole Attacks

Hackers compromise webpages that the target audience will likely visit to target particular user groups. For instance, hackers may compromise websites associated with a certain sector or government organization (Krithika, 2017).

7.10.3.3. Zero-Day Exploits

These assaults infected a user's device using previously undiscovered software flaws.

7.10.4. Consequences of Drive-by Download Attacks

For people and businesses, drive-by installation attacks can have major repercussions, including:

- Theft of private data, including financial and personal information.
- Installing further malware may cause the device to run slowly or introduce new security holes.
- If the gadget is hijacked, the attacker may be able to operate it remotely.
- A decrease in productivity since users might have to devote resources to cleaning malware or recovering their devices.

Did you Know?

In May 2020, vendor Sophos reported that the global average cost to remediate a ransomware attack (considering downtime, people time, device cost, network cost, lost opportunity and ransom paid) was $761,106. Ninety-five percent of organizations that paid the ransom had their data restored.

7.11. RANSOMWARE

The malicious program known as ransomware encrypts a victim's files, rendering them unavailable, and then requests money in exchange for the decryption. It is one of the most important security risks that people and companies face today because it may seriously harm one's finances and reputation (Gaurav et al., 2022). These details relate to ransomware are discussed in subsections.

7.11.1. Working of Ransomware

Phishing e-mails, malicious advertising, or taking advantage of flaws in technology or systems are the most common ways ransomware is propagated. It encrypts files after infecting a machine, rendering them unavailable. The victim is then shown a message alerting them that their data have been encrypted and requesting payment in return for the decryption key, typically in a pop-up window or text file (Ali, 2017).

7.11.2. Impact of Ransomware

Attacks with ransomware can potentially seriously harm people's finances and reputations. Critical data and systems may become inaccessible to victims, causing downtime and lost production. The organization's reputation could suffer due to the ransomware assault and the high expense of both repaying the ransom and rehabilitating from it.

7.11.3. Prevention of Ransomware Attacks

The strongest defense against ransomware attacks is prevention. Companies can adopt robust security measures like firewalls, anti-virus, and detection systems for intrusions to lower the chance of infection. Frequent data backups are also crucial since they enable victims to recover their files without ransom. It's also essential to teach staff members how to spot phishing e-mails and the dangers of ransomware.

7.12. EXPLOIT KITS

A programming tool called an exploit kit lets someone without experience programming software code create, alter, and spread malware. Other names for exploit kits are infection kits, crimeware kits, DIY attack kits, and malware toolkits. Cybercriminals use these toolkits (Figure 7.7).

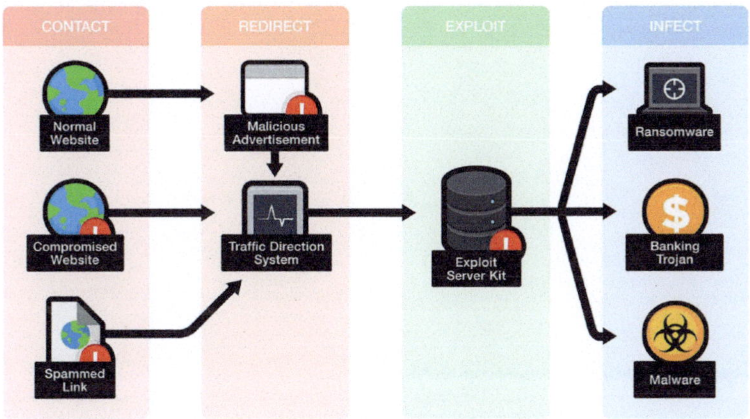

Figure 7.7. Picture of exploit kit.

Source: Trendmicro, Creative Commons License.

7.13. ADVANCED PERSISTENT THREAT (APT) ATTACKS

A targeted cyberattack known as an advanced persistent threat (APT) occurs when an unauthorized intruder breaches a network and does so while going unnoticed for a considerable amount of time. An APT attack aims to observe network activity and steal data to acquire access, using exploit kits and malware rather than harming a system or network. Cybercriminals generally use APT attacks to steal data from high-value targets like large businesses and nation-states over an extended period (Alshamrani et al., 2019).

ACTIVITY 7.1.

You are an employee at a large corporation, and you receive an email from what appears to be your company's IT department asking you to click on a link to update your password due to a recent security breach. The email looks legitimate, and you are worried about the security of your account, so you click on the link and enter your login credentials. A few days later, you notice some unauthorized transactions on your company credit card. Was this a case of phishing? How could you have avoided falling for this scam?

7.14. SUMMARY

This chapter focuses on the importance of ethical and security considerations in the development and implementation of ISs. The chapter highlights the ethical concerns related to privacy, accuracy, property, and accessibility. It also discusses various security issues such as unauthorized access, hacking, and malware attacks, and the measures to mitigate them. Overall, the chapter stresses the significance of addressing ethical and security issues in ISs to protect individuals' rights and maintain the integrity of the system. It encourages organizations to adopt ethical principles and implement robust security measures to prevent any breaches that can harm individuals or organizations.

REVIEW QUESTIONS

1. What are the main ethical concerns surrounding the use of information systems in modern society? Provide examples of how these concerns have been addressed in practice.
2. What are the primary security threats facing information systems today? Describe some of the most common forms of cyberattacks and explain how organizations can protect themselves.
3. How do businesses ensure that the use of informative systems adheres to ethical standards and legal regulations?
4. What measures can organizations take to protect sensitive data and prevent cyber-attacks on their informative systems?
5. How can the use of informative systems impact individual privacy and data protection?
6. What are some of the challenges associated with balancing the benefits.

MULTIPLE CHOICE QUESTIONS

1. Which of the following is an ethical issue that can arise in information systems when individuals or organizations claim ownership of creative works or ideas that are not their own?

a. Accessibility
b. Accuracy
c. Intellectual property
d. Phishing

2. What is the term used to describe the principle that information systems should be designed to be usable by all individuals, regardless of their abilities or disabilities?

a. Accessibility

b. Accuracy
c. Intellectual property
d. Phishing

3. **Which of the following is a security issue that can arise in information systems when the information contained within them is not correct or up to date?**
   a. Accessibility
   b. Accuracy
   c. Intellectual property
   d. Phishing
4. **What is the term used to describe a type of cyber-attack where an attacker attempts to trick individuals into divulging sensitive information through fraudulent e-mails or websites?**
   a. Phishing
   b. Denial of service
   c. Botnets
   d. Intellectual property
5. **Which of the following is a security issue that can arise in information systems when an attacker attempts to overwhelm a computer system or network with traffic, preventing legitimate users from accessing it?**
   a. Phishing
   b. Denial of service
   c. Botnets
   d. Accessibility
6. **What is the term used to describe a collection of compromised computers or devices that are controlled by an attacker and used to carry out various cyber-attacks?**
   a. Phishing
   b. Denial of service
   c. Botnets
   d. Intellectual property

Answers to the Multiple-Choice Questions

1. (c); 2. (a); 3. (b); 4. (a); 5. (b); 6. (c)

REFERENCES

1. Akiyama, M., Iwamura, M., Kawakoya, Y., Aoki, K., & Itoh, M., (2010). Design and implementation of high interaction client honeypot for drive-by-download attacks. *IEICE Transactions on Communications, 93*(5), 1131–1139.
2. Ali, A., (2017). Ransomware: A research and a personal case study of dealing with this nasty malware. *Issues in Informing Science and Information Technology, 14*, 087–099.
3. Alshamrani, A., Myneni, S., Chowdhary, A., & Huang, D., (2019). A survey on advanced persistent threats: Techniques, solutions, challenges, and research opportunities. *IEEE Communications Surveys & Tutorials, 21*(2), 1851–1877.
4. Bansal, G., Muzatko, S., & Shin, S. I., (2021). Information system security policy noncompliance: The role of situation-specific ethical orientation. *Information Technology & People, 34*(1), 250–296.
5. Bélanger, F., & Crossler, R. E., (2011). Privacy in the digital age: A review of information privacy research in information systems. *MIS Quarterly,* 1017–1041.
6. Bosch-Capblanch, X., Ronveaux, O., Doyle, V., Remedios, V., & Bchir, A., (2009). Accuracy and quality of immunization information systems in forty-one low income countries. *Tropical Medicine & International Health, 14*(1), 2–10.
7. Culnan, M. J., (1984). The dimensions of accessibility to online information: Implications for implementing office information systems. *ACM Transactions on Information Systems (TOIS), 2*(2), 141–150.
8. Culnan, M. J., (1985). The dimensions of perceived accessibility to information: Implications for the delivery of information systems and services. *Journal of the American Society for Information Science, 36*(5), 302–308.
9. Dhillon, G., & Backhouse, J., (2000). Technical opinion: Information system security management in the new millennium. *Communications of the ACM, 43*(7), 125–128.
10. Frank, C., Nance, C., Jarocki, S., & Pauli, W. E., (2018). Protecting IoT from Mirai botnets; IoT device hardening. *Journal of Information Systems Applied Research, 11*(2), 33.
11. Gaurav, A., Gupta, B. B., & Panigrahi, P. K., (2022). A comprehensive survey on machine learning approaches for malware detection in IoT-based enterprise information system. *Enterprise Information Systems, 1*, 1–25.
12. Joloudari, J. H., Haderbadi, M., Mashmool, A., GhasemiGol, M., Band, S. S., & Mosavi, A., (2020). Early detection of the advanced persistent threat attack using performance analysis of deep learning. *IEEE Access, 8*, 186125–186137.
13. Kalloniatis, C., Mouratidis, H., Vassilis, M., Islam, S., Gritzalis, S., & Kavakli, E., (2014). Towards the design of secure and privacy-oriented information systems in the cloud: Identifying the major concepts. *Computer Standards & Interfaces, 36*(4), 759–775.

14. Kovach, K. A., & Cathcart, Jr. C. E., (1999). Human resource information systems (HRIS): Providing business with rapid data access, information exchange and strategic advantage. *Public Personnel Management, 28*(2), 275–282.
15. Krithika, N., (2017). A study on WHA (watering hole attack)–the most dangerous threat to the organization. *Int. J. Innov. Sci. Eng. Res. (IJISER), 4*, 196–198.
16. Lavenue, L. M., (1997). Technical data rights in government procurement: Intellectual property rights in computer software and the indicia of information systems and information technology. *USFL Rev., 32*, 1.
17. McGraw, G., & Morrisett, G., (2000). Attacking malicious code: A report to the infosec research council. *IEEE Software, 17*(5), 33–41.
18. Onsrud, H. J., Johnson, J. P., & Lopez, X., (1994). Protecting personal privacy in using geographic information systems. *Photogrammetric Engineering and Remote Sensing, 60*(9), 1083–1095.
19. Paradice, D., Freeman, D., Hao, J., Lee, J., & Hall, D., (2018). A review of ethical issue considerations in the information systems research literature. *Foundations and Trends® in Information Systems, 2*(2), 117–236.
20. Paulson, R. A., & Weber, J. E., (2006). Cyberextortion: An overview of distributed denial of service attacks against online gaming companies. *Issues in Information Systems, 7*(2), 52–56.
21. Peabody, J. W., Luck, J., Jain, S., Bertenthal, D., & Glassman, P., (2004). Assessing the accuracy of administrative data in health information systems. *Medical Care, 1*, 1066–1072.
22. Rogerson, S., Miller, K. W., Winter, J. S., & Larson, D., (2019). Information systems ethics–challenges and opportunities. *Journal of Information, Communication and Ethics in Society, 17*(1), 87–97.
23. Sharma, P., Dash, B., & Ansari, M. F., (2022). Anti-phishing techniques–a review of cyber defense mechanisms. *IJARCCE, 11*(7), 153–160.
24. Siponen, M. T., & Oinas-Kukkonen, H., (2007). A review of information security issues and respective research contributions. *ACM SIGMIS Database: The DATABASE for Advances in Information Systems, 38*(1), 60–80.
25. Smith, H. J., Dinev, T., & Xu, H., (2011). Information privacy research: An interdisciplinary review. *MIS Quarterly*, 989–1015.
26. Sood, A. K., & Zeadally, S., (2016). Drive-by download attacks: A comparative study. *IT Professional, 18*(5), 18–25.
27. Stock, M., & Stock, W. G., (2006). Intellectual property information: A comparative analysis of main information providers. *Journal of the American Society for Information Science and Technology, 57*(13), 1794–1803.
28. Thapa, K., & Bossler, J., (1992). Accuracy of spatial data used information systems. *Photogrammetric Engineering & Remote Sensing, 58*(6), 835–841.

29. Wright, R. T., & Marett, K., (2010). The influence of experiential and dispositional factors in phishing: An empirical investigation of the deceived. *Journal of Management Information Systems, 27*(1), 273–303.

30. Zimba, A., Chen, H., Wang, Z., & Chishimba, M., (2020). Modeling and detection of the multi-stages of advanced persistent threats attacks based on semi-supervised learning and complex networks characteristics. *Future Generation Computer Systems, 106*, 501–517.

31. Zlomislić, V., Fertalj, K., & Sruk, V., (2017). Denial of service attacks, defenses and research challenges. *Cluster Computing, 20*, 661–671.

CHAPTER 8

EMERGING TRENDS IN INFORMATION SYSTEM

UNIT INTRODUCTION

The information systems (IS) business is experienced enormous growth, and more and more companies are seeking expansion opportunities in this sector due to its great potential. Information technology (IT) has a variety of uses, which is why it has proved to be an essential element of the current structure of enterprises. Due to the increasing importance of this business, it is crucial to comprehend its most vital parts and the main features which make it the innovative instrument that it is. Every year, latest ideas emerge in this field, making it vital for professionals to be aware of these trends and all that they include. Regardless of one's career, familiarity with these may enhance one's professional position and help one comprehend the possibility of technological advancements in their current field (Mancini, 2016).

Learning Objectives

At the end of this chapter, the reader will be able to understand:

- The significance of could computing;
- The concept of artificial intelligence and virtual reality;
- The importance of block chain data and cybersecurity;
- The significance of zero trust security.

Key Terms

- Artificial intelligence
- Automation
- Blockchain data
- Could computing
- Internet of things (IoT)
- Virtual reality
- Zero trust security

8.1. CLOUD COMPUTING

Cloud computing is an emerging trend in information systems (IS) that refers to the delivery of on-demand computing resources over the internet. These resources can include servers, storage, databases, software, and networking.

The cloud computing model provides a convenient, scalable, and cost-effective way for businesses and organizations to access and use computing resources without having to build and maintain their own infrastructure.

There are several types of cloud computing models, including public, private, and hybrid clouds. Public clouds are available to anyone over the internet and are managed by third-party service providers.

Private clouds are operated within an organization's own data center and are managed by internal IT staff. Hybrid clouds combine both public and private clouds to provide a flexible and scalable infrastructure that can be customized to meet the specific needs of an organization (Wu et al., 2013). One of the key advantages of cloud computing is its scalability.

Another advantage is the flexibility it provides. Users can access cloud resources from anywhere with an internet connection, making it easier to work remotely or collaborate with others (Peiyu & Dong, 2011).

Despite its benefits, cloud computing also poses several challenges and concerns, including data security and privacy, vendor lock-in, and the risk of service disruptions or downtime. Organizations need to implement robust security measures and carefully select cloud service providers to ensure the protection of their data and systems (Alali & Yeh, 2012).

Real-world examples of cloud computing include popular cloud service providers like Amazon Web Services, Microsoft Azure, and Google Cloud Platform, which offer a wide range of cloud-based services and solutions to businesses and organizations of all sizes. Many organizations are adopting cloud computing to streamline their operations, reduce costs, and improve their competitiveness in today's digital economy (Masrom & Rahimli, 2014) (Figure 8.1).

TIPS

Cloud resources can be easily scaled up or down to meet changing business needs, which can help organizations reduce costs and improve efficiency.

Figure 8.1. Illustration of cloud computing.

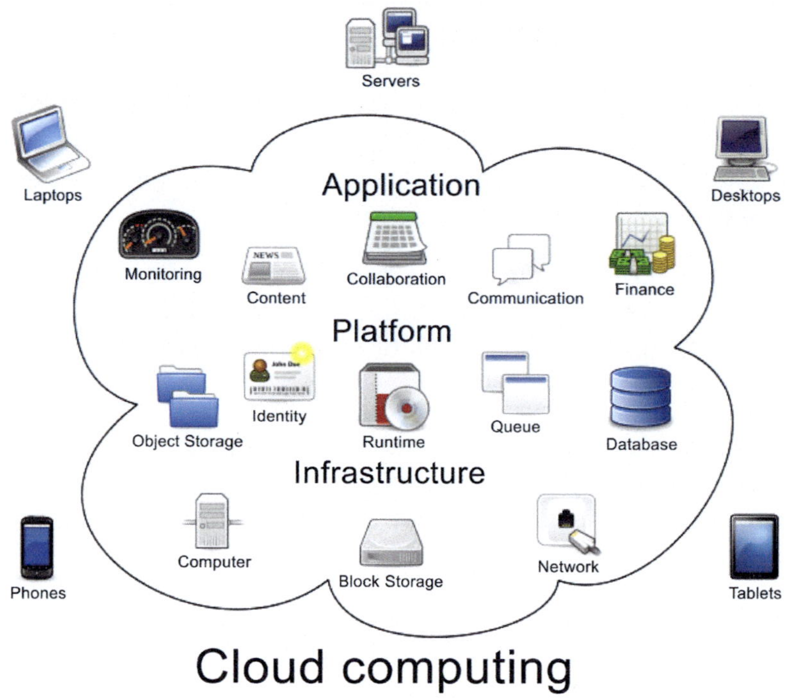

Source: SpringerLink, Creative Commons License.

8.2. BIG DATA ANALYTICS

Big data analytics is an emerging trend in ISs that involves the collection, processing, and analysis of large and complex data sets to extract insights and make better decisions. With the exponential growth of data in recent years, organizations are increasingly turning to big data analytics to gain a competitive edge and drive innovation (Novak et al., 2021).

The key components of big data analytics include data storage and management, data processing, data analysis, and data visualization. To effectively analyze large data sets, organizations often use advanced technologies such as machine learning, natural language processing, and predictive analytics. These technologies enable organizations to identify patterns and trends in their data and make data-driven decisions that can improve their business processes, products, and services (Huerta & Jensen, 2017).

One of the key advantages of big data analytics is its ability to provide valuable insights that were previously hidden or inaccessible. By analyzing large and diverse data sets, organizations can gain a deeper understanding of their customers, market trends, and operational inefficiencies. This information can be used to optimize business processes, improve customer experiences, and identify new business opportunities (Müller et al., 2016).

However, there are also several challenges and concerns associated with big data analytics. These include data security and privacy, data quality and integrity, and the need for specialized skills and expertise to analyze and interpret large data sets. Organizations need to implement robust security measures and data governance policies to ensure the protection of their data, and they need to invest in the necessary tools and resources to effectively analyze and interpret their data (Bi & Cochran, 2014).

Real-world examples of big data analytics include companies such as Amazon, Facebook, and Google, which use big data analytics to optimize their operations and provide personalized experiences to their users. Many organizations across various industries are adopting big data analytics to improve their decision-making processes, reduce costs, and gain a competitive edge (Watson, 2014) (Figure 8.2).

Figure 8.2. Picture of big data.

Source: Learntek, Creative Commons License.

8.3. AUTOMATION

Automation is an emerging trend in ISs that refers to the use of technology to perform tasks or processes that were previously done manually by humans. Automation can be applied to a wide range of industries and functions, including manufacturing, logistics, customer service, and finance. The use of automation technologies can lead to several benefits, including increased efficiency, reduced costs, and improved accuracy. Automation can help businesses streamline their operations, increase production rates, and improve their bottom line. Automation can also help reduce the risk of human error, which can be costly and time-consuming to correct. One area where automation is making significant strides is in the use of robotics and artificial intelligence (AI). Robotics and AI are being used to automate tasks such as packaging, assembly, and transportation in manufacturing and logistics industries. In the healthcare industry, robots are being used to perform surgery and assist with patient care (Stohr & Zhao, 2001).

Another area where automation is gaining traction is in the use of chatbots and virtual assistants for customer service. Chatbots can be programmed to answer frequently asked questions, provide product recommendations, and assist with customer inquiries, freeing up customer service representatives to focus on more complex issues (Kopec et al., 2003).

Did you Know?

AI gradually restored its reputation in the late 1990s and early 21st century by finding specific solutions to specific problems. The narrow focus allowed researchers to produce verifiable results, exploit more mathematical methods, and collaborate with other fields (such as statistics, economics and mathematics).

While automation offers many benefits, it also presents challenges and concerns. One of the main challenges is the potential for job loss as tasks and processes become automated. This has led to discussions about the need for retraining and reskilling workers for jobs that require more complex and creative thinking. There are also concerns about the potential for automation to reinforce biases or perpetuate inequalities if not developed and implemented carefully. Real-world examples of automation can be found in industries such as automotive manufacturing, logistics, and transportation, and customer service. As automation technologies continue to advance and become more accessible, it is expected that more industries and functions will be transformed by automation in the coming years (Zhai et al., 2009).

8.4. ARTIFICIAL INTELLIGENCE (AI)

Artificial Intelligence (AI) is an emerging topic in ISs that refers to the creation of computer systems that can do activities that traditionally require human intellect, including visual perception, voice search, decision-making, and language translation. AI technologies are reshaping how companies and organizations work and are anticipated to have a substantial influence on a variety of sectors over the next few years. There are several sorts of AI, such as machine learning, processing natural languages, robotics, and deep learning (Vuong et al., 2019). Using algorithms and statistical models, machine learning allows machines to acquire knowledge from information and enhance their efficiency over time. Natural language processing allows robots to comprehend and interpret human language, while robotics includes the creation of machines capable of doing physical activities (Vuong et al., 2019).

One of the key advantages of AI is its ability to automate repetitive and time-consuming tasks, which can help organizations improve efficiency and productivity. For example, AI-powered chatbots can handle customer inquiries and support requests, while AI-powered predictive analytics can help businesses make better-informed decisions. Despite its benefits, AI also poses several challenges and concerns, including job displacement, bias, and ethical issues related to the use of AI in decision-making. Organizations need to carefully consider these issues and take steps to address them in their AI strategies (Ågerfalk, 2020).

Real-world examples of AI include virtual assistants like Siri and Alexa, which use natural language processing to understand and respond to user requests, and self-driving cars, which use machine learning and computer vision to navigate roads and avoid obstacles. Many organizations are investing in AI to gain a competitive edge and improve their operations, and AI is expected to play an increasingly important role in the future of business and technology (Collins et al., 2021) (Figure 8.3).

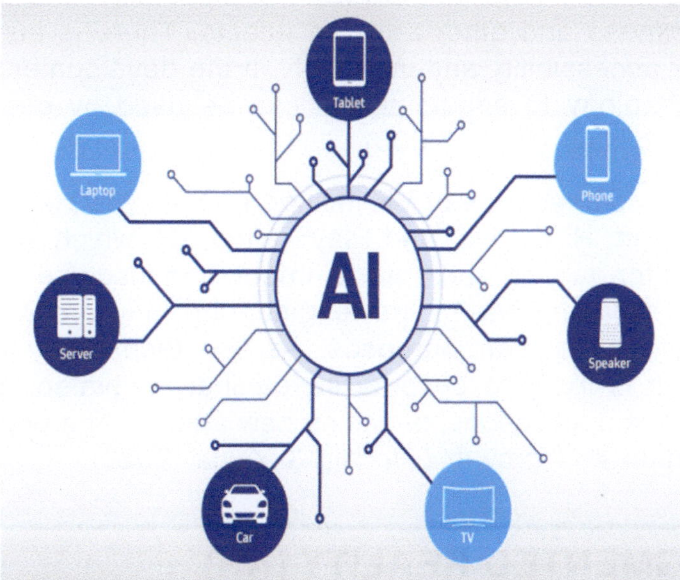

Figure 8.3. Image of artificial intelligence.

Source: Brainware University, Creative Commons License.

8.5. VIRTUAL REALITY (VR)

Virtual reality (VR) is an emerging trend in ISs that involves the use of computer technology to create immersive and interactive digital environments that simulate real-world experiences. VR technology typically includes a headset or other device that allows users to enter and interact with virtual environments using sensory input such as sight, sound, and touch.

One of the key advantages of VR technology is its ability to provide highly immersive and realistic experiences that can be used for a wide range of applications. For example, VR can be used for training and simulation purposes in industries such as healthcare, aviation, and military. It can also be used for entertainment, such as in gaming and theme parks. Another advantage of VR is its potential to enhance communication and collaboration. VR can enable remote teams to work together in a virtual environment, providing a more immersive and engaging experience than traditional video conferencing or phone calls. It can also be used for remote learning and education, allowing students to explore virtual environments and engage with learning materials in new and innovative ways (Walsh & Pawlowski, 2002).

KEYWORD

Software compatibility is a characteristic of software components or systems which can operate satisfactorily together on the same computer, or on different computers linked by a computer network.

Despite its benefits, VR technology also poses several challenges and concerns, including the cost and complexity of development, hardware and software compatibility, and the risk of motion sickness and other adverse effects. There is also a need for greater accessibility and inclusivity in the development and use of VR technology to ensure that it can be used by people of all ages and abilities (Batty, 2008).

Real-world examples of VR include popular VR platforms such as Oculus Rift, HTC Vive, and PlayStation VR, which are used by consumers for gaming and entertainment. It is also used in various industries, including healthcare, engineering, and architecture, for training and simulation purposes. As VR technology continues to evolve, it is likely to become increasingly prevalent in various industries and applications, providing new and exciting opportunities for innovation and growth (Dincelli & Yayla, 2022).

8.6. AUGMENTED REALITY (AR)

Augmented reality (AR) is an emerging trend in ISs that enhances the real-world environment with digital information and virtual objects. AR technology allows users to interact with digital content in a natural and intuitive way, enhancing the user's experience by providing additional information and context in real-time. AR technology uses computer-generated graphics, sounds, and other sensory inputs to overlay digital content onto the user's view of the physical world. This technology can be used in a variety of applications, including entertainment, gaming, education, healthcare, and manufacturing (Chen et al., 2014).

One of the key advantages of AR is its ability to provide a more immersive and engaging user experience. AR technology can be used to enhance educational content by providing students with interactive learning experiences that bring subjects to life. In healthcare, AR can be used to provide doctors and nurses with real-time information about patients, allowing them to make more informed decisions about their care. In manufacturing, AR can be used to provide workers with digital instructions and assistance, reducing errors and improving productivity (Berkemeier et al., 2019).

However, there are also several challenges and concerns associated with AR technology. One of the main challenges is the need for high-quality hardware and software to support AR applications. Additionally, there are concerns around privacy and security, as AR applications may collect sensitive information about users.

Real-world examples of AR include popular applications like Pokemon Go and Snapchat, which use AR technology to provide users with interactive and engaging experiences. AR is also being used in industries like healthcare, where it is being used to provide medical professionals with real-time information about patients during surgery (Abdi & Meddeb, 2018).

In conclusion, AR is an emerging trend in ISs that has the potential to transform a wide range of industries and applications. While there are challenges and concerns associated with this technology, the benefits of AR are significant and offer exciting opportunities for innovation and growth.

KEYWORD

Digital instruction is delivered via technology, such as video and smart software that offers students a personalized sequence of learning experiences, and does not include live interaction with a teacher.

8.7. BLOCKCHAIN DATA

Block chain technology is becoming an increasingly popular tool for managing and securing data, and its use in data management has emerged as an important trend in recent years. Block chain data refers to any data that is stored on a blockchain, a decentralized, distributed ledger that records transactions across a network of computers (Brandon, 2016).

Remember

The block chain data is encrypted, time-stamped, and stored across the network, making it highly secure and tamper-proof.

One of the key benefits of using blockchain technology for data management is its ability to enhance data security. The decentralized nature of the blockchain means that no single entity controls the data, making it difficult for hackers or cyber criminals to gain access to sensitive information. The encryption of the data also makes it virtually impossible to tamper with, ensuring the integrity of the data. This is particularly important for industries such as healthcare and finance, where data security is of the utmost importance (Berdik et al., 2021).

Another benefit of using blockchain data is its ability to streamline data management processes. The blockchain is a shared database that can be accessed by multiple parties simultaneously, reducing the need for intermediaries and improving the efficiency of data sharing and exchange. This can be particularly useful in supply chain management (SCM), where blockchain technology can be used to track the movement of goods from one location to another, ensuring transparency and accountability (Ghosh, 2019).

The use of blockchain data is also emerging as a way to address the issue of data privacy. Many people are becoming increasingly concerned about the amount of personal data that is being collected and shared by companies and are looking for ways to control their own data. Blockchain technology allows individuals to own and control their own data, and to share it with others on a need-to-know basis. This can help to address privacy concerns and give individuals more control over their personal information.

In addition to these benefits, the use of blockchain data is also becoming more popular due to the increasing availability of blockchain platforms and tools. As more companies develop and adopt blockchain technology, the barriers to entry are becoming lower, and it is becoming easier for businesses of all sizes to implement blockchain data solutions (Sarwar et al., 2021).

Overall, the trend of using blockchain data is likely to continue to grow in the coming years as more businesses and industries recognize the benefits of this technology for managing and securing data. It has the potential to revolutionize data management, making it more secure, efficient, and transparent, and could have a significant impact on a wide range of industries, from finance and healthcare to SCM and beyond (Figure 8.4).

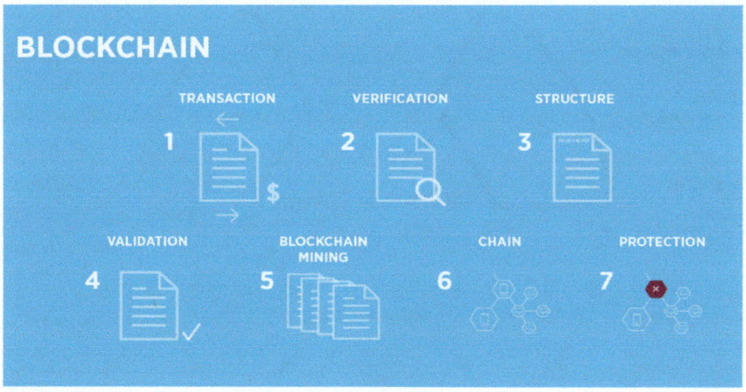

Figure 8.4. Schematic of blockchain data.

Source: Cloud DNA, Creative Commons License.

8.8. CYBER SECURITY

Cybersecurity is the practice of protecting computer systems, networks, and sensitive data from unauthorized access, use, disclosure, disruption, modification, or destruction. In today's interconnected world, cybersecurity has become a critical concern for businesses, governments, and individuals alike. As the frequency and sophistication of cyber threats continue to increase, the field of cybersecurity is evolving rapidly to keep pace with new threats and technologies (Diwan, 2021).

Did you get it?

The global cost of cybercrime is expected to reach $10.5 trillion by 2025, up from $3 trillion in 2015, according to a study by cybersecurity ventures.

8.8.1. Internet of Things (IoT) Security

As more devices become connected to the internet, the potential attack surface for cybercriminals increases. IoT devices, such as smart home appliances, wearable technology, and industrial control systems, are often not designed with security in mind, making them vulnerable to attack. Emerging trends in IoT security include the use of blockchain technology to secure IoT devices and networks and the development of security standards for IoT devices (Figure 8.5).

Figure 8.5. Explanation of internet of things.

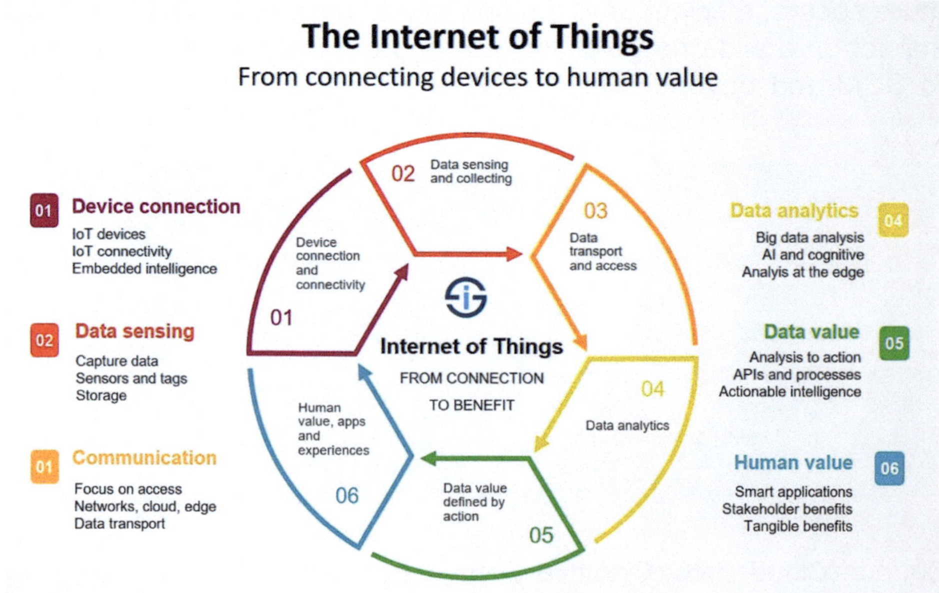

Source: Elena Georgescu, Creative Commons License.

ACTIVITY 8.1.

A small e-commerce business is experiencing rapid growth and needs to scale up their online store to accommodate the increased traffic and sales. They are considering migrating their website and database to a cloud computing platform. What are the potential benefits and drawbacks of using cloud computing for their e-commerce business? What factors should they consider when selecting a cloud service provider?

8.8.2. Cybersecurity Awareness Training

One of the weakest links in cybersecurity is human error. Employees can unwittingly click on a phishing e-mail or download a malicious attachment, providing cybercriminals with a foothold in an organization's network. To address this issue, many organizations are investing in cybersecurity awareness training to educate their employees about the risks of cyber threats and how to prevent them (Ansari, 2022).

8.8.3. Zero Trust Security

Zero Trust Security is an emerging security model that assumes that every user and device accessing a network is untrusted, regardless of their location or credentials. In a Zero Trust Security model, access to resources is granted on a need-to-know basis, and all traffic is inspected for threats. This approach is becoming increasingly popular as traditional perimeter-based security models become less effective in protecting against modern cyber threats (Campbell, 2020).

8.9. SUMMARY

These emerging trends are transforming the way businesses operate, enabling them to be more efficient, productive, and innovative. Cloud computing allows businesses to scale up or down their IT resources as needed, while big data analytics helps organizations make better-informed decisions based on data insights. Automation and AI are helping companies automate tasks, improve decision-making, and reduce errors.

Virtual and AR technologies is providing new ways for businesses to engage with customers and enhance the user experience. Blockchain data is offering a secure and transparent way of sharing information, and cyber security is becoming increasingly important as organizations become more reliant on digital systems.

Overall, these emerging trends are changing the way we work, communicate, and interact with technology, and organizations that embrace these technologies are likely to have a competitive advantage in the marketplace.

REVIEW QUESTIONS

1. What is cloud computing and how does it differ from traditional computing methods?
2. What is automation and how is it being applied in different industries?
3. What are some examples of artificial intelligence and how are they being used in business and society?
4. How can virtual reality and augmented reality technologies be used in different fields such as education, healthcare, and entertainment?
5. What are the different types of cyber threats and how can organizations protect themselves from them?
6. What are the potential benefits and drawbacks of these emerging trends in information systems and how can organizations manage them effectively?

MULTIPLE CHOICE QUESTIONS

1. Which of the following is an emerging trend of information systems that provides on-demand access to shared computing resources over the internet?

a. Virtual reality
b. Big data analytics
c. Automation
d. Cloud computing

2. What is the term used to describe the process of analyzing large and complex data sets to identify patterns, insights, and trends?

a. Cloud computing

b. Big data analytics
c. Artificial intelligence
d. Automation

3. **Which of the following is an emerging trend of information systems that involves using technology to perform routine tasks and processes?**
   a. Virtual reality
   b. Cyber security
   c. Automation
   d. Blockchain data
4. **Which of the following is an emerging trend of information systems that involves the simulation of human intelligence in machines?**
   a. Artificial intelligence
   b. Blockchain data
   c. Virtual reality
   d. Automation
5. **What is the term used to describe a computer-generated simulation of a three-dimensional image or environment that can be interacted with by a person?**
   a. Augmented reality
   b. Virtual reality
   c. Blockchain data
   d. Big data analytics
6. **Which of the following is an emerging trend of information systems that enhances the real world with computer-generated sensory input?**
   a. Artificial intelligence
   b. Blockchain data
   c. Augmented reality
   d. Cyber security

Answers to the Multiple-Choice Questions

1. (d); 2. (b); 3. (c); 4. (a); 5. (b); 6. (c)

REFERENCES

1. Abdi, L., & Meddeb, A., (2018). Driver information system: A combination of augmented reality, deep learning and vehicular Ad-Hoc networks. *Multimedia Tools and Applications, 77*, 14673–14703.
2. Ågerfalk, P. J., (2020). Artificial intelligence as digital agency. *European Journal of Information Systems, 29*(1), 1–8.
3. Alali, F. A., & Yeh, C. L., (2012). Cloud computing: Overview and risk analysis. *Journal of Information Systems, 26*(2), 13–33.
4. Ansari, M. F., (2022). A quantitative study of risk scores and the effectiveness of AI-based cybersecurity awareness training programs. *International Journal of Smart Sensor and Ad Hoc Network, 3*(3), 1.
5. Batty, M., (2008). Virtual reality in geographic information systems. *The Handbook of Geographic Information Science* (Vol. 1, pp. 317–334). Oxford, Blackwell Publishing.
6. Berdik, D., Otoum, S., Schmidt, N., Porter, D., & Jararweh, Y., (2021). A survey on blockchain for information systems management and security. *Information Processing & Management, 58*(1), 102397.
7. Berkemeier, L., Zobel, B., Werning, S., Ickerott, I., & Thomas, O., (2019). Engineering of augmented reality-based information systems: Design and implementation for intralogistics services. *Business & Information Systems Engineering, 61*, 67–89.
8. Bi, Z., & Cochran, D., (2014). Big data analytics with applications. *Journal of Management Analytics, 1*(4), 249–265.
9. Brandon, D., (2016). The blockchain: The future of business information systems. *International Journal of the Academic Business World, 10*(2), 33–40.
10. Campbell, M., (2020). Beyond zero trust: Trust is a vulnerability. *Computer, 53*(10), 110–113.
11. Chen, C. Y., Chang, B. R., & Huang, P. S., (2014). Multimedia augmented reality information system for museum guidance. *Personal and Ubiquitous Computing, 18*, 315–322.
12. Collins, C., Dennehy, D., Conboy, K., & Mikalef, P., (2021). Artificial intelligence in information systems research: A systematic literature review and research agenda. *International Journal of Information Management, 60*, 102383.
13. Dincelli, E., & Yayla, A., (2022). Immersive virtual reality in the age of the metaverse: A hybrid-narrative review based on the technology affordance perspective. *The Journal of Strategic Information Systems, 31*(2), 101717.
14. Diwan, T. D., (2021). An investigation and analysis of cyber security information systems: Latest trends and future suggestion. *Information Technology in Industry, 9*(2), 477–492.
15. Ghosh, J., (2019). The blockchain: Opportunities for research in information systems and information technology. *Journal of Global Information Technology Management, 22*(4), 235–242.

16. Huerta, E., & Jensen, S., (2017). An accounting information systems perspective on data analytics and big data. *Journal of Information Systems, 31*(3), 101–114.
17. Kopec, D., Kabir, M. H., Reinharth, D., Rothschild, O., & Castiglione, J. A., (2003). Human errors in medical practice: Systematic classification and reduction with automated information systems. *Journal of Medical Systems, 27*, 297–313.
18. Mancini, D., (2016). Accounting information systems in an open society: Emerging trends and issues. *Accounting Information Systems in an Open Society: Emerging Trends and Issues, 1*, 5–16.
19. Masrom, M., & Rahimli, A., (2014). A review of cloud computing technology solution for healthcare system. *Research Journal of Applied Sciences, Engineering and Technology, 8*(20), 2150–2153.
20. Müller, O., Junglas, I., Brocke, J. V., & Debortoli, S., (2016). Utilizing big data analytics for information systems research: Challenges, promises and guidelines. *European Journal of Information Systems, 25*(4), 289–302.
21. Novak, A., Bennett, D., & Kliestik, T., (2021). Product decision-making information systems, real-time sensor networks, and artificial intelligence-driven big data analytics in sustainable industry 4.0. *Economics, Management and Financial Markets, 16*(2), 62–72.
22. Peiyu, L. I. U., & Dong, L. I. U., (2011). The new risk assessment model for information system in cloud computing environment. *Procedia Engineering, 15*, 3200–3204.
23. Sarwar, M. I., Iqbal, M. W., Alyas, T., Namoun, A., Alrehaili, A., Tufail, A., & Tabassum, N., (2021). Data vaults for blockchain-empowered accounting information systems. *IEEE Access, 9*, 117306–117324.
24. Stohr, E. A., & Zhao, J. L., (2001). Workflow automation: Overview and research issues. *Information Systems Frontiers, 3*, 281–296.
25. Vuong, Q. H., Ho, M. T., Vuong, T. T., La, V. P., Ho, M. T., Nghiem, K. C. P., & Ho, R. C., (2019). Artificial intelligence vs. natural stupidity: Evaluating AI readiness for the Vietnamese medical information system. *Journal of Clinical Medicine, 8*(2), 168.
26. Walsh, K. R., & Pawlowski, S. D., (2002). Virtual reality: A technology in need of IS research. *Communications of the Association for Information Systems, 8*(1), 20.
27. Watson, H. J., (2014). Tutorial: Big data analytics: Concepts, technologies, and applications. *Communications of the Association for Information Systems, 34*(1), 65.
28. Wu, Y. U. N., Cegielski, C. G., Hazen, B. T., & Hall, D. J., (2013). Cloud computing in support of supply chain information system infrastructure: Understanding when to go to the cloud. *Journal of Supply Chain Management, 49*(3), 25–41.
29. Zhai, D., Goodrum, P. M., Haas, C. T., & Caldas, C. H., (2009). Relationship between automation and integration of construction information systems and labor productivity. *Journal of Construction Engineering and Management, 135*(8), 746–753.

INDEX

A

Abstracted programming 98
Accessibility 187, 189, 192, 201, 203
Accounting function 179
Accounting information systems 173
Accounting system information 179
Acquisition phase 97
Action diagrams 98
Additional semantics 4
Advanced persistent threat (APT) 200
Aerodynamic thrust 4
Aid management 176
ALU (Arithmetic/logic unit) 40
American National Standards Institute (ANSI) 131
Annual data growth rate 49
Application program 129
Application program interface (API) 64
Application software 61, 62, 65, 71, 73, 74, 77, 78, 80, 81, 82, 83, 84, 87
Artificial Intelligence (AI) 166
Audio communication 162
Audio player 60
Augmented reality (AR) 165
Authorization 187, 189
Automotive manufacturing 212

B

Better collaboration 167
Biased data 193
Big data analytics 210, 219, 220, 221, 222
Billing information 158
Billing system 6
Block chain data 207, 215, 216
Block chain technology 215
Bluetooth 159, 168
Blu-ray high-definition video disc 51
Botnets 188, 202
Buckland 4, 31
Business application 15
Business context 172
Business entities 157
Business environment 2, 10
Business intelligence (BI) 8, 20, 32, 34
Business knowledge 38
Business landscape 172
Business management 158
Business operations 89
Business opportunity 57
Business planning 171
Business stakeholders 15
Business support systems 174
Business-to-Business (B2B) 16
Business-to-Consumer (B2C) 16

C

Cabinet housing 40
Campaign management 139

Cargo rate 10
CASE (Computer-aided software engineering) 107
Cathode-ray tube 58
CD burner 50
CD-recordable (CD-R) 50
CD-rewritable (CD-RW) 50
CD-ROM (Compact disc read-only memory) 50
Centralized management 163, 167
Central server 46
Change Analysis 94
Cirrus computer 38
Classic malware attacks 197
Clerical-level transaction processing 175
Client relationships 18
Client retention 139
Client-server architecture 14
Client service 38
Cloud-based platform 133
Cloud computing 133
Collective decision-making 175
Common system 6
Communication channel 155, 159, 161
Competition data 11
Competitive edge 177, 210, 211, 213
Complex infrastructures spanning 157
Comprehensive database 15
Comprehensive storage-management system 49
Comprehensive validation 90
Computational power 196
Computer benchmarks 45
Computer calculations 47
Computer-generated graphics 215
Computer hardware functions 61, 63
Computer implementation 98
Computer interface design 98
Computer networking 66
Computer pointing device 53
Computer programs 93
Computing experience 67
Conceptual data model 101
Conceptual model 101
Conceptual process models 101
Confidential information 197
Confidentiality 172, 179
Confidentiality breach 189
Consecutive access 47
Constructed system 94
Contemporary society 179
Contemporary technology 171
Control decision 157
Correlation method 44
Cost-effective database 133
CPU architecture 61
Customer data 18, 23
Customer misinformation 190
Customer relationship management (CRM) 15, 31, 35
Customer satisfaction 139, 145
Customer segmentation analysis 139
Customer service 6, 19, 22
Customer support 155
Customization 158
Cyberattack 200
Cybersecurity attack 165
Cybersecurity awareness 218, 221
Cyber threat 195

D

Data accuracy 120
Data analysis 45, 75
Data analyst 20
Data availability 193
Data backup system 49
Database administrator (DBA) 120
Database application 128, 132
Database-as-a-service (DaaS) 133
Database environment 120
Database-equipped computer system 14
Database infrastructure 121
Database management solution 134
Database management system\" (DBMS) 119
Database modification 128
Database plan 125
Database system 121

Data breaches 156
Data-cleansing systems 137
Data cleanup 147
Data definition language 147
Data design techniques 103
Data dictionary systems 107
Data entity 123, 149
Data entry 93
Data loss prevention (DLP) 141
Data management 121, 122, 124, 125, 129, 136, 152
Data manipulation language (DML) 130
Data mart 138, 150
Data mining 121, 139, 140, 142, 152
Data mining techniques 139
Data-mining technology 140
Data normalization language 147
Data-oriented work 94, 95
Data output 98
Data processing framework 101
Data process model 101
Data resources 92, 171
Data security 93, 191
Data sharing 155
Data system 38
Data visualization 210
Data warehouse 121
Decent system 95
Decision automation 12
Decision making 2, 29, 32, 33, 34
Decision-making rules 11
Decision Segmentation 12
Decision support system (DSS) 10
Decoding program instructions 40
Deep learning 212, 221
Degree of predictability 5
Denial of service 188, 202, 205
Denial-of-service (DoS) attack 195
Design process 91, 93, 95, 111, 112
Desirable system 97
Development methods 91
Development phase 89, 93
Development stages 91
Digital advertising agency 133
Digital age 187, 189, 203
Digital data 120, 121
Digital economy 209
Digital society 181
Digital storage data 43
Dimensional information 14
Direct access storage device 48
Disastrous repercussions 195
Disk drive 50, 51, 79
Distributed system architectures 157
Diverse team 90
Documentation 93
Drive-by download attacks 188, 197, 204
Dual booting 69
Dual-core processor 44
DVD (Digital video disc) 50
Dynamic Forecasting 12

E

Effective knowledge management system 177
Effective management 158
Effective Technical and Human Implementation of Computer-based Systems (ETHICS) 109
Elastic Cloud service 133
Electrical current 42
Electric charge 42, 59
Electro-luminescent light 59
Electronic data 56, 195, 196
Electronic gadgets 1
Electronic health records database 125
Electronic system 174
Element management 158
Emergency response 155
End-User License Agreements 61
Engine power 37
Enterprise collaboration system 173, 182
Enterprise resource planning (ERP) 15, 28, 32, 33, 34
Enterprise resource planning software 183
EPROM (Erasable programmable read-only memory) 57
Eternal storage 43

Ethernet 161, 168
Ethical challenges 189
Ethical dilemmas 191
Ethical implications 191
Evaluation phase 100
Exabyte 43
Exception report 96
Execution speed 100
Executive information systems (EIS) 174
Executive support system (ESS) 10
Expenditure data 128
Expert systems 173, 177, 184
Exploit kit 199
Exponential growth 210
Extensive network 62

F

Fahrenheit 4
False information 193
Fault detection 158
Fault, performance, accounting, and security (FCAPS) 157
FBI (Federal Bureau of Investigation) 123
Feasibility research 97
Feasibility study 97
Federated database system 144
Feedback mechanism 6
File design 93
File management 67
Finance information systems 173
Financial decision 179
Financial information 132
Financial statements 179
First generation (FG) 106
First-generation methods 103
First-level design 101
Flat file 121, 127
Flat file databases 127
Flexible systems 38
Food Allergen and Consumer Protection Act 130
Formal communication 96
Formal report 96
Four-tiered management pyramid 8
Fraud Detection 12
Functional business systems 173
Functional coherence 104
Functioning storage area 42

G

Geographical data 14
Geographic analysis 14
Geographic data 57
Geographic distribution 12, 14
Geographic information 12, 13, 31
Geographic information systems (GIS) 12, 13
Geometric analysis 14
Geometric information 13
Gigabyte 43
Global conceptual framework 101
Google Cloud Platform 209
Greater flexibility 37
Grid computing 46
Groundwork 89
Guest feedback 38
GUI (Graphical user interface) 64

H

Hacked website 197
Hard disc 51, 63, 65
Hardware components 1, 29, 30
Hardware decisions 37, 38
Harmful software 194
High reliability 168
High-resolution digital camera 55
High-speed communications channels 49
Human analysis 177
Human-computer interface 100
Human resource information systems (HRIS) 179
Human resource planning 158

I

IEA (International Energy Agency) 119
Information demands 92
Information development 89

Information management development 94
Information storage 14
Information system development 2
Information systems (IS) 1
Information Systems Work and Analysis (ISAC) 109
Information technology (IT) 187, 189
Informative system 188
Infrared 168
Input documents 93
Intellectual property 188, 189, 191, 192
Intellectual property protection 191
Intelligent decision-making systems 166
Intended system 97, 98
Interaction style 98
Inter-departmental agreement 93
Interdepartmental communication 93
Interface complexity 104
Internal Integrity 94
Internal representation 101
International Data Corporation (IDC) 120
International Organization for Standardization (ISO) 157
International Telecommunications Union (ITU) 157
International Underwriting Association (IUA) 144
Internet-connected devices 196
Internet of Things (IoT) 165
Internet phone service 142
Inventory number 122
IS applications 3, 15
IS challenges 3
IS evaluation 3
IS evolution 3
IS security 3
IS typology 3

J

Jackson Systems Development (JSD) 109
Jackson systems programming (JSP) 109
Job displacement 213
Judgment, assessment 10
Just-in-time strategy 17

K

Kilobyte 43
Knowledge 4, 5, 19, 30, 31, 32, 33
Knowledge management (KM) 15, 30, 177
Knowledge sharing 177
Knowledge systems 173

L

Land use plan (LUP) 27
Language translation 212
Laser printer 59
Leadership 96
Legal liability 164
Lingo programs 5
Liquid crystals 58
Local Area Network (LAN) 160
Logical access path (LAP) 129
Logical capacity 5
Logical design 91, 98, 117
Login process 66
Lost data 49

M

Machine cycle time 41
Machine learning 166
Magnetic discs 47, 48
Magnetic ink character recognition (MICR) 56
Magnetic tape 47
Mail-order business 124
Main circuit board 43
Main memory 45, 47
Malicious advertising 194, 198
Malicious programs 188, 194
Malicious software 194
Malvertising 188, 194, 197
Malware 164
Manageable code 103
Management control 96
Management information systems (MIS) 7, 174, 175
Managements structure 94

Managerial decision making 174
Managerial level 7, 28
Manufacturing department 178
Manufacturing process 17
Manufacturing technique 21
Marketing and sales system 178
Marketing automation software 183
Market share 25
Megabyte 43
Memory chips 51
Memory-management 65
Metadata 136
Metropolitan area network (MAN) 161
Mobile computing devices 68
Mobile technology 14
Modeling approach 90
Modeling information management 90
Modern digital era 194
Modern printer 59
Modern screen technology 55
Modular design 103
Modular programming 103
Multicore microprocessor 44
Multidimensional analysis 142
Multimedia services 158
Multiprocessing 44
Multiuser database systems 128

N

Natural language processing 166, 213
NCSA (National Cyber Security Alliance) 191
Negative effect 193
Neighborhood attraction information 38
Network downtime 164
Networking capability 63
Networking equipment 1
Network management 157, 158, 159, 169
Network monitor 46
Network virtualization 46
NORA (non-obvious relationship awareness) 190
Normalization 104
Numerous schemes 4

O

Object-oriented database management 121, 146
Object-relational database management system (ORDBMS) 143
OCR (Optical character recognition) 55
Office information systems 175
One-to-one marketing 139
Online computer service 66
Online database service 128
Online education 172, 180
Online fraud 195
Online processing 135
Online transaction processing (OLTP) 136
OPEC (Organization of Petroleum Exporting Countries) 119
Open-source database systems 132
Open systems interconnection (OSI) 158
Operating Integrity 94
Operating system (OS) 2
Operational control 96
Operational management 8
Operation control 96
Operation control systems 174
Optical discs 47
Optical media 51
Optimal strategy 62
Order processing system 24
Organic light-emitting diode (OLED) 59
Organizational environment 96
Organizational performance 52
Organizational structure 7, 8
Organizational transformation 4
Output devices 38, 40, 48, 52, 53, 55, 60, 78, 80, 81, 82, 83, 84, 87
Output documents 93
Overwhelming 195

P

Parallel computing applications 45
Parallel processing 45, 46
Peer-to-peer based systems 157
Performance Optimization 12

Peripheral cards 43
Peripheral devices 40, 64
Permanent storage 47
Persistent storage 47
Personal entertainment 195
Personal information 181
Personality trait 95
Pertinent data 124
Petabyte 43
Phishing scam 195
Phosphorescent substance 58
Physical access path (PAP) 129
Physical database 93
Physical design 99, 113, 118
Plant disease management 10
Plasma display 58
Population segment 193
Potential problems 90, 111
Power consumption 59
Practical application 37
Predetermined process 5
Predictive analysis 140
Primary key 123
Primary transaction data 9
Printing data 56
Privacy inflation 190
Private clouds 209
Private data 198
Problem definition 97
Procedural Integrity 94
Process control system 175
Process design 91
Processing capacity 40, 44
Processor access 42
Production budget 178
Production information systems 173
Productive administration 7
Productivity 24
Productivity software 147
Profitability 6, 10, 17
Program code consistency 100
Program logic 93
Programming language 100
Programming software code 199
Programming style 103
Program modules 103
Project inception 97
Project planning 90

Q

QBE (Query by example) 130
Quad-core chips 44
Quality control cycle 171
Quality of service assurances 158
Query language 131, 143

R

Ransomware 197, 198, 199
Rapid Application Development (RAD) 110
Read-only memory (ROM) 43
Real-time position data 57
Record keeping 9
Redundant data 137
Redundant storage method 49
Regulatory repercussions 187, 193
Relational databases 131, 133, 144, 146
Relationship management 17
Reliability 187
Remote work 155, 163, 172, 180
Requirements acquisition 97
Requirements analysis 97
Resource description framework (RDF) 136
RFID (Radio frequency identification) 57
RIA (Rich internet application) 62
Robust security 164, 165
Routing services 14
Run click-fraud operations 197

S

Sales forecasting 178
Sales information systems 173
SAN (Storage area network) 49
Satellite-based internet connections 160
Satellite communication 156
Scalability 66
Schema 147

Secondary storage 38, 40, 47, 67, 78, 79, 82, 83, 85
Second-generation methods 103, 106
Security mechanisms 93
Semantic level 4
Semi-structured decision-making 176
Sensitive information 192, 194, 202
Service management 158, 169
Service-oriented methodologies 14
Single database system 144
Single software system 15
Single-user databases 128
Slower communication 167
Social Security 120, 195
Soft Systems Methodology (SSM) 109
Software design 90
Software packages 15
Software vulnerability 195
Sole ownership 191
Solid-state storage (SSD) 51
Solution Configuration 12
Spatial information 14
Speech-input device 54
Speech-recognition technology 54
Spreadsheet 127
Storage devices 1
Strategic implementation 7
Strategic management 8
Strategic planning 96
Structural recognition model 14
Structured programming 103
Structured Query Language (SQL) 130
Structured Systems Analysis and Design Methodology (SSADM) 109
Structure element 98
Supply chain management (SCM) 15, 28, 35
Supply chain management system 183
Swift data 48
System conversion 93
System description 93
System design 91, 93, 101, 113, 117
System disruption 164
System functioning 100
System Integrity 94
System performance 22, 28
Systems repositories 107
Systems software 61
Systems theorist 4
System unit 40, 41
System verification 93

T

Tactical management 8
Task-management 65
Task management software 65
Technical assistance 25
Technical information 138
Tedious process 179
Telecommunication 155, 156, 157, 159, 160, 162, 164, 167, 168
Telecommunication management network (TMN) 157
Terabyte 43
Test marking 55
Thematic analysis 14
Third-generation methods 103
Time Machine 69
Time sharing 65
Timesheet data 128
Top-Down Functional Decomposition (TDFD) 105
Top management 11
Total cost of ownership (TCO) 25, 49
Total system performance 37
Transaction flow 9
Transaction processing systems (TPSs) 7, 136
Transfer rates 47
Transmission media 156
Treasury management 9
Trouble ticketing 158

U

Ultimate system 99
Unauthorized entry 93
Unauthorized intruder breaches 200
Unified Database 126

Urbanization process 27
USB flash drive 52, 79
User centric development 92
User-implementation organizations 100
User profiling 158
Utility software 70

V

Valuable data 4
Video conferencing 156
Virtual models 45
Virtual reality gaming 183
Virtual reality headset 183
Virtual reality (VR) 165
Virtual tape 49
Visual perception 212
Vital business data 48
Voice-recognition technology 54
VR memory 65
VR technology 214

W

Walmart database 125
Web browser interface 62
Web-delivered software application 62
Wide Area Network (WAN) 160
Windows manipulation features 68
Wired communication 156
Wired telecommunications 159
Wireless communication 156
Word-processing programs 127
Workgroup productivity 175
World Wide Web Consortium (W3C) 136

Y

Yourdon Systems Method (YSM) 108

Z

Zero-day exploits 188
Zero trust security 207